the originals. Variant texts are provided for comparison.

These tales are placed in ethnographic and folkloristic context by a lengthy general Introduction, and each tale is accompanied by a note indicating (where known) the source, collector, date and location of the recording, and summarizing the relevant comparative and interpretive data. Bibliographic references are unobtrusively provided throughout and are gathered into a useful Bibliography.

Swedish Folktales and Legends fills the gap of Swedish folklore available in English and offers comparatists, folklorists and the general reader a valuable collection of migratory legends, international folktales, and memorates collected in rural Sweden.

JOHN LINDOW is a member of the Department of Scandinavian at the University of California, Berkeley.

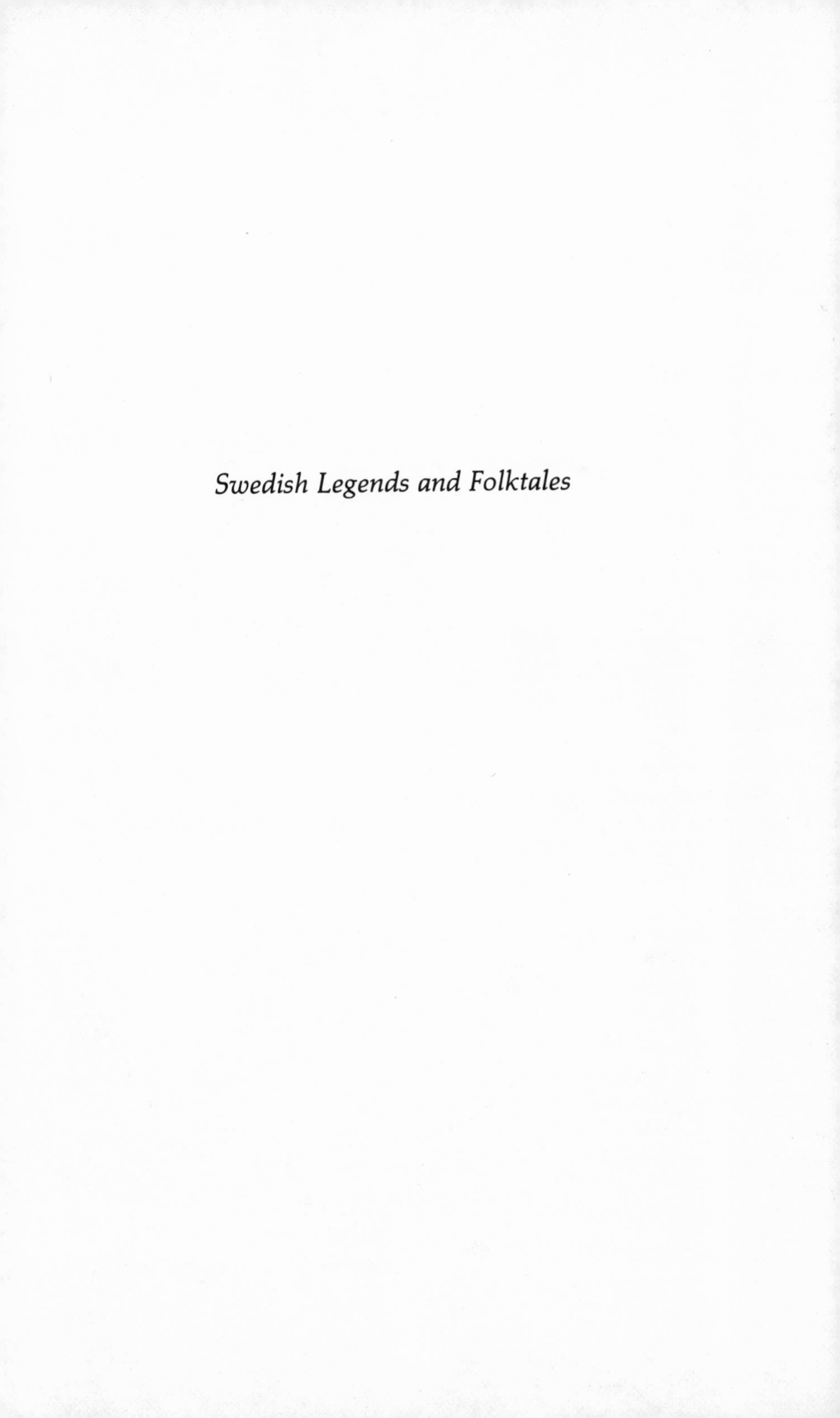

Swedish Legends and Folktales

Swedish Legends and Folktales

John Lindow

University of California Press

Berkeley • Los Angeles • London

University of California Press
Berkeley and Los Angeles, California

University of California Press, Ltd.
London, England

ISBN 0-520-03520-8
Library of Congress Catalog Card Number: 77-78380
Printed in the United States of America
Designed by Dave Comstock

1 2 3 4 5 6 7 8 9

To Kitty, Megan, and Devin
with love, as always

Contents

Preface xi
Introduction 1
Texts 57

This World

1. Investigation of a Grotto 59
2. Sounding at Vassdal (*Bohuslän*) 60
3. Delsbo's Churchbell (*Hälsingland*) 61
4. The Man Who Drowned in a Washbasin (*Småland*) 64
5. Twelve Children on a Platter (*Dalsland*) 65
6. The Piece of Straw (*Västergötland*) 66
7. Retribution (*Skåne; Gotland*) 67
8. Folk Beliefs about Portents (*Bohuslän*) 68
9. Portent from the Nissar (*Skåne*) 71
10. Plague Omens (*Skåne*) 71
11. Buried Alive to Stop the Plague (*Småland*) 72
12. Plague Victims Dig Their Own Graves (*Östergötland*) 74
13. The Survivors (*Bohuslän*) 74
14. An Old Troll Is Tricked Into Revealing His Treasure (*Bohuslän*) 75
15. Tokarsberget's Treasure (*Västergötland*) 76

The Other World

16. The Giant from Klasahall (*Blekinge*) 79
17. A Toy for the Giant (*Halland*) 80
18. Save It for Tomorrow (*Värmland*) 82
19. The Giant Who Moved (*Västergötland*) 82

20. The Big Boulder North of Torstuna Church (*Uppland*) 84
21. It's a Long Way to Gamla Uppsala (*Uppland*) 85
22. A Giant Builds a Church (*Västergötland*) 86
23. The Old Man from Håberg (*Bohuslän*) 88
24. Trolls Take Over the Farm (*Värmland*) 89
25. The Bear Trainer and the Trolls (*Västergötland*) 90
26. Beating the Changeling (*Värmland*) 91
27. The Changeling Speaks on the Way to Baptism (*Småland*) 92
28. Changing a Housewife (*Skåne*) 93
29. Communion Wine in the Troll Food (*Halland*) 94
30. Bergtagen (*Västmanland*) 96
31. The Silver Mountain (*Småland*) 97
32. Stealing for the Trolls (*Småland*) 98
33. The Pan Legend (*Västergötland*) 99
34. A Message for the Cat (*Västergötland*) 101
35. Ljungby Horn and Pipe (*Skåne*) 102
36. Retrieving the Cup (*Gotland*) 103
37. Encounters with the Skogsrå (*Västergötland; Värmland; Östergötland; Västmanland*) 105
38. The Rå Helps a Charcoal-Burner (*Västmanland*) 107
39. Tibast and Vändelrot (*Öland*) 109
40. Garlic and Tar (*Värmland*) 111
41. Shooting the Skogsrå (*Dalsland*) 111
42. A Rude Awakening (*Skåne*) 112
43. Tricking a Christian (*Småland*) 113
44. Oden Was a Sunday Hunter (*Dalsland*) 114
45. The Woman Was Tied Behind the Horse by Her Braids (*Jämtland*) 115
46. The Näck's Reel (*Småland*) 117
47. The Näck Pulls the Plow (*Östergötland*) 119
48. Riding the Bäckahäst (*Skåne*) 120
49. The Strömkarl at Garphytte (*Västmanland*) 121
50. The Näck Longs for Salvation (*Östergötland*) 123
51. The Mill Spirit (*Hälsingland*) 124
52. The Sjörå Warns of an Impending Storm (*Blekinge*) 126
53. Helping the Sjörå (*Värmland*) 126
54. The Sjörå in Helgasjön (*Småland*) 127
55. "Binding" and Driving Off a Sjörå (*Värmland*) 128

56. A Handout for the Merman (*Skåne*) 130
57. Håvålen (*Bohuslän*) 131
58. The Blind Sea Captain (*Småland*) 132
59. Encounters with Tomtar (*Skåne; Öland; Närke*) 136
60. The Tomte Carries a Single Straw (*Småland*) 138
61. New Clothes for the Tomte (*Västergötland*) 139
62. The Tomte Learns to Rest (*Halland*) 140
63. The Missing Butter (*Halland*) 141
64. The Tomte's Favorite Horse (*Bohuslän*) 142
65. Exorcising the Tomte (*Bohuslän*) 143
66. A Ship's Tomte (*Bohuslän*) 144

The World of Religion

67. The Devil as a Black Dog (*Värmland; Småland*) 147
68. The Hårga-Dance (*Hälsingland*) 148
69. Dancing in Dalarna (*Lappland*) 150
70. The Dance at Frisagård (*Halland*) 151
71. The Cardplayers and the Devil (*Skåne*) 152
72. The Devil Advises Suicide (*Värmland*) 154
73. The Girls at the Parsonage Get Help Sewing Crinoline (*Västmanland*) 155
74. Giving the Devil a Ride (*Bohuslän*) 156
75. The Devil as the Fourth Wheel (*Skåne*) 157
76. Outwitting the Devil (*Värmland*) 158
77. The Devil in the Church (*Småland*) 159
78. Old Erik in the Mill (*Dalarna*) 161
79. The Easter-Hag Put a Water-Trough in Her Place (*Dalsland*) 163
80. With Her Godmother to Josefsdal (*Dalarna*) 164
81. The Witch at Tådås (*Bohuslän*) 165
82. The Magic Horn (*Uppland*) 168
83. Following the Witch (*Småland*) 169
84. Milking Others' Cows (*Småland*) 170
85. Captain Eli (*Småland*) 172
86. The Devil and Kitta Grå (*Småland*) 174
87. Werewolf and Nightmare (*Skåne*) 176
88. Becoming a Werewolf (*Värmland*) 179
89. The Identity of the Nightmare (*Bohuslän; Västergötland*) 180

90. The Farm Hand Tied Sharpened Scythes over the Horse's Back (*Västmanland*) 182
91. A Haunting (*Uppland*) 183
92. A Ghost Gets a Free Ride (*Västergötland*) 184
93. Strand-Ghosts (*Halland*) 185
94. The Parson Could Not Say "Our Daily Bread" (*Värmland*) 187
95. Peace in the Grave (*Hälsingland*) 188
96. The Hanged Man Seeks His Pine Tree (*Värmland*) 189
97. The Power of Sorrow (*Swedish Finland*) 190
98. The Dead Bridegroom (*Ångermanland*) 191
99. The Christmas Service of the Dead (*Värmland*) 193
100. A False Ghost (*Uppland*) 195

Abbreviations 197
Bibliography 199
Index of Tale Types 211
General Index 213

Preface

Two important factors stand behind this book.

The first is my observation that within Scandinavian folklore Swedish tales have in general not been well known in English, despite the large importance of the theoretical and practical contributions of Swedish folklorists in the founding of the study of folklore and its continued growth. Swedish tales that have found their way into English have virtually without exception come from the realm of the wonder tale or Märchen (Swedish *saga*), despite the overwhelming importance in numbers and relevance to folklife of the more casual tales usually known as legends (Swedish *sägner*). Many Norwegian legends are available in Reidar Th. Christiansen's admirable edition of *Folktales of Norway,* translated by Pat Shaw Iversen, in the series *Folktales of the World.* No such service has been performed for Swedish legends, however, and so this book concentrates on them, although some wonder tales are included as well. Sweden is unique in the history of folktale collecting in that the importance of word-for-word recording early became established there, decades before electronic recording was feasible. One therefore finds tales relatively close to oral tradition, and I have attempted to retain the breathless, constantly moving quality of the language of the originals. This is a far more difficult proposition than rendering the material into faceless academic prose, and only the reader will be able to judge whether the game was worth the candle.

The second factor is a book. I first began to contemplate a book of translations based on Swedish legends when Bengt af Klintberg's *Svenska folksägner* came into my hands four years ago. This excellent volume, containing over four hundred texts, folkloristic and bibliographical notes, and a lengthy introduction, has been at my side throughout the work on this book. My debt to it will be obvious to anyone who is familiar with it. Besides translating some of the tales printed there, I have found helpful Klintberg's organization and coverage, and I have frequently followed his bibliographic guide. Finally, certain of my comments are based primarily on his. My debt is so great that it was impossible to indicate individual cases.

Much of the strength of Swedish folktale scholarship is based on the archives, whose vast holdings provided early models of organization and ample grist for the folklorists' mill. I have been unable to visit Sweden during the period of my work on this book, and so my texts are all chosen from printed sources. I have no doubt that I would have chosen different texts if I had had access to the Swedish archives, but I hope the material I have been able to find and present here will not give too distorted a picture of Swedish legend tradition.

The Introduction and notes to the individual tales are provided for the benefit of the general reader and the scholar not working actively within the area of Swedish legends. Both should bear in mind that the picture of Sweden presented in the Introduction is of necessity somewhat general; many of the details are valid for certain districts or periods only. The notes to the tales are intended to present, in as brief but readable a form as possible, some basic bibliographic guidelines and suggestions for interpretation. The reader is warned that certain of the rationalizations of the mysterious and supernatural are mine alone and might provoke scepticism or ire on the part of some folklorists. To them I offer my apologies and the excuse that I have in most cases based my rationalizations on the model long in favor in Scandinavia, described in Lauri Honko's terms in the Introduction.

In citing bibliographical items I have tried to be as unobtrusive as possible without sacrificing overall breadth of coverage. I hope my efforts will be regarded as an invitation to further study, not as an exercise in pedantry. To make my citations more useful, I have gathered most of them into the Bibliography, and there I have added some additional material, primarily important editions, not cited in the text of the book. My goal has not been to provide exhaustive coverage, but merely to offer a representative sample.

Certain of the texts were translated and distributed to my classes in Scandinavian Folklore at the University of California from 1973 through 1976. I have always learned from my classes, not least in the case of the tales printed here, and I am glad to offer my thanks to the students who made teaching them such a pleasurable learning experience for me.

A portion of the bibliographic work, and some of the initial classification of tales, were done with the aid of the Committee on Research at the University of California, Berkeley, to whom I owe my warmest thanks. I was fortunate in being able to employ Agneta Bendsjö-Schipper for this work; she did much and contributed significantly to the final result. The typescript was prepared skillfully and cheerfully by Sally Fiske, and I had some help in proofreading and checking references from Mary Visher. My thanks to them all.

Finally, my thanks and love to my family, who have learned to live with the constant clatter of a typewriter and to ignore the frequent mental lapses of a husband and father whose mind has all too often been thousands of miles away.

Introduction

The legends, folktales, and memorates printed in this book are with one exception collected from rural oral traditions of the nineteenth and twentieth centuries in Sweden.* Such legends were told daily in rural Sweden for centuries before they were collected, and they made up the largest part of oral narrative material in pre-industrial Sweden. They were an important part of everyday life, which they reflected and helped shape. An understanding of them, therefore, requires at least some acquaintance with the society which produced and used them, as well as a feeling for the oral traditions and folk beliefs they represent.

It is difficult to generalize about a country stretching fifteen hundred kilometers from north to south and in places over four hundred kilometers from east to west, ranging from uninhabited mountainous areas north of the Arctic Circle to densely populated, intensively cultivated regions situated further south than Glasgow, Edinburgh, and even Copenhagen. It is, however, possible to describe Sweden accurately as a land covered by vast forests alternating with arable land, a land falling geographically into two basic areas of approximately equal size. South of an imaginary line joining Värmland, Närke, Dalarna, and Gästrikland, Sweden is a relatively flat, arable country, with geographically older surfaces. North of this line lie newer surfaces, culminating in the northwestern mountains. There is far

*Memorates are purely personal narratives told by people about their own experiences. This and other terms are discussed in more detail below, pp. 25–28.

SWEDEN
International boundary
Provincial boundary
200 meter contour
0 100 KM
10°
20°
65°
60°
55°
LAPPLAND
NORRBOTTEN
VÄSTERBOTTEN
ÅNGERMAN-LAND
JÄMTLAND
HÄRJE-DALEN
MEDALPAD
FINLAND
NORWAY
HÄLSING-LAND
DALARNA
GÄSTRIKLAND
SVEALAND
Uppsala
VÄRMLAND
VÄSTMAN-LAND
UPPLAND
Stockholm
DALS-LAND
NÄRKE
SÖDERMANLAND
BOHUSLÄN
VÄSTER-GÖTLAND
ÖSTER-GÖTLAND
GÖTALAND
GOTLAND
SMÅLAND
HALLAND
ÖLAND
DENMARK
SKÅNE
BLEKINGE
USSR
Lund
Malmö
BALTIC SEA

less contiguous arable land here, and the climate is relatively harsh, with a growing season as low as 140 days. Most of the population still lives in the southern area, although industrialization and urbanization have reduced the rural population throughout the country.

In prehistoric times the dense forests effectively cut off communication, and so cultures arose in three different areas in the southern region (the northern region was not settled until somewhat later). These three regions were South Sweden, until the seventeenth century a part of the Danish kingdom; Götaland, with settlement on the plains and by the shores of Lakes Vänern and Vättern; and Svealand, centered in the valley of Lake Mälaren. Originally these seem to have been separate kingdoms, but, by the Viking Age, Götaland and Svealand were consolidated into one kingdom. The northern area should also be regarded as a separate unit, although it was settled primarily from Svealand and has close associations both with Svealand and with Finland to the east.

The Swedish provinces, no longer administrative units but still of cultural importance, presumably represent early centers of population. The provincial laws, originally oral but recorded on parchment during the late Middle Ages, were important expressions of the unity of each province. For the traditions recorded in this book, however, certain broad groupings of the provinces are useful. Skåne, Halland, and Blekinge, the three provinces obtained from Denmark in 1658, may be called South Sweden; this designation should also include part of southern Småland and for certain purposes must be extended as far north as southern Götaland. The term Southwest Sweden would include the areas around Vänern, namely Bohuslän, Dalsland, Värmland, and part of Västergötland. Central Sweden encompasses Östergötland, Södermanland, Västmanland, Närke, and Uppland, and is therefore a fairly vague distinction. Similarly vague is the designation North Sweden, which includes the culturally conservative Dalarna (Dalecarlia), the Norwegian-influenced provinces of Jämtland and Härjedalen, and the coastal provinces extending from Gästrikland to Norrbotten, ending with the largely uninhabited Lappland. Given the sparseness of the population in northern Sweden, the provinces were never as culturally important as divisions in the south, and the inclusive term Norrland is often used for them; Dalarna must be excluded from this designation. The island of Gotland, off the east coast, has long been a separate cultural and linguistic area. There are also large numbers of Swedish speakers in Finland, where Swedish shares the status of an official language. Although their numbers have been rapidly dwindling, there are still many Swedish enclaves along the Finnish west coast. With one exception, texts from Swedish Finland have not been included in this book, which has been limited to the political boundaries of modern Sweden. The exception is story no. 97, "The Power of Sorrow," taken from a diary entry from seventeenth-century Helsinki. At that time Finland was no more than a Swedish territory, and the upper classes were all Swedish.

Until the Industrial Revolution, which took more than a century to reach Sweden, most of the population there, as in the rest of Europe, was engaged in agriculture, combined with fishing in coastal regions. The fertile plains of the south were the most intensively cultivated, but nearly all arable land was in use. In forested areas a one-field system was common, while two- and three-field systems, including crop rotation and grazing on fallow land, were employed on the plains. The size of farms varied from large estates to small crofters' holdings on the edges of moderate farms and manors, but most of the farms were privately owned or rented and of sufficient size to function independently. Until 1827 much of the country was characterized by villages with independent farmsteads, but then a new law of redistribution split up the villages into more dispersed but centralized farms by reducing or eliminating the complex patchwork of the farmstead system. This affected the plains areas more strongly than the forested areas, where farms had always been located further apart.

The primary crops were the grains and root vegetables, with grazing often taking place on uncultivated meadows. In the northern area shielings were used, some members of the household accompanying the livestock up into the mountains for grazing during the summer months. In all areas farming was carried out by traditional means, using only traditional tools, primarily handmade. Most households had to be self-sufficient, particularly in areas of minimal settlement.

In the rural areas, therefore, a division into the following social classes might be made. At the top stood the large landowners, many of them members of the hereditary nobility, who owned and worked the large estates. Some were absentee landlords, however, and not a few estates, particularly in the more distant past, were crown or church property. The nobility and urban middle class, an increasingly important factor in Swedish society, controlled virtually all the movable wealth and were the only ones with any real access to education or "higher" culture. As a result, most of the society functioned orally, an important factor in the shaping and maintaining of the cultural traditions represented in this book.

Beneath the wealthy landowners came the peasantry, a vast class with many important internal divisions. One speaks of rich peasants and poor, and the range between them could really be quite great. The rich peasant might approach the wealthy landowner in the size of his farm, number of livestock, and so forth, whereas the poor peasant might eke out a subsistence only with difficulty; rich peasants might produce enough to sell to others, poor peasants not enough to feed their own families. Generally a farm would consist of several buildings, various fields, some cattle, and, besides the farmer and his family, some hired hands to help work the land. A large family was almost a necessity, given the amount of labor required to run a farm of even modest size. The farmer was in charge of the work in the fields, other heavy work, horses, and the male servants; the farmer's wife took charge of many of the domestic activities, like spinning, weaving, sewing, cooking, preserving, and so forth, and she also was in charge of the female servants. The farmer's children were in a sort of intermediate stage between servant and farmer; they worked like servants but had certain additional rights. The eldest son could expect to inherit the farm after his father, but the other sons had to make their own way. They could enter the church, become soldiers or artisans, or try to find work on other farms.

The distinction between farmer and servant was originally based on the ability to pay taxes: those who could pay were farmers (Swedish *bönder*, singular *bonde*), those who could not were classified as farm hands. Full-time servants were regular household members who were paid in room and board. In addition they could expect to receive some clothing, some seeds to plant for their own use, and, rarely, money. For example, in the 1820s in Skåne a regular farmhand (*dräng*) typically received the following as annual wages: one blue or white sweater, one pair each of leather and flaxen pants, one leather jacket, one linen shirt and one wool shirt, two pairs of socks, two pairs of shoes or one pair of boots, and four to six barrels of seeds and the use of a small patch of land to plant them in.

There was, naturally, much complexity in this social class. In Skåne four classes of male farm hands were distinguished: grown man, younger man, boy, and older man. Female servants, who were of somewhat less importance, were divided into two classes: grown women and girls. The household of a moderately large farm might consist of the farmer, his wife and children, two male farm hands, two female servants, and seasonal help. The latter were employed only at periods of peak activity when time was short, such as harvesting or haymaking. Otherwise these men were on their own. Some became craftsmen, some beggars, some, sad to say, starved.

This, then, was the social nucleus of early rural Swedish society. In the forested areas, where farms were dispersed, it is an adequate picture of society. On the more densely populated plains, however, where villages had grown up, the social system was more complex. There one must reckon with artisans, occasional shopkeepers (in the bigger towns only), soldiers, beggars, and peddlers. Of these the soldier probably enjoyed the highest social status. Often a given unit of population, so-and-so many farms or households, had to provide the crown with a soldier. When not on campaign, he lived in his own house on land provided him, and he might function as a rudimentary schoolteacher, since he often had some book learning. Soldiers were important in the spreading of oral traditions through their regular travel from the village in military service and subsequent returns with news of the rest of the world. Most parts of Sweden, particularly in the war-torn southern provinces over which Denmark and Sweden repeatedly fought, have tales about warfare and famous battles, and legends about the warrior-king Charles XII make up a regular legend cycle. In our collection we have one tale told by a soldier: no. 4, "The Man Who Drowned in a Washbasin," from the soldier Karl Snygg.

As opposed to the respectable soldier, craftsmen often had to wander from place to place, accepting seasonal work when available and trying to sell their talents at other times. They were still, however, more highly regarded than the peddlers, who wandered with their sacks from village to farm and were often regarded as little more than scoundrels. In Sweden they have entered oral tradition as the well-known Västgöteknalle, a trickster figure who appears in many humorous tales. Peddlers would frequently gather in markets, which would provide an excellent opportunity for the transmission of folktales, including particularly the migratory legends and international folktales presented in this book. A quieter but probably equally effective factor in the dissemination of traditional lore was the visit of the peddler, artisan, or craftsman to the individual farm, particularly in the less densely settled plains and northern areas.

At the bottom of the social scale stood a rather large class of beggars, those who went around without work and were cared for either by relatives, the wealthy, or the church. Some members of this class were genuinely unemployed, victims of a growing population in a relatively unstable economy. Others were simply too old, ill, or feeble to work. There was much variety in this segment of the population, as there was among the group of hired hands. A description of Skåne in the 1840s, for example, left by Eva Wigström, one of the most vigorous folklore collectors from that area, includes seven different kinds of beggars. One class was the village's own beggars, who were generally known to all and treated kindly. A second group was composed of more or less professional beggars, who wandered from parish to parish, often on horseback, and seem to have made a successful business enterprise out of begging. A third group was the insane or those who feigned insanity for the benefit of the charity that might come to them. A fourth group was similar to the professional beggars but made less of a business of their begging and might justly be regarded as wanderers. The fifth and sixth groups were ethnically defined: gypsies might take odd jobs but for the most part were engaged in magic, and sometimes the line between them and common thieves was not clearly drawn by the community; and Finns and Lapps were regarded primarily as magicians, to be treated circumspectly because of the danger they represented. Finally, a last class of "beggars" in mid-nineteenth-century Skåne was composed of minstrels and other traveling musicians. In other parts of Sweden the groups might be somewhat different—Lapps and Finns played a much larger role in northern Sweden, for example—but everywhere there was this large group of people wandering about, dependent on others for food and shelter. Everywhere they went they brought traditional lore with them.

Thus, early rural Swedish society might be described as basically stable, with some elements of movement, for two thousand years before the Industrial Revolution. The balance was ideal for the maintenance, transmission, and spreading of oral folk traditions. Most people were born, raised, and buried in the very same farm or village. Children were constantly with their parents, and with primogeniture they were on a farm that had belonged to their family for many years, often for centuries. In a self-sufficient household little came from without, and work techniques, tools, social values, and stories were all handed down from one generation to the next, and there was ample opportunity for reinforcement of cultural traditions within generations. At the same time, the frequent visits of wanderers of one sort or another infused new life into traditions through variation and contrast, and whatever was truly new came generally from these outsiders. This society was primarily an oral one, with virtually no book learning outside of the rudiments required for church membership. Oral culture tends to be remarkably conservative, and stories change little as they are handed down from one generation to the next. They are told with different words, but the cluster of details which makes up the essence or plot of a story tends to be stable.

The household or extended family, then, was the basic social unit. Local social organization, however, was of course based on a somewhat broader scale. Organization was by parish (Swedish *socken,* abbreviated *sn.*), a number of which would be grouped in a district (*härad,* abbreviated *hd.*). The ancient division into provinces was replaced by a division into counties (Swedish *län*), and the symbol of local government was the sheriff (*länsman*), usually a rich local landowner appointed from above. His powers were awesome and in some local matters close to absolute. The central government, a parliamentary monarchy, had little immediate effect on the lives of the ninety percent or so of the population who were engaged in agriculture.

What did affect the people's lives, in virtually every phase, was the church. During the Reformation the international Catholic Church, which had counted Swedes among its members since the late Middle Ages, was replaced by a state Lutheran Church. Although it had a hierarchy of bishops and archbishops, culminating like the government in the king, for the most part the church, like the government, had a direct effect on the lives of the people only on a local level. Generally each parish had a parson, although some of the more outlying parishes, particularly in the north, often had to share the services of a single rotating parson. A parson had some university training and was ordinarily the only person in the parish who could read and write. Besides serving as spiritual shepherd of his parishioners and carrying out all the sacraments, his major duty was to preach a sermon during service every Sunday. Since such sermons had an important influence on the oral traditions presented in this book, it is worth examining the circumstances of the sermon. In brief, dramatic subject matter and a thundering delivery were preferable for several reasons. To begin with, there often might be a tavern in the vicinity of the church and many members of the congregation might be less than sober during the service. Furthermore, the extreme importance of seating arrangements, where status was linked to the relative location of the pews, often erupted into fisticuffs. At such times the accepted technique, indeed perhaps the only sensible alternative under the circumstances, was for the parson to continue his sermon, perhaps seeking to make it even more interesting to lure attention away from the blows raining down under his nose. Of considerable importance, too, was the fact that churches were not heated. Although it was considered improper to wear more than one's ordinary indoor formal dress, efforts to keep the circulation going were acceptable, the most common being an almost constant stomping of the feet. Given the additional danger that those who were warm enough (perhaps from drink) and satisfied with their pews might drift off to sleep, it is no wonder that the most successful preachers were the best storytellers.

Story no. 97, "The Power of Sorrow," actually recounts a legend told from the pulpit, and it seems apparent that the content and form of many other stories might well follow the same route. That so many stories of Swedish oral tradition have to do with the devil is surely also a result of the influence of the sermon, and the humorous international tale, story no. 77, "The Devil in the Church," is an ironic indication of how tradition might regard an undisciplined congregation.

The parson was evidently an awesome figure in many cases. Because he could read and write, it was assumed he had understanding of or access to the Black Book. He functions as the hero in the many tales relating encounters between devil and clergy, where the positive value of Christianity regularly triumphs over the negative power of Satan, as in several of the stories printed here; but in as many others he is the butt of some sort of humor, often cruel. This ambiguous position of the parson is doubtless due to two factors, social and economic. Socially he was an outsider, either actually because he had been assigned to the parish from an entirely different part of the country, or symbolically because he had left the parish as a boy or young man to study at the university, an unknown and hence feared institution in rural areas. Economic friction between parishioners and parson was almost inevitable because of the way the parson got his living. In the older period he lived off his parish through the tithe and through offerings made in church, usually only on holidays. In addition there were often other special arrangements regarding payment in kind for the parson from harvests, dairy products, and so forth. From the point of view of the peasant the parson was quite well off, but still in reality he often was rather poor, since the principal burden of caring for the poor, housing travelers, and the like often fell on the parsonage.

The complement of local church figures was completed with the dean and the churchwarden (both in larger parishes only) and the sexton. The latter, although not sanctified and a man of little formal education, was a figure of high social standing because of his association with the church buildings and churchyard, the conduct of the clerical business of the parish, the ringing of the churchbells, and the education of the parish's young people. Since he was usually a local, and since most of his contacts with the parish were of a positive nature, he was generally in good standing with most of his neighbors. The contrast between parson and sexton has formed the subject of a number of humorous international folktale types throughout Europe, examples of most of which have been collected in Sweden.

Into this stable Christian society, people were born, and there they lived their lives as their parents had before them and as their children would after them, until the dissolution of traditional rural society in the twentieth century. Let us follow a typical individual through the life cycle.

Even before birth he was the object of traditional beliefs. With a high mortality rate for both infants and mothers, with a relatively large number of pregnancies not carried to term, it is not surprising that a number of traditional means developed to avoid trouble from the outset. For example, a pregnant woman was supposed to keep calm and avoid being frightened, for if she were frightened, for example, during the fifteenth week of pregnancy, her child would fall ill during his fifteenth year. If the fright were caused by an animal, the illness or its course would somehow resemble that animal. If she looked through a keyhole her child would be cross-eyed, and if she walked too far her child might be lame. All these elements of belief provided explanations where otherwise there were none and where the treatment of disease lay in the realm not of science but of magic.

At birth a woman was attended by a midwife, generally an older, experienced woman, quite often with a reputation for magic. Besides her obvious obstetric duties, the midwife had to see to it that the correct superstitions were observed, and not infrequently an assistant might be called in to chant magic formulas or the Lord's Prayer. An effective midwife could be in great demand, and a well-known migratory legend tells of the woman who was midwife to the trolls. A successful, safe delivery was cause for rejoicing, and often a woman's neighbors would gather around the bed for a quiet celebration. Storytelling frequently made up part of the festivities, and here was another opportunity for the transmission of traditional lore.

Consistent with Catholic doctrine, folk belief had it that the newborn infant was heathen until it had been baptized. This meant that steps had to be taken to protect it from evil spirits and the beings of the other world. The most frequent elements of protection were lights, fire, and steel, and sometimes herbs. Lights and fire kept constantly burning would make it difficult for trolls to steal the baby, and steel in the cradle, a cross carved on it, or herbs smeared on it would force the trolls to keep their distance. As an example of the very real problems people faced, one may cite the need to wash a newborn infant shortly after birth. If the water had not been fetched before the actual moment of birth it could not be used, for the *näck*, a water creature, might be lurking invisibly in it hoping to steal or harm the baby. And despite these precautions, the beings of the other world did manage to steal or harm a fair number of infants, according to folk tradition. The biggest danger was that of changing. When changing occurred, a troll mother substituted her brat for the human baby, which she took with her off to the other world. We know now that changing provided an explanation for ill, deformed, or retarded children, the most common conditions being idiocy, mongolism, hydrocephalus, cretinism, rickets, and atrepsy. But the danger of changing was real for all that to the people whose traditions we are studying here, and it had both positive and negative results. Among the more positive were the nearly constant observation and scrutiny applied to the infant; among the negative were the beatings and other mistreatment accorded such unfortunate children because of the folk belief that threatened or actual mistreatment of a changeling would cause the troll mother to return the human child and rescue her troll child from its misery. Stories of such incidents perhaps had positive didactic value, too, since the troll mother's statement that she was better to the human child than the human mother was to the troll child (see story no. 26, "Beating the Changeling") casts a bad light on child abuse, but they must also have led to the actually recorded incidents of abuse of "changelings." However, several changeling stories were apparently used primarily for entertainment; these stories are of the sort which involve tricking the changeling into revealing his identity, like story no. 27, "The Changeling Speaks on the Way to Baptism."

Besides the child, the newly delivered mother was also regarded as heathen. Her re-entry into the church was formalized at a special ceremony known in Sweden as, literally, the "church-reception" (*kyrkotagning*), which took place at an established time after birth.

The individual's first sacrament, and the one that in theory ended the threat of a changing, was baptism. To reduce that threat the sacrament might be celebrated on the very day of birth and was only seldom postponed more than a few days. Godparents were appointed, and the choice might involve some consideration, for somehow the child was thought to acquire some of the characteristics of the godparent. On the good side this meant that a godparent could pass special skills or qualities of personality on to a child; on the bad side it might doom a child to witchcraft in later life (see story no. 80, "With Her Godmother to Josefsdal"). Because the child was in theory vulnerable up until the very moment of baptism, means of protection were often used, such as a piece of steel in the swaddling clothes. The actual ceremony must have seemed, in its ritual, similar to numerous other magic ceremonies of which the populace had knowledge or use.

The child then grew up in the household or on the farm of his parents. When he was little, play occupied much of his time, but as soon as he was old enough, chores were assigned. Such education as he received was provided by the sexton, a retired soldier, the godparents, or perhaps his parents, but whoever did the teaching the principal aim was the same: he had to familiarize himself with Christian doctrine and learn the proper responses for participation in Christian ceremony. In practice this meant learning the Lord's Prayer and the Catechism, usually by rote. Thus he could not expect to become anything more than a functional illiterate familiar with the dogma and traditions of the Swedish Lutheran Church, although some members of rural society, particularly from the mid-eighteenth century onward, did learn the rudiments of reading and writing. Even so, the culture remained predominantly oral.

Confirmation occurred when, according to tradition, the child had mastered the elements of Christianity and thus was prepared for formal entry into the Christian fellowship. During the early centuries of Christianity this was taken to be the age of seven, but by the nineteenth century fourteen was the accepted age. This was an important and therefore dangerous time, rather like baptism. Now, however, the danger was posed not so much by the trolls as by the devil and temptation. Story no. 73, "The Girls at the Parsonage Get Help Sewing Crinoline," warns against the sin of pride at precisely this time.

After confirmation the individual was in theory a regular member of the church and an adult, and indeed the age of majority for boys came at fifteen, but in practice most individuals stayed on at home for a number of years longer. These were the transition years, from childhood through youth to adulthood, and they were, from the point of view of tradition, the most vulnerable years of all. If ever a boy or girl were to meet a troll, in legend it would be at just this point, and the troll might well be on the lookout for a human spouse. A number of the legends in this book deal with this problem, such as nos. 38–43, which tell of erotic encounters with the *skogsrå,* and no. 98, "The Dead Bridegroom." Usually the human manages to escape the danger, but some stories tell of marriage between this world and the other world, as in part of story no. 87, "Werewolf and Nightmare."

Legend tradition notwithstanding, a number of persons managed to marry, settle down, and have families. Marriage was regularly arranged by families with an aim toward increasing wealth or consolidating property, and romantic love played but a small role. Ideally, newlyweds would set up their own farm, either inherited or on newly broken and hence less desirable land. Before marrying, they might first spend a limited amount of time with their in-laws, but subsequently if no farm could be found, there was no real possibility of marriage. Thus marriage was an economic and social matter, and as such socially desirable. Because marriage implied economic respectability and a measure of independence, it was regarded positively, and bachelordom or spinsterhood were regarded negatively. The strongest symptom of this point of view concerned witchcraft, which tended to be laid at the door of unmarried or widowed older women.

Whether one did or did not marry, the later years were occupied by hard work in a clearly established social position. Those who had married were expected to have children, and childless marriages were regarded suspiciously, as story no. 5, "Twelve Children on a Platter," indicates. The final sacrament was the funeral, and death was, if anything, fraught with more danger than birth. The great problem was to effect a smooth transition from this world to the world of the dead, a transition summarized in the funeral customs but involving a great deal more. Those who did not make the transition smoothly (perhaps because of business left undone in this world, as in story no. 95, or because of improper burial, as in story no. 93, or because of crime in this world, as in story no. 96, or because of simple orneriness, as in story no. 91) became ghosts. The ghosts of Scandinavian folk tradition were regarded far more concretely than the shades of Anglo-American literary tradition, and should more accurately be referred to as the living dead. A tradition of the living dead in Scandinavia extends as far back as there are written records, and anyone familiar with the Icelandic sagas will recall the *draugar,* revenants who terrorize the living and pose a constant threat of death and destruction. The most famous is probably the chillingly malevolent Glámr of *Grettis saga,* at last laid to rest by Grettir himself. Swedish folk tradition makes a distinction between ghosts whose identity is known, called *spöken* (singular *spöke*), and ghosts of unknown identity, called *gastar* (singular *gast*). The latter, following the rule of fear of the unknown, are more terrifying than the former and share certain characteristics of the nature-beings.

Stories often identify the cause of haunting, or they stress the encounter with the revenant, but additionally there were numerous customs that had to be carried out correctly in order to avoid the possibility of the dead coming back again. One of the more common aspects of folk belief, for example, was that the revenant could only re-enter a house the way he left it, so if a haunting appeared imminent it was sometimes wise to knock a hole in the wall, carry off the corpse to the graveyard, and then rebuild the wall. Similar customs are found throughout the world and reflect a basic fear of the dead that all men seem to share.

Like the individual, the year had its own cycle, and following it through will give added understanding to the people whose traditions fill this book. The calendar was, in effect, an attempt to regulate the weather and seasons and the activities of the population, primarily agricultural, but also to a certain extent religious. The arrival of the Julian calendar in the late Middle

Ages had several effects: the pre-Christian folk festivals were relocated on days of Christian celebration, for example, and so the midwinter ceremony became the birthday of Christ. If no important saint's day were available, a folk festival might die out, as did the autumn festival. In England it was aligned with St. Michael's day, but in most of Scandinavia the harvest took place much earlier and no important saint's day was conveniently available. This process of aligning important activities with saints' days became common, although folk tradition also used "signal days," Swedish *märkesdagar*, a given number of days before or after an important day, to regulate agricultural activities.

A sampling of important days will give some indication of the way this sometimes confusing but internally consistent system functioned. Midwinter was aligned with various saints' days, depending on location, ranging from Henrik (19 January) in the south, to Candlemas (2 February) in the north. The arrival of Spring generally coincided with Annunciation Day (25 March), and the rules for planting various crops often were measured in weeks from that day until midsummer. The date of Easter could of course vary; excepting Christmas, it was the most important religious festival and its celebration stretched over several days. Because it was one of the most important Christian holidays, it was inversely regarded as an important pagan holiday, and Easter was particularly sacred to Satan and witches, many of whom were referred to as Easter-hags. This was the time when witches flew off to Blåkulla, traditionally regarded as the site of the Black Mass. A secular holiday, borrowed ultimately from France, was the first of May, the day of St. Valborg (St. Walpurga, an English nun who founded religious houses and engaged in missionary activity in Germany, and died in 777). Celebrated the evening before, the ceremony involved the lighting of fires and other festivities. A few weeks later came St. Erik's day (18 June), an important day for planting, though the crop varied from place to place. The big summer festival was midsummer, traditionally celebrated on June 24. At this time all the crops had been planted and it was not yet time for slaughtering, reaping, or the fall planting, and thus the prominence of this festival was not due to chance. Midsummer was commonly celebrated by night-long bonfires, dancing, feasting, and drinking, and it was the biggest secular holiday of the year. The custom of dancing around the Maypole, now a prime feature of the Swedish midsummer celebration, was borrowed from Mayday celebrations elsewhere, which accorded better climatically with the Swedish midsummer than with Mayday. Presumably the loan was enacted originally by the upper classes. After midsummer, farm activities were resumed, the timing being determined by traditional rules affixed to certain dates. Harvest and slaughter were the primary activities, and among the rules were local notions that, for example, fall harvest should not begin before St. Olof's day (29 July) and should be completed by St. Bartolomeus (24 August). Following the harvest there was no general harvest celebration, except sporadically, and a fall planting, if undertaken at all, was likely to be a risky proposition. The important fall festival affiliated in much of Europe with the slaughter on St. Martin's day (11 November) was generally unknown in Sweden, winter weather already having set in, but in Denmark and Skåne goose was eaten, and this custom spread to the north during the nineteenth century and now has become a nearly universal Swedish holiday. During the weeks before Christmas the last important activity, threshing, was carried out, and by Christmas it was ordinarily finished. The Christmas holiday, usually thirteen days long but sometimes as long as twenty, coincided with the culmination of the agricultural year; threshing, the last outdoor activity, was finished, and no outdoor work would be done until the spring planting. Celebration of the holiday centered on good food and drink, though its religious significance was not overlooked. A measure of its importance is the frequency with which encounters with nature beings are recorded in oral narrative tradition; examples from within this collection are, among others, stories nos. 24–25, which detail the overrunning of a farm or household every Christmas Eve. Because Christmas is the greatest Christian holiday, it is simultaneously the time when the non-Christian beings are at their most active.

The above ethnographic description has been of necessity rather general. Those interested in more specific detail or further reading will enter a bibliographic jungle, sometimes bewildering in its size and complexity. Among the material I have found useful, a few items may be mentioned; they represent personal taste but at least offer something of a guideline. Axel Sømme, ed., *A Geography of Norden* (Oslo, 1960), contains excellent maps and useful texts by various experts on all the Nordic lands. Similar but more technical is W. R. Mead, *An Economic Geography of the Scandinavian States and Finland* (London, 1965), and more general is Roy Millward, *Scandinavian Lands* (London, 1965). More to the immediate points is Sigurd Erixon, "Svensk byggnadskultur och dess geografi," *Ymer*, 42 (1922), 249–290. A recent work is Hans W:son Ahlman et al., eds., *Sverige: Land och folk* 1–3 (Stockholm, 1966). Among the many histories, the most recent is that of Franklin Scott, *Sweden: The Nation's History* (Minneapolis, 1977). Ingvar Andersson, *A History of Sweden*, translated by Carolyn Hannay (London, 1955), is also useful, as is Lennart Jörberg, *The Industrial Revolution in Scandinavia*, The Fontana Economic History of Europe, 4:8 (London, 1970). A standard Swedish reference work remains Emil Hildebrand, ed., *Sveriges historia till våra dagar* 1–15 (Stockholm, 1919–45), and the most interesting social history is Gösta Johannesson, *Skånes historia* (Stockholm, 1971).

Scandinavian peasant life is treated extensively in Troels-Lund, *Dagligt liv i Norden i det sekstende århundrede* 1–7 (Copenhagen, 1879–1901), a massive work which remains fertile ground for the ethnographer and folklorist. A lengthy description of Norwegian conditions is K. Visted, *Vår gamle bondekultur* 1–2 (Kristiania, 1971). For Denmark one may cite H. F. Feilberg, *Dansk bondeliv, saaledes som det i mands minde førtes, navnlig i Vestjylland* (Copenhagen, 1889), which C. W. von Sydow termed the best account of the common people in any language. A similar volume for Sweden is Tobias Norlind, *Svenska allmogens lif: 1. folksed, folktro och folkdiktningen* (Stockholm, 1912), outmoded but still useful and occasionally humorous, but not so humorous as L. Lloyd, *Peasant Life in Sweden* (London, 1870). Recent sound and reliable textbooks are Sigfrid Svensson, *Introduktion till folklivsforskning* (Stockholm, 1966), and its successor, Nils-Arvid Bringéus, *Människan som kulturvarelse: en introduktion till etnologi*, Handböcker i etnologi (Lund, 1976), which incorporates the latest work and viewpoints.

Most Swedish ethnographic discussions, however, tend to treat a single area or subject. A representative sample would include Gideon Danell, "Folklivet i en gammal svensk by," *FmFt*, 12 (1925), 33–41; August Ehrenberg, *Allmogen i Albo härad under 1880-talet* (Kristianstad, 1945); Levi Johansson, *Bebyggelse och folkliv i det gamla Frostviken*, Skrifter utg. genom Landsmåls- och folkminnesarkivet i Uppsala, B3 (Uppsala, 1947); A. Kullander, "Några drag ur det forna skogsbyggarlifvet i Edsvedens skogstrakter," *SvLm*, 11:10 (1896), 3–50; Lars Levander, *Övre Dalarnes bondekultur under 1800-talets förra hälft* (Stockholm, 1943); Linnar Linnarsson, *Bygd, by och gård*, Skrifter utg. genom Landsmåls- och folkminnesarkivet i Uppsala, B4 (Uppsala, 1948); P. Möller, "Allmogeliv i Göingebygden vid adertonhundratalets början," *FmFt*, 3 (1916), 179–190; Martin P:n Nilsson, "Byalaget i sydsvensk kultur," *Saga och Sed*, 1943, pp. 54–63; Yngve Nilsson, *Bygd och näringsliv i norra Värmland: en kulturgeografisk studie*, Meddelanden från Lund Universitetets Geografiska Institutionen, Avhandlingar, 18 (Lund, 1950); Anna-Maja Nylén, "Svensk landsbygd i omvandling," *Rig*, 47 (1964), 1–9; Carin Phil, "Livet i det gamla Överkalix," *SvLm*, 1955, pp. 83–187; Anna Sandström, *Natur och arbetsliv i svenska bygder: Götaland* (Stockholm, 1948), and *Natur och arbetsliv i svenska bygder: Norrland* (Stockholm, 1924); Johannes Sundblad, *Gammaldags seder och bruk* (Stockholm, 1917), which itself seems rather old-fashioned; Edvin Thorsén, *Uppländsk torparliv* (Stockholm, 1949); and Eva Wigström, "Allmogeseder i Rönnebergs härad i Skåne på 1840-talet," *SvLm*, 8:2 (1891).

Two invaluable reference works deserve special mention. The first is *Nordisk Kultur* (Copenhagen, Oslo, Stockholm, 1931–55). Its thirty volumes, issued under the general direction of Sigurd Erixon, contain technical articles by experts on many important aspects of medieval and modern Scandinavia, each volume treating a different subject. Among the more important for the culture we have been discussing here is the four-volume sub-series entitled *Teknisk kultur*, and other individual volumes of particular interest are: Edvard Bull and Sverre Steen, eds., *Byer og bebyggelse*, Nordisk Kultur, 18 (Oslo, 1933); Martin P:n Nilsson, ed., *Tideräkningen*, Nordisk Kultur, 21 (Stockholm, 1934); and K. Rob. V. Wikman, ed., *Livets högtider*, Nordisk Kultur, 20 (Stockholm, 1949). The second important reference source is the *Kulturhistorisk lexikon för nordisk medeltid* (Copenhagen, Malmö, Oslo, 1956 et seq.), which contains short articles on a wealth of subjects dealing with the Scandinavian Middle Ages, including many on folkloristic topics.

Books dealing specifically with annual customs are: Martin P:n. Nilsson, ed., *Årets högtider,* Nordisk Kultur, 22 (Stockholm, 1938); Sigfrid Svensson, *Bondens år: kalender, märkesdagar, hushållsregler, väderleksmärken,* revised ed. (Stockholm, 1972); and Nils-Arvid Bringéus, *Årets festseder* (Stockholm, 1976).

Stories very much like the ones in this book have been told in Sweden and throughout northern Europe for many centuries, in all probability for at least two millenia. Story no. 33, "The Pan Legend," for example, has a direct affinity with a story recorded by Plutarch and may safely be regarded as two thousand years old in Sweden.* With the exception of some early antiquarian activity, however, it was not until the nineteenth century that sustained interest in collecting and writing down these oral tales developed. In Sweden as elsewhere in Europe this was a direct result of the romantic movement, which through the rose-tinted glass of burgeoning nationalism saw the oral tales and songs of the peasantry as valid expressions of a national soul and as poetry of true power and beauty. The earliest collections were thus aimed not for scholarly use or for archiving but rather for intellectuals, educated readers who had thrown off their taste for the measured neo-classicism of the eighteenth century. The earliest collectors were, in effect, artists who borrowed raw material from the peasantry and reworked it for their own uses. Even the Grimm brothers, who called for fidelity to the collected texts as they stood and basically disapproved of the uses and alterations poets like Brentano would subject material to, were subject to this call, as Wilhelm Grimm's careful, patient, and constant stylistic honing of the *Kinder- und Hausmärchen* demonstrates. In Sweden the literary reworking of material collected from oral literature, or simply inspired by it, was all but universal in the earliest collections. Publication of this material began in 1814, with the first volume of *Svenska folkvisor från forntiden* ("Swedish Folksongs from Ancient Times") by Arvid August Afzelius and E. G. Geijer, although ballad collecting had been undertaken earlier by Leonhard Fredrik

*See my discussion following story no. 33, pp. 100–101.

Rääf. The edition was largely due to the efforts of Afzelius (1785–1871), and it has the virtue of being taken for the most part from oral tradition; contemporary ballad collections from other parts of Europe depended heavily on uncritical use of manuscripts. A few of Rääf's texts were included in Afzelius's edition, but most of them were only published, along with some other material, in the edition of A. I. Arwidsson, *Svenska fornsånger* ("Ancient Swedish Songs"), 1834–42. Afzelius was also responsible for some of the earliest printing of legends and folktales, which he employed in part of his massive *Swenska folkets sago-häfder* ("Legendary History of the Swedish People"), in nine volumes, 1844–68. However, most scholars regard that work as too deficient in source criticism and basic annotation to be of much value.

Scientific collection and printing of Swedish prose traditions, and indeed perhaps the modern study of folklore in Sweden, begins with Gunnar Olof Hyltén-Cavallius (1818–89), the subject of a study by Nils-Arvid Bringéus, *Gunnar Olof Hyltén-Cavallius som etnolog: en studie kring Wärend och wirdarne* (Stockholm, 1966). First inspired by the ballad collection of Afzelius and Geijer, Hyltén-Cavallius began collecting ballads in the late 1830s, and in 1853 he and the Englishman George Stephens, an antiquarian who left his mark on many aspects of Nordic philology and folklore, published a collection entitled *Sveriges historiska och politiska visor* ("Historical and Political Ballads of Sweden"). The two also collaborated on Sweden's first important edition of wonder-tales (fairy-tales), *Svenska folksagor och äfventyr* ("Swedish Fairy-Tales"), of which the first volume appeared in 1844 and the second in 1849. The remainder of the collection remained unpublished until 1937–42. Influenced as it was by the contemporary editions of Asbjørnsen and Moe in Norway and Christian Molbech in Denmark, and by the Grimms' pioneering collection (the first volume was dedicated to them), *Svenska folksagor och äfventyr* follows the practice of presenting the content of the field recording unchanged but leaving its form in the hands of the editor. A truly gifted stylist like Asbjørnsen could create a work of lasting beauty and great significance for the development of the Norwegian language, primarily through his use of contemporary spoken forms and the consequent break with the fixed Danish writing tradition in Norway, but Hyltén-Cavallius chose a different direction and his deliberately archaic style never appealed to popular taste. Besides collecting himself, Hyltén-Cavallius relied on reports from others in the field, and one of his more important reporters was Sven Sederström, from whose pen we have story no. 58, "The Blind Sea Captain," intended for publication in the abandoned *Svenska folksagor och äfventyr.*

Hyltén-Cavallius also published important editions of riddles and proverbs, and his greatest work, the massive *Wärend och wirdarne,* is nothing less than an attempt at a complete ethnography of Värend, his native district, and its inhabitants. Work on this project lasted more than a quarter of a century and included, seemingly near the beginning, the collection of a number of legends from Värend and elsewhere, probably under the inspiration of the earliest Nordic legend collection, that of the Dane, J. M. Thiele, *Danske folkesagn* ("Danish Folk Legends"). An edition, "Folksägner från Värend," was prepared, but it remained unpublished until 1968, serving as a sort of draft for parts of *Wärend och wirdarne.* Two of these legends from "Folksägner från Värend" have been included in this book, stories no. 27 and 54, and some attempt has been made to capture in the translation the wordy and sometimes archaic literary style in which Hyltén-Cavallius dresses the tales.

Although he refashioned his tales according to definite literary aims, a practice followed by nearly all editors of wondertales in Sweden, Hyltén-Cavallius also left a harbinger for the future more scientific collecting that was to begin in the late nineteenth century. This was his doctoral dissertation, *Vocabularium vaerendicum,* defended at Uppsala in the late 1830s. This study of the local dialect of Värend shows that even at the onset of modern scholarship in Sweden the study of local dialects was already linked with the study of folklore. Indeed, the link was common to most of the early Scandinavian folklorists, not just Swedes. It comes forth clearly, for example, in the collection of short biographies of Scandinavian folklore pioneers, edited by Dag Strömbäck, *Leading Folklorists of the North* (Oslo, 1971; reprint of *Arv,* 25–26 [1969–71]). Today the fields have been split, but the historical association between them is attested by the housing of both linguistic and folkloristic records in a single archive at Uppsala, Landsmåls- och Folkminnets-Arkivet ("The Dialect and Folklore Archives"); and the Gustav Adolf Academy for Research in Popular Lore (Gustav Adolfs Akademi för Folklivsforskning), the most important such body in Sweden, encompasses both linguists and folklorists. The linking of the two subjects had significant consequences for the collection of folklore, since collection of dialect materials required painstaking accuracy. As a result, word-for-word collecting, with close attention to phonological, morphological, and syntactic detail, became the rule within the scholarly community. The central organ for the publication of such material was a journal with the ambitious title *Nyare Bidrag till Kännedom om de Svenska Landsmålen och Svenskt Folklif* ("More Recent Contributions to the Knowledge of the Swedish Dialects and Swedish Folklife"), usually shortened to *Svenska Landsmål.* It began publication in 1878 under the direction of J. A. Lundell, a young linguist who had worked out the alphabet used to record Swedish dialects. The early numbers of this journal contain a great many recordings of Swedish oral legend tradition, containing just what the informant said, no more and no less, in his own words and using his own dialect. Clearly this is a necessity for folktale research, and it is a tribute to the young Swedish scholars of the late nineteenth century that they put it into effect relatively early and despite the opposition of established folklorists like Nils Gabriel Djurklou, who was supported by the most famous folklorists from Denmark and Norway, Svend Grundtvig and Asbjørnsen. Indeed, it was in a review of an edition of folktales by Djurklou, *Sagor och äfventyr, berättade på landsmål* ("Fairy Tales, Narrated in Dialect"), that the principle of word-for-word presentation of folktales was first articulated in Sweden. The reviewer, Vilhelm Wadman, writing not surprisingly in *Svenska Landsmål* (6: smärre meddelanden [1885], pp. xxxvi–xlii), praises the tone and style of the collection but notes that these are the work of Djurklou, not his informants, and therefore are a kind of falsification. Only a true word-for-word rendition is acceptable as a true representation of oral tradition.

The study of folktales had entered the university, and one result was greatly increased possibilities for collection. Previously workers like Hyltén-Cavallius had worked largely independently, occasionally utilizing friends or family as reporters in the field but for the most part doing all their collecting alone. Now students were organized to collect when in their home districts on vacation, and a system of more or less permanent reporters was set up in certain circumstances in some areas. The material from this collecting, in some cases still ongoing, was housed in the various archives, the most important being those at Uppsala, Lund, Göteborg, and the Nordic Museum in Stockholm, and these offer the patient researcher a tolerably complete picture of Swedish folktale tradition. They are described by Carl-Herman Tillhagen, "Folklore Archives in Sweden," *Journal of the Folklore Institute*, 1 (1964), 20–36.

Individual items in these vast repositories of tradition each represent a "performance," a telling of the tale (or proverb, riddle, bit of folk belief, etc.) by the informant to the collector. Background information is regularly limited to the name, date, place of birth, and residence of the informant, the date and location of the collecting, and the name of the collector. For linguistic purposes these data are sufficient, since they place the informant's dialect and idiolect into perspective. For the folklorist, however, they may be insufficient, since they omit the extra-textual factors of context and the non-linguistic "texture" of the text (the terms are from Alan Dundes, "Texture, Text and Context," *Southern Folklore Quarterly*, 28 [1964], 251–265). The ordinary collecting situation is often far removed from the dynamics of narrative tradition, and the dynamics of that tradition are simply not recorded in the archives, large as they are. Since legend tradition of the sort recorded in this book is for all practical purposes extinct in present-day Sweden, we can do no more than regret our loss and restrict ourselves, as Swedish folklorists traditionally have, to the texts themselves, in printed form.

Perhaps as a result of the practical need of classification for archiving, Swedish folklorists have taken a leading role in the discussion concerning genre divisions and terminology, with the result that a sometimes confusing plethora of terms and distinctions has evolved. Much of the debate is of purely academic interest, but an understanding of some of the more important terminology and generic distinctions is helpful in understanding the legend traditions that fill this book.

A first basic distinction among prose traditions is that between wonder-tale (also called fairy-tale, *Märchen*, and occasionally folktale) and legend, perceived as early as by Jakob Grimm. As he saw, the distinction had to be relative: "Das Märchen ist poetischer, die Sage historischer." The wonder-tale is more "poetic"; that is, it makes regular use of the fantastic and fabulous, exaggeration, abrupt transitions, magic, surprise endings, and so forth. Although the fairy-tales of English tradition are not directly from oral tradition, they offer a good approximation of some of the tales of the best narrators. We should stress, however, that these tales were told by and for adults, and only made their way secondarily into the nursery.

The legend is, according to Grimm, more "historic" than the wonder-tale. This is true, but not in the way Grimm meant it. For him, and for many other early nineteenth-century folklorists, legends were relics of earlier eras, rather like archaeological artifacts, which if interpreted correctly held the key to a people's history. Today no one would doubt that legends sometimes do contain material that is anomalous because retained from an earlier cultural stage; but the legends themselves are told because they are relevant to the culture of the storyteller and his listeners. Legends are "more historical" because some of them are believed to be true by the tradition-bearers. As a consequence, they appear far less fabulous and do not tend to appeal to the fantastic. Excesses of style are uncommon, although good narrators may tell legends, particularly migratory legends, in a style quite like that they use for wonder-tales. Legends also tend to be shorter and less complex than wonder-tales, and the average Swedish legend, at least as it was collected in tradition or reported from the field, fills no more than half a printed page and would not require more than a few moments to tell.

The distinction between wonder-tale and legend is discussed by Stith Thompson, *The Folktale* (New York, 1946), pp. 7–10, and is explicit in the discussion of Max Lüthi, *Märchen*, 5 Aufl., Sammlung Metzler, 16 (Stuttgart, 1964) and Lutz Röhrich, *Sage*, 2 Aufl., Sammlung Metzler, 55 (Stuttgart, 1971). Important essays by Nordic scholars are gathered in C. W. von Sydow, ed., *Folksägner och folksagor*, Nordisk Kultur, 9B (Stockholm, 1931), including von Sydow's classic "Om folkets sägner" (pp.

96–112). A similar, more recent collection is by Anna Birgitta Rooth, ed., *Folkdikt och folktro,* Handböcker i etnologi (Lund, 1973). A useful essay by Rooth is "Saga och sägen," in her *Lokalt och globalt* 1 (Lund, 1969). Definition and systematization are discussed by Carl-Herman Tillhagen, "Was ist eine Sage? Eine Definition und ein Vorschlag für ein europäisches Sagensystem," in G. Ortutay, ed., *Tagung der Sagenkommission der International Society for Folk-Narrative Research, Budapest, 14–16 Oktober, 1963 (Acta Ethnographica Academiae Scientiarum Hungaricae,* 13: 1–4 [1964], 9–17).

Legends are themselves a vast group and must be subdivided, as they exhibit such variety in tradition. Closest to the wonder-tales are the so-called migratory legends, generally the longest of legends, sometimes approaching the wonder-tales in length, but dealing with situations more or less familiar to the tradition-bearers in contexts familiar to their culture. What makes them migratory is the fact that, like wonder-tales, they exist in several variants widely diffused in time and space. This suggests a definite geographic and temporal development for each of these migratory legends; in the case of Scandinavia, nearly all must have come from the south. It should be stressed, however, that once a legend has been accepted locally in a given tradition, it may become quite localized; that is, it may be told as having happened to a person known to the tradition-bearers in a place known locally to them.

Since each migratory legend tends to follow a given plot whose basic components are more or less stable, it is possible to categorize them and establish for each an archetype or standard form. This has been carried out by Reidar Th. Christiansen, using Norwegian legends: *The Migratory Legends: A Proposed List of the Types with a Systematic Catalogue of the Norwegian Variants,* FFC, 175 (Helsinki, 1958). The numbering begins with 3000, taking up where the standard catalogue of wonder-tales, originally compiled by Antti Aarne and now used in the revised English translation of Stith Thompson, *The Types of the Folktale,* FFC, 184 (Helsinki, 1961), leaves off. Given the basic homogeneity of legend tradition within Scandinavia, Christiansen's catalogue is reasonably helpful in the study of Swedish texts, and ML numbers have been indicated where relevant in this volume. The broad categories covered in this catalogue are:

(1) The Black Book of Magic. The Experts; (2) Witches and Witchcraft; (3) Legends of the Human Soul, of Ghosts and Revenants; (4) Spirits of Rivers, Lakes, and the Sea; (5) Trolls and Giants; (6) The Fairies; (7) Domestic Spirits; and (8) Local Legends of Places, Events, and Persons. These categories give a rough indication of the kinds of material included in migratory legend tradition.

Opposed to migratory legends are local legends, which lack the means and/or motivation to travel from one place to the next as complete tales, although the motifs composing them migrate. The most obvious example of local legends is provided by etiological legends—that is, those which explain a local place name, a feature of the landscape, a custom, or a belief. Obviously, local legends are similar throughout the world, but the similarity is due more to polygenesis than to migration. Few true local legends have been included in this book, for the simple reason that they depend so strongly for their appeal on local knowledge or conditions, but the opening tales, dealing with investigation of the environment, might be classified as local legends and give at least some idea of the genre.

Not all legends which explain things are local legends. Any legend and most wonder-tales may be made explanatory simply by adding an etiological slant. In Sweden the migratory legend "Ljungby Horn and Pipe," ML 6045, stories nos. 35 and 36, is frequently used to explain the decline of the giants or trolls locally, and many tales about giants are used to explain local features of the landscape, physical and cultural. Story no. 22, "A Giant Builds a Church," for example, is very often told to explain the origin of the local church, but it is one of the more widespread migratory legends in Scandinavia.

The distinction between migratory and local legends is, then, in one sense not applicable to the bulk of the traditions in Swedish oral culture and in this book. Legends are often migratory in that they exist in variants diffused throughout all or part of the country, and they are local in that they are always tied to the culture of the tradition. The characters are often known personally to the tradition-bearers or were known to their parents or grandparents. If not, they bear names like those of the tradition-bearers and live the same sort of life the tradition-bearers live. What happens to the characters in legends might happen to anyone in the culture, and it is this possibility that gives the legends their relevance. They may tell of local eccentrics, the history of local families, the participation of local men in recent wars, the journey of a local person to the big city, or other unusual or noteworthy events. Many of them describe meetings with the beings of folk belief, with nature-beings or witches, ghosts, or the like. I have emphasized such legends in this book primarily because they are the most studied and because they relate to the areas of folk belief most likely to be of interest to a non-Swedish audience.

Legends detailing encounters with beings of the other world presuppose belief in the existence of these beings and the possibility of encountering them, and Swedish folklorists have made many worthy contributions to the study of the relationship between folk belief and legend. C. W. von Sydow, holder of the first chair in folklore and ethnography at Lund, was an important pioneer whose influence is still felt strongly today. In 1934 in a famous essay, "Kategorien der Prosavolksdichtung" (reprinted in his *Selected Papers on Folklore* [Copenhagen, 1948], pp. 60–88), he coined the term *memorate,* which is distinct from a legend of a supernatural experience. A memorate contains no elements of fiction and is outside of legend tradition. It may be repeated by close friends or family members of the person whose experience it relates, but it will only enter tradition if it has the strength and inherent interest to appeal to others. If a memorate enters tradition, the rules of tradition quickly come into force: extraneous material is eliminated, possible contradictions with general folk belief are removed, motifs traditionally adhering to the particular belief complex of the experience are added, and the result is a traditional legend. Two important papers dealing with the distinction between legend and memorate are Gunnar Granberg, "Memorat und Sage: einige methodische Gesichtspunkte," *Saga och Sed,* 1935, pp. 120–127, and Juha Pentikäinen, "Grenzprobleme zwischen Memorat und Sage," *Temenos,* 3 (1968), 136–167.

Von Sydow also was the first to champion the theory, still followed in its essentials, that supernatural experiences result from actualization of folk beliefs during dreams, hallucinations, or fatigue, or during periods when an individual is under stress. A recent paper by the Finnish folklorist Lauri Honko offers a model for such experiences and the memorates which result from them ("Memorates and the Study of Folk Belief," *Journal of the Folklore Institute*, 1 (1964), 5–19; c.f. Lauri Honko, *Geisterglaube in Ingermanland*, FFC, 185 [Helsinki, 1962]). The basic requirements for a supranormal experience are reduced sensory perception and/or psychic stress; a person wandering lost at night in the woods, for example, would have both. The experience begins when some sensory stimulus is only partially observed. It becomes supranormal if the subject complements the partial stimulus with an internal stimulus leading to interpretation of the object as a supernatural being. The internal stimuli used to complement partial external stimuli are drawn from the sum of experiences undergone by the individual and the traditional beliefs of his culture, which together Honko calls the frame of reference. The frame of reference dictates which beings are encountered, when they are encountered, and their appearance. A Swedish peasant would, for example, be unlikely to see a troll wearing a tuxedo seated at the dinner table, but wandering lost in the woods he might well see several shabby, slightly sinister-looking beings he would know were trolls. The psychic stress is another important factor in the supernatural experience. The wanderer lost in the woods sees nature-beings, the farm hand mistreating the horses sees domestic spirits, and the card shark sees the devil. The resulting description of the encounter, reinforced by discussion with others familiar with the tradition, is a memorate. A traditionalized account lacking first-person immediacy is a legend, and the path from one to the other would seem to be fairly clear. In the notes for certain of the stories printed here, e.g. no. 64, "The Tomte's Favorite Horse," I have provided a brief sketch of the application of the model.

What was this frame of reference like? The stories themselves provide the best indication, but a brief general survey of beliefs touching on the texts chosen may be useful. Those desiring further reading are directed to Nils Lid, ed., *Folketru*, Nordisk Kultur, 19 (Stockholm, 1935), in particular the essay by von Sydow, "Övernaturliga väsen" (pp. 95–159). A collection of recent essays on supernatural beings is Åke Hultkranz, ed., *The Supernatural Owners of Nature* (Stockholm, 1961).

The texts in the first portions of the present book relate directly to "This World," the world of the tradition-bearers.

Nos. 1 and 2, which describe attempts to investigate the physical environment, imply that such investigation is a dangerous proposition and further indicate that some things are best left alone. Such a belief is fairly typical of traditional societies and is at once a cause and effect of stability.

The texts in no. 3, "Delsbo's Churchbell," are included primarily to indicate the persistence of individual legends through generations of oral tradition and to give some idea of the effects of that tradition on the texts which pass through it. It is, however, also a good example of a local "historical" tradition, and it demonstrates how history is reformulated according to traditional rules and folk belief.

Fate and portents were a favorite subject of legends and have obviously been so for many centuries. Predestination could invite a kind of stoicism, and such stoicism might be helpful in the face of adversity. Portents have a large role to play in any pre-scientific society, although a desire to see into the future has hardly been limited to such societies. Methods of seeing the future are widespread, and in Sweden almost any occurrence in the least bit out of the ordinary might be regarded as an omen. I have included here accounts which relate more obviously to the supernatural, since they provide an interesting parallel to other legends of supranormal experiences, but almost any action could be interpreted, if only one knew how. In practice, difficult cases of interpretation were routinely given to those with special powers who were known as *de kloka*; the literal translation of "the wise ones" hardly begins to indicate their powers. They were the local experts on almost everything not associated with material culture or the church, including illness, prophecy, magic, and a great many other important factors. Traditionally "the wise ones" were regarded positively and were accorded friendship and trust, as opposed to Finns and Lapps, who shared some of their powers but were outsiders and hence potentially dangerous. The ability to have visions, apparently possessed, for example, by the woman known to the informant of story no. 9, "Portent from the Nissar," was a frequent characteristic of the wise ones.

Besides illustrating a world view, legends helped reinforce it, and nowhere is this clearer than in legends used didactically. The view of fate, for example, was that it was inexorable, a view which accords well with the socially positive notion that one must not shirk one's duty or place, whatever it may be. Of the many legends illustrating this belief, story no. 5, "Twelve Children on a Platter," is perhaps the most striking. A great number of the others also have at least implicit didactic power, in that they pose standards of behavior for various situations.

The few legends of the great plague included here illustrate several factors, among them folk beliefs about disease, retention of historical events in oral narrative, and traditional attitudes toward catastrophe. The legends usually refer to the Black Death of the mid-fourteenth century, which harried the population in Scandinavia, as elsewhere, with awesome ferocity. However, the disease was a fairly common visitor, and during its last sojourn in Sweden, in 1710–11, it carried off around fifteen percent of the population. Thereafter other epidemics, of diseases like typhus and cholera, helped people retain the terror that accompanied every dangerous epidemic. Perhaps for that reason, plague legends have retained their currency and sense of immediacy. See further Carl-Herman Tillhagen, "Sägner och folktro kring pesten," *Fataburen*, 1967, pp. 215–230.

If epidemic represented the invisible threat to life always posed by the environment, buried treasure represented the riches it offered. To an impoverished rural population treasure must have offered a strong inducement to fantasy, and buried treasure legends made up a regular part of the legend inventory in virtually all parts of the country, as attested by Tobias Norlind, *Skattsägner* (Lund, 1918). One may speculate that they rose with the middle class, currency, and consumer products, but they must always have been a kind of escape literature. A concession to reality is that in most of them the treasure remains buried, or at least out of the hands of the human hero; this should be compared to the traditional ending of the wonder-tale, where the hero winds up with a fortune of half the kingdom. That treasures were so often associated with beings of the other world, even, not infrequently, with dragons, is further indication of their ultimate role in fantasy.

The legends in the second portion of the book I have termed those of the other world, by which I mean the world of the nature-beings. As the tales themselves demonstrate, this world is essentially the one in which the tradition-bearers live, and the term "other world" must therefore not be understood as referring to some sort of never-never land on the far side of the rainbow. It is, rather, the "other" world of the tradition-bearers, the part of their own world they know least well, including mysterious places like deep forests, mountains, graveyards, and watercourses. Under certain circumstances even familiar ground may become unfamiliar and "other." Such circumstances would include darkness, bad or stormy weather, the period following a birth or death, the evening of great holidays, the visit of a stranger, or virtually anything else out of the ordinary. Under these circumstances, or at almost any time out on the periphery of their environment, belief in nature-beings might be actualized, and for that reason I sometimes refer to such beings as otherworldly beings or simply otherworlders.

Traditionally regarded as the oldest among them are the giants (Swedish *jätte,* plural *jättar*). In most areas they seem to be regarded as the generation preceding the current nature-beings one is likely to encounter, having been driven off either by lightning bolts (a relic of Thor the giant-killer in Old Norse mythology?) or by the coming of Christianity. Personal encounters with giants are rare, the stories tending rather to fall into two basic categories. The first is the purely entertaining migratory legend, stressing either the giant's size or his lack of wit, and the second is an origin legend ascribing some feature of the physical landscape, ordinarily a rather large one, to the activities of some primeval giant. Typical is the *jättekast* or "giant's toss," describing how a giant threw a large boulder at something, thus accounting for the boulder's present location. More extensive labors are also posited, however, such as the construction of a church. In areas where for one reason or another active giant belief still lived, giants might play any of the roles ordinarily taken by other nature-beings, as demonstrated by story no. 16, "The Giant from Klasahall." The standard work on giants remains that of C. W. von Sydow, "Jättarna i mytologi och folktro," *FmFt,* 6 (1919), 52–96, which stresses their role in modern tradition as those who, long ago, helped form certain aspects of the physical environment. Secondary impulses for popular fantasy included their large size and their occasional good or bad relations with men, presumably long ago, all of which have been included in legends. For further discussion, not based on Swedish traditions, see John R. Broderius, *The Giant in Germanic Tradition* (Chicago, 1932), and Valerie Höttges, *Typenverzeichnis der deutschen Riesen- und riesischen Teufelssagen*, FFC, 122 (Helsinki, 1937).

Scholarly tradition agrees with popular tradition that giants are old. They are the *jötnar* (sing. *jötunn*) of Old Norse, and they were found in England as well, where the Old English term is *eoten*. Although it has not been exempt from challenge, the standard etymology has it that the term is related to the verb "eat," and hence that the term originally meant something like "eater, devourer," a meaning clearly not relevant to the modern usage of the term.

Also found in Old Norse are the trolls, one of the major groups of otherworldly beings in recent Swedish tradition. Swedish *troll* (Neuter; plural *troll*) is of uncertain etymology but is certifiably ancient, showing attestations in Old Swedish manuscripts from the Middle Ages. Although belief varies from area to area, in general trolls are those nature-beings who live farthest from human habitation, usually with some form of social organization; this distinguishes them from solitary beings like the *rå* and *näck*. Unlike their counterparts in the illustrations accompanying modern editions of fairy-tales, the trolls of Swedish popular belief were no larger than normal and generally not of hideous appearance. They looked very much like the men and women one knew, the primary differentiating factors being that one did *not* know them and that they were not Christian. As a result they were ultimately dangerous, however well they seemed to get along with the Christian community on any given occasion. Story no. 29, "Communion Wine in the Troll Food," shows just how antithetical Christianity and the trolls were thought to be. The stories chosen here emphasize several sorts of threats against humans, including overrunning a farm, changing, and *bergtagning* ("kidnapping"). Overrunning a farm or household provides one of the older story patterns in Germanic story tradition and may be traced at least as far back as the Old English epic *Beowulf*, where the monster Grendel's visits make the splendid hall Heorot stand empty out of fear. In modern tradition the overrunning is usually done by collective beings; in Norway it is the *oskorei*, in Sweden the trolls, and Christmas Eve is the time favored for their visits. Just as the poem *Beowulf* emphasizes not the harryings of Grendel but the cleansing of the hall by Beowulf, so the modern tales stress the moment when the trolls are driven off. Of the two tales below concerning such visits, one, no. 24, "Trolls Take Over the Farm," describes the use of traditional Christian means to drive off the non-Christian trolls, and is evidently closer to folk belief than the following "The Bear Trainer and the Trolls," an international migratory legend with a humorous intent. Tales of changing show a similar variety, ranging from the straightforward no. 26, "Beating the Changeling," through the humorous migratory legend no. 27, "The Changeling Speaks on the Way to Baptism," to the chilling no. 28, "Changing a Housewife." As mentioned above (p. 12), belief in changing has its origins in abnormal or deformed children, whose condition was blamed on the trolls.

Another tragedy blamed on the trolls was *bergtagning*, literally "taking into the mountain"; a person was *bergtagen* (adjective) if he or she was thought to have been kidnapped by the trolls. In most cases, of course, the person was probably lost somewhere in the nearby woods or mountains, not an uncommon occurrence among a rural population whose density was among the smaller in Europe and who lived in a land rich in thick forests, with occasional forbidding mountains. Once a person had become lost, any number of factors contributed to a belief in *bergtagning*. The victim himself, wandering hungry and frightened in unfamiliar territory, was under the sort of psychic stress likely to lead to a supranormal experience, and interest dominance would lead to activation of the belief in trolls and their dwelling places in the mountain. Strong visions, hallucinations, or dreams might easily beset the wanderer and would be all too realistic. Those at home, meanwhile, would traditionally attribute the wanderer's tardiness to the trolls, and then would counter with the strongest power they had, the power of Christianity, and would vigorously ring the churchbells. This was supposed to break the power of the trolls, but in reality it surely provided a means of orientation for the wanderer if he was within earshot, and thus helped him to find his way home. Once he had returned, his recounting of any encounters he may have experienced with the trolls would be added to the evidence demonstrating *bergtagning*. Furthermore, any lasting infirmities, such as lameness (from a fall) or lack of wits (from hunger or fear) would also be blamed on the trolls. Story no. 32, "Stealing for the Trolls," demonstrates such a case, and additionally blames altered behavior (stealing) on the influence of the trolls. Given a firm belief in *bergtagning,* imaginative narrative was able to assign a more active role to the trolls, and in some tales of *bergtagning* they are said to come to the village or household and drag off the victim, in some cases with a fierce struggle, as in story no. 30, "Bergtagen."

Trolls are a sort of all-purpose otherworldly being, equivalent, for example, to fairies in Anglo-Celtic traditions. They therefore appear in various migratory legends where collective nature-beings are called for. Two of these, represented here, are the so-called "Pan-legend" and "Ljungby Horn and Pipe," the tale of retrieving the cup. The two demonstrate the fluidity of characters in migratory legends: trolls and cats alternate in stories nos. 33–34, trolls and "little people" in 35–36. For the "little people" in story no. 36, "Retrieving the Cup," I have employed the term *vättar,* which is used in South Sweden for certain underground beings very much like trolls. Similar beings in the north are called *vittror.* By and large, however, such differences are primarily terminological and are significant only in certain cases.

Important works on trolls and similar beings are Elisabeth Hartmann, *Die Trollvorstellungen in den Sagen und Märchen der skandinavischen Völker,* Tübinger Germanistische Arbeiten, 23 (Stuttgart-Berlin, 1936); H. F. Feilberg, *Bjærgtagen,* Danmarks Folkeminder, 5 (Copenhagen, 1910); J. S. Møller, *Moder og barn i dansk folkeoverlevering,* Danmarks Folkeminder, 48 (Copenhagen, 1940), 233–260; Ella Ohlson, "Naturväsen i ångermanländsk folktro," *FmFt,* 20 (1933), 70–112.

In a survey of nature-beings in Swedish folk belief intended for field workers, C. W. von Sydow stressed the basic difference between collective beings and solitary beings ("Naturväsen: en översikt till ledning för samlare," *FmFt,* 11 [1924], 33–48). Giants, trolls, *vättar* and *vittror* are all essentially collective beings who inhabit nature. They have families, farms, and human foibles; they work their land, tend their cattle, and brew their beer just as their human neighbors do. By contrast, certain solitary beings inhabit nature without families or ordinary households, although some do pursue ordinary household affairs and own cattle which is occasionally sighted by humans. These solitary beings tend to be defined exclusively by their place of residence: forest, lake, or stream. Foremost among them is the *skogsrå* (plural *skogsrån*).

The term *rå* refers to a solitary nature-being or spirit and is often affixed to a term of location: *skogsrå,* for example, uses the word *skog* "forest" as its first component and refers to a forest being; *sjörå* uses *sjö* "lake" and refers to a water being; and *gårdsrå* uses *gård* "farm" and refers to a household spirit. The most likely etymology for *rå* associates it with the root of the verb *råda* ("counsel, decide") and suggests that the term originally meant "the ruling one," or something of the kind. Another etymology postulates a development from "boundary marker" to "being or spirit tied to a specific locality." Whatever the etymology, in recent tradition the *rå* is generally regarded as a female figure, usually rather attractive, with jurisdiction over a specific area of nature. The *skogsrå* was strongly represented in all parts of Sweden except the north, where a similar figure was said to be one of the *vittror.* The *skogsrå* appears in many sorts of narratives, ranging from stark memorates to elaborated migratory legends. One of her more dangerous attributes was the ability to lead people astray when they were out in the forest, her domain, and anyone who lost his way in otherwise familiar territory could be fairly certain that he was dealing with the *skogsrå.* Sometimes the victim might witness the *skogsrå* in a supranormal experience; on other occasions she could remain invisible, but even then the victim's confusion would be ascribed to her. When the *skogsrå* was encountered, memorates were likely to stress her physical beauty, and scholars have been quick to point out that this is a tradition created and passed by men, frequently by men whose work caused them to spend long periods of time in isolation at their work in the forest. Under such circumstances it is not surprising that some experienced erotic fantasies, and that these were molded by tradition into a more or less unified body of belief about the *skogsrå.* She granted success in hunting and help in such activities as charcoal burning, her price generally being no more than a place in the man's bed. Since such encounters were experienced as reality, the human victims must sometimes have experienced feelings of guilt and remorse, and so a popular subject of *skogsrå* legends was how to rid oneself of a *skogsrå* with whom one had had an erotic liaison. Here the migratory legend ML 6000, "Tricking the Fairy Suitor," was frequently employed; it tells of a man who pried from his *skogsrå* lover an herbal formula against which no supernatural being has erotic power. This he did by tricking her into believing she was advising him about one of his cows who was being bothered by a supernatural bull. Other methods, described in stories nos. 38 and 41, were more direct, since they simply involved leaving the *skogsrå* behind somewhere or shooting her. Stories nos. 42 and 43 are more entertaining accounts of encounters with the *skogsrå*. In no. 42, "A Rude Awakening," the sexual implications of the meeting have been subordinated to the *skogsrå*'s ability to change the outward appearance of things in the forest. No. 43, "Tricking a Christian," seems to provide the *skogsrå* with a motivation for her amorous adventures with the Christian community, a motivation based ultimately on hostility. As in so many entertaining and somewhat humorous accounts of such encounters, the quick-witted hero emerges safe from his brush with the other world.

The most notable work on the *skogsrå* has been done by Gunnar Granberg. Most important are his "Skogsrået: en folkminnesgeografisk orientering," *Rig*, 1933, pp. 145–197, and *Skogsrået i yngre nordisk folktradition*, SKGAAF, 3 (Uppsala, 1935). All of the *skogsrå* stories in this book have been taken from the latter.

In certain parts of Sweden, primarily the south and southwest, the *skogsrå* is regarded as the quarry of the supernatural hunter in tales of the wild hunt. Most scholars accept that beliefs in the wild hunt, popular in Scandinavia and Germany, derive from the noises of nature, either flocks of birds or the wind whistling in the treetops. Typical of such beliefs in Norway is the *oskorei*, a wicked band of spirits, sometimes regarded as the dead, rushing about on important holiday evenings. Sometimes they kidnap innocent victims, who are badly treated during their wild ride; a few do not survive. In Sweden (and Denmark) the conceptions are somewhat different, in that they focus on a single spirit who is ordinarily said to hunt the beings of the other world. Here the international migratory legend ML 5060, "The Fairy Hunter," is applied (story no. 45, "The Woman Was Tied Behind the Horse by Her Braids").

Just as the *skogsrå* has jurisdiction over the forest, so a water spirit holds sway over water. The most important water spirit is the *näck,* usually regarded as a solitary male being living in and ruling a specific watercourse. Two important conceptions regarding this being are manifested in stories, namely his musicality and his taking on the form of a horse and interacting with the human community. His musicality is commonly regarded by scholars as a derivation from the splashings and gurglings of the brooks in which he usually lives, which has been carried over to the music of the tradition, usually dance music played on a fiddle. Many fine musicians were said to have learned to play from the *näck,* as exemplified by story no. 49, "The Strömkarl at Garphytte," an international migratory legend which somewhat humorously denies full competence to the learner, who only masters tuning his instrument. Because of his association with music, the *näck* has been drawn into two other important story complexes, the ceaseless dance, of which story no. 46, "The Näck's Reel," is an example, and the nature-being's desire to enter the Christian community (no. 50, "The Näck Longs for Salvation"). The ceaseless dance complex was for the most part used didactically, with the devil as the musician, and at this point in narrative tradition the *näck* and the devil approach one another closely. As a result, the *näck* is sometimes found in other stories characteristic of the devil, and the expression *ta mig näcken* ("*näck* take me") evidently employs a euphemism for Satan. Such identification with the devil contrasts sharply with the melancholy being who wails with grief at the news that he has been denied eternal salvation; such a conception is based on the theological notion that the nature-beings are fallen angels.

The term *näck,* related to Greek, Sanskrit, and Old Irish verbs meaning "wash," is well attested among the older Germanic languages and even at such early stages shows association with water monsters, particularly those with the form of a horse. Old High German attests *nihhus* ("crocodile"), and Old English *niccor* may mean both "water monster" and "hippopotamus," apparently with the etymological sense of the latter, namely "river horse," a sense which Icelandic *nykur* has retained. Thus an association of the *näck* with horses is ancient and well established. Two sorts of stories accrue to this association, those in which the *näck* is a workhorse and those in which humans ride him. The latter seem to be centered in the south, where a white horse called a *bäckahäst* ("brook-horse") replaces the *näck*. In some areas riding the *näck* leads to disaster, but for the most part the riders are not carried off helpless into the stream, but manage to escape, as in story no. 48, "Riding the Bäckahäst." The *näck* as workhorse is common in many areas of Scandinavia, and stories about this subject tend more toward memorates than more elaborate legends. One assumes that such stories reflect the occasional use of a strange or wild horse; perhaps, too, wish fulfillment of overworked farmers is involved. See story no. 47, "The Näck Pulls the Plow."

Another sea creature, about whom conceptions tended to be less specific than those about the *näck*, was the *sjörå*. The term is a compound noun composed of *sjö* ("lake, sea") and *rå* ("supernatural being"). The *sjörå* may inhabit any body of water, including an ocean, and may be either male or female, although females tend to predominate. The *sjörå* lacks the *näck*'s association with music and horses and tends rather to fall into patterns typical of the *skogsrå* and other nature-beings. If treated respectfully, she may help her human neighbors, as in stories 52–53, where she warns of an impending storm. Warnings of this nature represent the most common sort of help offered by the *sjörå*, who shows far less tendency to involve herself in the day-to-day activities of the humans with whom she occasionally comes into contact than does the *skogsrå*, who sometimes helps men burn charcoal. Like the *skogsrå*, however, the *sjörå* has jurisdiction over the "game" of the sea, and she helps in fishing just as the *skogsrå* helps (or interferes) in hunting. Perhaps the unwillingness of the *sjörå* to become involved in the everyday lives of men is due to the degree of isolation imposed by her element, the sea, as opposed to the greater intimacy of the forest.

Not all *sjörån* are female, however. Males tend to be more like trolls, and like trolls they can be both benign and threatening. Story no. 54, "The Sjörå in Helgasjön," for example, tells of a lake troll who nearly drags the human protagonist and his boat down to a certain doom. No. 58, "The Blind Sea Captain," on the other hand, describes in some detail the undersea residence of a rather friendly if reserved *sjörå* with vast holdings on the sea bottom. The brooding threat to the humans, however, which lurks just under the surface of the story, is realized in the end when the *sjörå* at last takes the captain's eyesight. And positive interaction between the human and sea-troll community, including intermarriage, was apparently also possible, as demonstrated by the sea figure called Håvålen, known in most of the coastal regions around Göteborg, who lived a full and productive life among humans before returning to the sea to die (see story no. 57, "Håvålen").

There is no satisfactory general study of sea-beings in Nordic or Swedish folk tradition. Important articles treating various aspects of the problem include Maja Bergstrand, "Näcken som musikaliskt väsen," *FmFt,* 23 (1936), 14–31; Brita Egardt, "De svenska vattenhästsägnerna och deras ursprung," *Folkkultur,* 4 (1944), 119–166; and H. Fernholm, "Fiskelycka: studier över valda delar av fiskets folklore," *Folkkultur,* 3 (1943), 242–283.

As one moves closer to human habitation, otherworldly beings tend to become more friendly. Accordingly the being best disposed toward men is the household spirit, known in Sweden as the *tomte* (plural *tomtar*) or, in parts of the south, as the *nisse,* a hypercoristic form of the name Nikolas. The term *tomte* is regarded as elided from compounds whose first component is the noun *tomt* ("plot of land") and whose second component is some nature-being. Beliefs concerning the *tomte* were fairly consistent throughout Sweden, generally according with the following utterance of belief by an informant from around Karlstad in Värmland, whose identity was not stated in the printed text:

> *Tomtar* are small, wear red caps, and are usually quite shabby. They are very strong, so it is not good to cross them. They can be either a help or a nuisance. If you treat them well they can be of much use to you, but if you treat them badly they can do you much harm. If you take care of your horses and cows properly, they will help you; often you will find the feeding already done in the barn and stalls when you arrive there in the morning. But if you mistreat your cattle, they torment them, and they [the cattle] end up bony and miserable. The *tomtar* never like people to swear, get into fights or drink too much. For that reason it sometimes happens that they may give a farm hand a good box on the ears if he comes into a stall and swears or is drunk. (ULMA 42:9, pp. 235–236.

Printed in J. A. Lundell et al., "Sagor, sägner, legender, äventyr och skildringar av folkets levnadssätt på landsmål," *SvLm,* 3:2 (1881–1946), 257–258).

As this utterance clearly shows, the functional essence of belief in the *tomte* was a sort of folk conscience, which would see to it that household duties were carried out correctly and that social proprieties were not abused. Such a notion is particularly discernible in the international migratory legend represented by story no. 64, "The Tomte's Favorite Horse." It also informs a good many other legends and, particularly, memorates concerning *tomtar.* In a more abstract way it stands behind tales like story no. 60, "The Tomte Carries a Single Straw," which teach respect for the beings of the other world, a didactic point common to many stories describing encounters with the household spirits. As the *tomte* was believed to punish deviation from a social norm or moral ideal, so too he rewarded correct or proper behavior. In the service of migratory legends this belief could be put to many humorous uses, as stories nos. 61 and 62 amply demonstrate. The first, "New Clothes for the Tomte," is almost entirely humorous in intent, but may have at least some didactic value in that it reinforces social immobility. The second, however, "The Tomte Learns to Rest," shows virtually no moralizing or didactic tendency, and its humorous intent may be compared with that of story no. 18, "Save It for Tomorrow." Similar jokes are also told about the devil, and one has the impression that they are not central to folk belief, despite their wide distribution.

A feature of virtually all beings of the other world is that they are convenient scapegoats for things that go wrong in the human community. *Bergtagning,* changing, and hauntings provide the most dramatic examples. Perhaps because he is an inherently less dramatic being, the *tomte*'s role in the problems of everyday life is less dramatic, often focusing on missing tools and the like. The most important instance is his role in one's neighbor's prosperity, alluded to in particular in the memorates of story no. 59, "Encounters with Tomtar." Epic crystallization is provided by the motif of the *tomte*'s theft of a neighbor's cow. It is frequently used humorously, as in story no. 63, "The Missing Butter," but in an agrarian society like the one which used these tales it is probably difficult to exaggerate the importance of cattle, an importance attested in particular by the role of cows as the object of witchcraft.

Unlike trolls and *rån,* the *tomte* seems to be basically benevolent unless crossed. *Tomtar* who bring a neighbor prosperity are regarded as a part of the neighbor's sphere, not deliberately hostile to other neighboring farmers, merely loyal to their own masters. A case of pure benevolence is provided by the seagoing *tomte* of story no. 66, "A Ship's Tomte," who saves his "household," the ship, from a problem of very tricky navigation. Not every *tomte* is regarded with friendship or humorous tolerance, however. Certain stories, generally regarded by scholars as products of the influence of the church, tell of the casting out of the *tomte* in a way which makes it clear that in these cases at least he shares certain features with the devil. Here we are in all probability in the presence of a clash between the organized Christian faith, whose tenets were imposed from above, however widely they may have been accepted, and the conservative traditions of folk belief, whose tenacity has sometimes been astounding. In the case of the *tomte,* churchly tales like no. 65, "Exorcising the Tomte," were doomed to remain in a minority position among *tomte* beliefs, for the simple reason that belief in the *tomte* served a valuable function in society as a force which upheld norms, punished the miscreant, and rewarded the good, always using prosperity as its currency.

The standard work on Scandinavian household spirits remains H. F. Feilberg's *Nissens historie,* Danmarks Folkeminder, 18 (Copenhagen, 1918), a study primarily based on Danish sources. Rich in material, it lacks a modern perspective. There are no major Swedish contributions to the subject. Articles dealing exclusively with the Swedish *tomte* are Helmer Olsson, "Tomten i halländsk folktro," *FmFt,* 24 (1937), 100–117, a survey of regional beliefs, including several legends, and J. Ejdenstam, "Är tomten ett dragväsen?," *FmFt,* 30 (1943), 8–17.

With the *tomte* we complete the list of prominent beings of the other world in Swedish folk tradition, omitting only beings of secondary importance or regional distribution. We may now turn to the beings who frequent the third part of this book, which I have termed "The World of Religion." These beings are almost members of the human community. They mingle in it and take an active part in it. One, Satan, is always there, appearing wherever sin is practiced or implied, and that is nearly everywhere. Others, like witches, werewolves, and nightmares, live what appear to be perfectly ordinary lives in the human community, punctuated only by ventures into their secret lives of sin or devastation. Another category, the dead, are inhabitants of a limbo world between this life and the next, parallel to but separate from and threatening to the human community which they once inhabited.

Conceptions of the devil are among the most widespread, important, and complex in European folk belief, and beliefs in Sweden were just as diffuse as elsewhere. In narrative tradition it is probably simplest to distinguish two figures. The first is an awesome Satan who interferes in men's lives, encourages and abets sinful behavior, leads the Black Mass, and presides over the sometimes vividly realized eternal torment of the damned. This figure is perhaps closer to folk belief than the second, who is characteristic of international migratory legends and wondertales. This Satan, *der gute, dumme Teufel* of German tradition, is a gullible, surprisingly good-natured fellow who can be tricked easily out of his due and manipulated into any number of humorous situations.

Characteristic of both conceptions of the devil is his ability to change his shape, a commonplace of European devil lore. In Sweden as elsewhere, Satan's most common guise is that of a well-dressed but slightly sinister-looking gentleman, sometimes with the typical European features of a cloven hoof or tail. When he adopts some other, more terrifying form, in Sweden it is most likely to be that of a black dog. The power of such a vision was extensive, as text A of story no. 67, "The Devil as a Black Dog," clearly shows: the mere presence of a strange black dog at a dance is enough to remind the dancers of the potential danger of their behavior, and the dance is quickly abandoned. Text B of the same story offers a far more terrible vision, since there the hellhound actively attacks a human, apparently without moral or ethical provocation, merely because it has been kicked. This vision remains despite the edifying end of the story with an exorcism.

The essential idea of the awesome Satan of folk belief is sin, any kind of which delights him. Typical activities which attract his presence are card playing and dancing, both of which were flourishing if not officially acceptable kinds of behavior in rural

Scandinavia. Story no. 71, "The Cardplayers and the Devil," paints a particularly frightening picture of the consequences of a thoughtless utterance during a card game: Satan seizes his victim bodily and drags him off helpless, until a quick-witted hero manages a rescue. Although it may strike a modern reader as exaggerated, such a story would have had considerable didactic power in the traditional society where it was told. The tale illustrates the proverb "Mention the devil and he is there," an item of folk belief with important consequences in devil nomenclature. To avoid mention of the devil, many taboo names were common, the more frequent including Shame, Old Erik, Horn-Per, That One (the old demonstrative pronoun *hin*, usually found in the phrase *hin onde*, "the evil one"), and so forth. Otherwise he might simply be referred to as Satan or the Devil.

Like the cardplaying tales are the legends of uncontrolled dancing, nos. 68–70. In them the role of Satan varies, but his presence is always a point of departure. Dancing probably did get out of hand from time to time, and some behavior accompanying dances may have displeased the church or shocked community norms, and thus the devil's role was assured. Once again the picture is a chilling one; the helpless dancers dancing themselves to death are surely paying the price for their sins even before they leave this world.

According to tradition, Satan was interested in all sins, greater or lesser. Examples of both are provided among our texts. In story no. 72, as the title suggests, the devil advises suicide, and hence a mortal sin is at the center of the story. But few sins seem to have been too small, as we learn from story no. 73, "The Girls at the Parsonage Get Help Sewing Crinoline." As I have suggested in my note to this story, however, the sin involved here is less insignificant than it might appear at first glance, since it involved preparation for the girls' first communion, an important rite of passage. Nevertheless, the tale demonstrates the devil's willingness to involve himself in sins at various levels of importance.

Although he seems to enjoy merely being present at sinful behavior (e.g., stories nos. 67A and 77), according to folk belief the devil was an active tempter. Those who succumbed would enter into a pact with Satan; such a pact would ensure them material advancement in this world at the cost of their eternal souls in the next. Although we encounter them today primarily in literature, in the world of the rural masses of pre-industrial Europe, including Sweden, such contracts were a part of everyday life. They might, for example, explain the unwonted rise in prosperity of a neighboring farm, particularly if the farmer there were not on good terms with his neighbors or attended church only sporadically. Such a case is found in story no. 74, "Giving the Devil a Ride," which assumes a pact with the devil. Given the difficult circumstances of poverty and subsistence farming that were the lot of much of the population, it is hardly surprising that some persons decided to forego the hereafter in favor of the here and now, and so we have actual records of attempted pacts with the devil. From the eighteenth century onward, as literacy became more common, written contracts were attempted, and a few have been retained from each of the Scandinavian countries (see Bente Gullveig Alver, *Heksetro og trolddom: et studie i norsk heksevæsen* [Oslo, 1971], pp. 37–38, for samples and discussion). From Sweden the longest and most detailed contract seems to have been left by a young Uppsala student named Daniel Salthenius. It ran as follows:

> I, Daniel Salthenius, desire from you, O Devil, the following items which you shall give me in exchange for payment. 1. You shall now at this time give me a purse which shall never run out of purely minted money, and that money shall remain in my possession or in that of the one I give it to. 2. You shall grant me particular success in the world with gentlemen and ladies of high station, as well as success in hunting and fishing, so that I never return empty-handed. 3. That all the arts I already have learned, or later shall learn, I shall retain.
> 4. That I now receive from you the Black Book.
> 5. That I can become visible or invisible whenever I wish. 6. You shall also now give me that thing, whatever it may be, that has the quality, that when I have it about my person, I may immediately come to any place I name. In return I promise to serve you during my lifetime as best I can and after my death to belong to you, body and soul. Anno 1718, this I affirm with my signature and blood.

The hapless student managed to lose this contract on the way to the appointed site, a tree in his home village, and so he wrote an abbreviated one and affixed it to the tree. The next morning when he returned, Bible in hand, to fetch his purse, Black Book, and magic transport device, he was met by the authorities, who had found both contracts. He was originally doomed to death, but the sentence was later commuted to eight days imprisonment, because of extenuating circumstances. One of these was his age, said to be less than fifteen at the time of the crime. This circumstance may also explain the somewhat puerile tone of the contract and its demands. The contracts are printed, with photographs and discussion, in K. Rob. V. Wikman, "Förskriving till djävulen," *Fataburen*, 1960, pp. 193–199.

Although giving oneself to the devil was serious business in reality, in story tradition it often serves as a means of establishing a sticky situation from which a quick-witted hero can extricate himself. Of the great many stories of this nature found in Swedish narrative tradition, one has been included here. Story no. 76, "Outwitting the Devil," tells of a wise Vänern skipper who manages to save himself from Satan in a humorous fashion. In this tale the devil is a rather impotent figure who weeps tears of frustration and shakes his fist in rage. Here we are closer to the humorous Satan of the wonder-tales, represented in this collection particularly by stories nos. 77, "The Devil in the Church," and 86, "The Devil and Kitta Grå." This devil is a foil against which human weaknesses are reflected, not without sympathy and good humor.

Common to nearly all stories concerning Satan, whether they portray the helpless Satan of wonder-tales or the awesome Satan of folk belief, is the structural pattern of his defeat. That he is defeated in wonder-tales and most humorous migratory legends reflects the structural demands of these genres and need concern us no longer here. But what of the defeat of the terrifying devil, like the black dog in story no. 67B, who may threaten a human being at any time? Two factors seem to lie behind this pattern. The first is simply that a world view in which the archfiend often got his way might simply be too gloomy to find expression in story; it is this natural optimism that leads to the nearly universal structural pattern of the overcoming of evil by good. A second and perhaps more substantive matter is the origin of the devil legends in Europe. It is assumed, surely correctly, that a great many devil legends were first promulgated from the pulpit, where they served as exempla in sermons. Many, like story no. 77, "The Devil in the Church," have become completely humorous and entertaining in modern tradition, but all are founded on the basic assumption that God and the church will always enjoy ultimate triumph over Satan. This point of theological dogma is most clearly represented within narrative tradition in the stories of encounters between devil and clergy. Clergymen, particularly those who had become famous in some way, perhaps by writing a book or taking part in an especially difficult exorcism, were regarded as the possessors of supernatural powers, represented concretely by the Black Book whose use they shared with the devil. Because of the theological background, encounters between devil and clergy frequently end in exorcism, as in many of the tales included in this book. In the larger context such encounters are similar to others between humans and otherworldly beings, a point amply demonstrated by story no. 78, "Old Erik in the Mill," where an ordinary human encounters a Satan virtually identical with the troll in story no. 51, "The Mill Spirit."

As a force inimical to God and his representatives on earth, the clergy, Satan stood at the top of a hierarchy parallel to the Christian church. The members of Satan's "church" were those who had entered into pacts with him, primarily witches. Worship was held at a so-called Black Mass, usually on important holiday eves, with Easter, the foremost Christian holiday after Christmas, taking a prominent position. Traditionally in Sweden the Black Mass was said to have been held at Blåkulla, which some scholars have identified with German Blocksberg or the Brocken, the mountain summit on which German witches worship the devil. At any rate, *Blåkulla* appears to be a compound of *blå* ("blue"; here: "dark-blue" or "black") and *kulle* ("hill"), and seems to have been used as a fantasy location despite the existence of two mountains in Sweden with that name.

People thought to have supernatural or magic powers have probably always existed in Scandinavia, as elsewhere. It was only by a peculiar set of circumstances within the international church during the fifteenth and sixteenth centuries that such persons came to be regarded as witches. The basic theological notion seems to have been that the practice of magic could only be possible through the aid of the devil; hence those who exercised some sort of supernatural powers were witches in league with Satan and were worthy of death. This notion was promulgated most strongly by Innocence VIII in 1487 in a papal bull entitled *Summis Desiderantes Affectibus.* Thereafter persecution of witches reached its height, ultimately to run its course by the eighteenth century. Since the tales in this book are collected from the late nineteenth and twentieth centuries, they focus on those aspects of witchcraft which exerted the strongest influence on popular imagination. Foremost among them was the Black Mass.

Accounts of the Black Mass given by confessed witches vary but ordinarily include an inverted Christian ritual, a feast, and revelry, often with a very strong sexual slant. Other confessions stress ordinary household activities, frequently those carried out before a large holiday, as in story no. 80, "With Her Godmother to Josefsdal." In either case one is dealing with fantasies of emotionally deprived women whose confessions often were extracted by torture. The familiar sociological patterns of witchcraft recognized elsewhere apply with equal veracity in Sweden: witches tended to be those women whose status in society was unclear, usually because they were unmarried, widowed, or childless. Suspected by their neighbors, such women lived in enforced, involuntary solitude, and hence were easy prey to feelings of inferiority and fantasies of another life where companionship, fine food, and erotic contact were available. Given a general belief in witchcraft, such fantasies were probably inevitable; they could be activated by entering a pact with Satan and using a magic salve to gain transportation to Blåkulla. The magic salve, which really was used, plays a major role in the reality of witchcraft, since it seems to have frequently included certain hallucinatory agents among the herbs and plants in the various recipes used for it. According to folk belief, the salve was rubbed on an object to give it the power to fly, as in story no. 82, "The Magic Horn," where it is used to grease a cart. Apparently it entered a witch's body when she "rode" the object, since "riding" was often a form of masturbation. This then led to the sometimes vivid accounts of sailing through the air to Blåkulla and the Black Mass held there. In story tradition such journeys have been exaggerated, as in stories nos. 82 and 83. In the former the cart greased with the magic salve flies off out of control, and in the latter, "Following the Witch," the magic salve has been completely omitted in favor of the humorous motif of misuse of a magic formula.

One implication of the hallucinatory value of the witches' salve is the belief, doubtless held by the witches themselves, that they could change the appearance of everyday household items. Thus the witch at Tådås (story no. 81) can make a basketful of manure and toads look palatable. The witch in story no. 79, "The Easter-Hag Put a Water-Trough in Her Place," is able to make a water-trough take on her form while she is off at Blåkulla; and the witch in no. 80, "With Her Godmother to Josefsdal," performs a similar trick on behalf of her goddaughter. The latter transformations solve the problem of how witches could be away at a Black Mass without being missed. These stories are otherwise typical of two aspects of the extensive story tradition concerning journeys to Blåkulla, a tradition that was extensive because of the central importance of the Black Mass in conceptions of witchcraft. "The Easter-Hag" concentrates on a basic problem the rest of the community faced when witchcraft was suspected. How could one identify a witch? The knife in the unresponding, sleeping woman provided a common answer in narrative tradition, even if one doubts the frequency of the test in real life. "With Her Godmother" explains how proselytizing could occur, even with an innocent victim. It may be recalled that the victim was taken at that vulnerable time before baptism, when she has not yet entered the Christian community by passing through the first rite of passage. The second portion of the text seems to satisfy the tradition-bearers' curiosity about what life at Blåkulla was like. It is apparent that this description derives ultimately from a witch cut off from most human contact, whose fantasies therefore ran more toward ordinary household activities in preparation for a great feast, where she might find companionship, than toward the more lurid sexual fantasies of other witches' confessions.

A witch's activity culminated in the journey to Blåkulla and the Black Mass, but in everyday life she was suspected of various sorts of minor magic acts, usually at the expense of her neighbors. In stories the most frequently attested of these is the milking of cows from other farms, as in the variants printed in story no. 84, "Milking Others' Cows." This was a quite genuine aspect of folk belief, which, like the intercession of the *tomte,* could account for a neighbor's prosperity, as well as the infirmity and lack of milk in one's own cows. Indeed, the importance of dairy farming is stressed by such conceptions: *tomtar* steal other farmers' cows and witches milk them from afar, a clear indication of the vital role of healthy cattle in this rural economy. Witches could actually steal off to some neighbor's stall, as in no. 84B, or they could use a garter to milk from afar, as in no. 85, "Captain Eli," or they could use a special device called a milk-hare, as in no. 84A. Although the formulae for producing milk-hares and similar magic objects varied from place to place, they were very widespread and are attested from the Middle Ages. Modern attestations include verbal expressions very much like the contracts with the devil discussed above. The socioeconomic background of beliefs in milking from afar and the milk-hare is evident. Tending the cattle was woman's work, and so problems with the cattle were assigned to women outside the Christian community.

Like the devil, witches could be employed in several sorts of narratives. The texts presented here include a memorate, several legends of various sorts, and a wonder-tale. The variety is evident in the cycle of "The Witch at Tådås," which contains an account of toads and manure made to look like appetizing food, a brief mention of her *tomte,* and a final section which approaches a wonder-tale in its length and complexity. Two other tales of famous known witches further exemplify this diversity: the story of Captain Eli, no. 85, is a grimly told tale of unrepentent witchcraft; whereas "The Devil and Kitta Grå," no. 86, is a humorous wonder-tale, light in tone, playing on both human and Satanic weaknesses.

The basic work on both the devil and witchcraft in Sweden is the lengthy study of Bror Gadelius, *Tro och öfvertro i gångna tider* 1–2 (Stockholm, 1912–13); the portions dealing with witchcraft have recently been reprinted as Gadelius, *Häxor och häxprocesser* (Stockholm, 1963). There is no overall study of Swedish devil legends, but Lutz Röhrich, "Teufelsmärchen und Teufelssagen," in *Sagen und ihre Deutung* (Göttingen, 1965), is useful. Studies devoted to witchcraft in Sweden are Albert Nilsson, "Övertro och häxprocesser," *Svenska folket genom tiderna*, 5 (Stockholm, 1939), 161–174, and Lauritz Gentz, "Vad förorsakade de stora häxprocesserna," *Arv*, 10 (1954), 1–39. Also useful is Bente Gullveig Alver, *Heksetro og troldom*, noted above.

As opposed to witches, who knowingly align themselves with the Devil, certain other transformed humans in Swedish folk belief act against their own will, sometimes without awareness of their supernatural activities. Two basic figures in this category are the werewolf and the nightmare, treated respectively by Ella Odstedt, *Varulven i svensk folktradition* (Stockholm, 1943), and Carl-Herman Tillhagen, "The Conception of the Nightmare in Sweden," in Wayland Hand and Gustav Arlt, eds., *Humaniora: Essays Honoring Archer Taylor* (Berkeley, 1960), pp. 317–329. Conceptions of the werewolf, literally "man-wolf," are similar to those prevalent throughout Europe, although the figure seems to have been present in Scandinavia for at least a thousand years. Swedish stories about werewolves, or the related man-bears, seldom stress the danger or devastation wrought by the being; rather they are concerned with his own lack of knowledge of his predicament or the pathos involved in living among the wolves. The only real point of danger to the human community seems to have been, according to folk belief, that the werewolf's nature forced him to try to rip the unborn child from a pregnant woman. This conception is consistent both with the notion that lycanthropy may be visited by a mother on her unborn son by certain socially unacceptable actions, and that pregnancy is a vulnerable period for all concerned. Folk belief also sometimes attributes the existence of the nightmare to actions during pregnancy that later redound on the child. The second component of the English term *nightmare* is cognate with Swedish *mara*. The etymology of this term is disputed but seems to have to do with crushing or pressing. This accords with the notion of the *mara* or nightmare in Swedish tradition; it is a being which afflicts people or cattle while they sleep. Those who have been "ridden" by the nightmare report feelings of constriction or physical oppression, difficulties in breathing, and so forth. Although the nightmare is seldom seen in her "supernatural" form, in certain stories she plays a role in her human form. In many cases she is similar to witches, and nightmare stories have borrowed much from stories of witchcraft. In one well-known migratory legend, however, she marries, in her human form, the man she was oppressing, and here one must reckon with the influence of other nature-beings, like the *skogsrå,* as well as erotic dreams.

The last important group of supernatural beings in Swedish folk tradition are the dead, a large group who play a major role in folk belief. Stories of the dead and conceptions regarding them are particularly accessible in Swedish tradition because of the very full survey of Louise Hagberg, *När döden gästar: svenska folkseder och svensk folktro i samband med död och begravning* (Stockholm, 1937). Important for analysis is Juha Pentikäinen, *The Nordic Dead Child Tradition: 1. Nordic Dead Child Beings,* FFC, 202 (Helsinki, 1968). A useful paper in English is Bengt af Klintberg, "'Gast' in Swedish Folk Tradition," *Temenos,* 3 (1968), 43–56. Scandinavian ghosts have far more physical presence than Anglo-American ghosts, and a conception of the "living dead" is ancient in Scandinavia. In narrative tradition, not surprisingly, the dead appear exclusively in encounters with the living. There are two major categories of the dead. The first is the *gast,* a term apparently borrowed from East Frisian *gāst* ("spirit"), cognate with English *ghost* and German *Geist.* The *gast* is the unknown dead person, and his primary habitat is nature, not the human community. He can be merely troublesome, as in story no. 92, "A Ghost Gets a Free Ride," a tale highly reminiscent of no. 74, "Giving the Devil a Ride." Any time a team had trouble pulling a cart, one might suspect that a *gast* had climbed aboard for a free ride; this would provide a convenient explanation for such ordinary phenomena as undernourished horses or ungreased axles. Many *gastar,* however, are about with a purpose, namely to find their way into hallowed ground. The vast majority of hauntings are motivated by something that has gone wrong in the human community and that the ghost has a major interest in. Among *gastar* the problem is often that they have not been buried in hallowed ground near a church, but have, rather, been lost at sea, perished in the forest far from human habitation, or perhaps been the victims of foul play. They have, therefore, not passed through the last rite of passage, the funeral, which is designed to transport them from the world of the living into the world of the dead. And so they hang around on the periphery of this world, not members of it but not members of the world of the dead, either. As soon as they reach hallowed ground the rite of passage is considered complete and the haunting ceases. The two variants presented in story no. 93, "Strand-Ghosts," provide examples of this vast category of narrative tradition. A related story is no. 94, "The Parson Could Not Say 'Our Daily Bread,'" which reverses the situation: the ritual cannot be carried out until the foul play in the girl's death is discovered.

The other sort of supernatural dead is called a *spöke*, a term related to English *spook* and which I have translated simply as "ghost." This is a known dead person, whose primary role in story tradition is to return as a revenant to haunt places of human habitation. Like all the supernatural dead, these ghosts find their motivation in aspects of their lives as humans. Some, like the ghost in the memorate "A Haunting," story no. 91, simply continue their evil ways after death; a very common motif in these cases is a quarrel which fails to cease with death. In other cases some specific piece of information has to be passed along to the living. In story no. 95, "Peace in the Grave," an old man wishes to clarify the location of some money he hoarded and failed to disclose to his son before death took him. The suicide of story no. 96, "The Hanged Man Seeks His Pine Tree," is apparently drawn by the nature of his crime to return to its scene, even when it has been moved. It is perhaps worth repeating that suicides were not buried in hallowed ground, and so one had every reason to expect them to haunt. Finally, in story no. 97, "The Power of Sorrow," the haunting is designed to correct matters in the world of the living by putting an end to excessive mourning for the departed. Here the ghost has virtually no aura of fear or terror about her, and her encounter with her living mother is melancholy rather than terrifying. Perhaps the sense of melancholy is what has made the story an appealing ballad subject. At any rate, the context of the story printed here, a sermon, marks clearly its didactic purpose.

Ghosts are also important characters in international migratory legends and wonder-tales. Here the awe and terror the dead could inspire are exploited to the fullest, and the result in the hands of a good storyteller can be quite gripping. Story no. 98, "The Dead Bridegroom," is an international wonder-tale whose basic premise is the change from love to malevolence toward the living, thought to accompany death. The dead bridegroom is the structural equivalent of the troll who tries to take a bride from the human community, but his peculiar situation enables the storyteller to play on the special fears people have of the dead and their world. It is worth noting, however, that the heroine is ultimately saved not only by her own bravery and wit but also by the intercession of a benevolent corpse. Thus not all the dead are hostile to the living.

The same occurs in story no. 99, "The Christmas Service of the Dead," in which the heroine's dead sister gives her the advice that saves her. The purpose of this migratory legend is clearly one of entertainment, but it must also have satisfied curiosity about the world of the dead. The tale postulates a world parallel to that of the living, usually invisible to us. What is somewhat anomalous about this particular legend is that the dead have nothing to gain by appearing to the living; they have no old accounts to settle, nothing to set right. The key to the appearance of the dead in this case is the timing; it is Christmas Eve, the night when all the spirits are active and abroad. Trolls roam the forests and mountainsides, the wild hunt roars overhead, and the service of the dead is, for once, visible to the living, if they are luckless enough to arrive early at the church for Christmas services.

It is appropriate that all the supernatural beings of folk belief should be abroad on the eve of the great Christian holiday, for what distinguishes them is, above all else, that they are not members of the Christian community. The nature-beings, particularly the collective ones, live lives very much like those of the tradition-bearers. Even the solitary *skogsrå* would like to marry a Christian, or at the least trick one; and according to one story, the *näck* in his watery isolation longs for eternal salvation. The witches are those who have renounced God and substituted worship of the devil, even though they still live within the Christian community. And the dead, although they evidently cling to Christianity after death, are those who have permanently left the Christian community for another world. Thus Christianity provides a touchstone for nearly all the folk beliefs of Swedish oral traditions, providing beliefs that can be activated in nearly any departure from the ordinary. Depending on the specific situation, blame might be assigned to the trolls (deformed or retarded children, lost wanderers in the forest), *skogsrå* (unacceptable erotic fantasies, lost cattle or sheep, lack of success in hunting), *näck* or *sjörå* (drownings, unsuccessful fishing), *tomte* (prosperity or failure on the farm), Satan (sin), witches (neighbors' prosperity, dry cows), or the dead (unexplained noises or sensations). In the case of one of the stories included in this book, we can literally see the actualization of folk belief and the incorporation of traditional narrative patterns into the account of the event. I refer to the "merman" of story no. 56, whom the collector later learned to be a perfectly ordinary man paying an unexpected visit to the area. By the same token we may imagine that the devil in story no. 74, "Giving the Devil a Ride," was perhaps originally simply a well-dressed stranger who was passing through the area.

The key word is "stranger." We are dealing with the stories of a traditional society, one in which the unchanged patterns were set long ago. These patterns include a world view, a set of beliefs which help to organize and interpret unfamiliar phenomena. The valence of familiarity and its opposite, the unknown, is perceived clearly in the degree of awe inspired by supernatural beings in relation to their place of residence. The giants live far from human habitation and are not likely to be encountered; they are regarded as having lived "long ago." The trolls, however, inhabit the mountains and forests, areas which people had to pass through from time to time but with which they were not closely familiar. Thus trolls are the least known of the nature-beings, and the ones who are most likely to do harm to humans they encounter. Certain parts of the forest, however, were better known, namely the areas where men carried out seasonal work, like charcoal burning. Here one might encounter a *skogsrå.* Unlike a troll, a *skogsrå* is likely to initiate an intimate encounter, despite her ultimately hostile attitude toward the human community as a whole. The water creatures are less likely to be encountered, perhaps, but one has the impression that the *näck,* who inhabits a small watercourse, is more likely to be friendly to humans than a *sjörå* encountered far out at sea, unless the *sjörå* is propitiated in some way. Closest to home one finds the *tomte*, who actually shares the homestead with the human inhabitants. He is the most well-disposed toward humans, working hard to maintain a farm's prosperity and punishing those actions that work against such prosperity. Finally, witches and Satan live among the tradition-bearers but have opened a spiritual gulf between themselves and the others. In some ways this makes them the most frightening. Here we should recall that the women actually identified as witches were precisely those who were unfamiliar to their neighbors or whose status was strange or unclear; in their lack of knowledge about what actually goes on in the households or minds of witches, good people imagined the most awful crimes, primarily by activating traditional beliefs accorded them by the Church. And the greatest mystery of all is death, which surely accounts for the conceptions of the dead seen throughout the world. In Sweden the living dead were for the most part those who left the Christian community of the dead, located physically in the churchyard, to haunt among the living; many had never found repose in that community and only encountered humans in their search for it. The pattern is consistent. Familiarity and cordiality go hand in hand, while the unknown inspires fear. With the breakdown of the rural society that produced the beliefs and tales found in this book, and the subsequent dissolution of these traditions, the tradition-bearers merely learned to be familiar with a different set of circumstances, and to fear a different set of unknowns.

Texts

This World

1. Investigation of a Grotto

In Tvåaker, just east of the church, is a ridge called Höråsen. On its north side is a rather large precipice, at the bottom of which is a grotto formation said to extend some distance into the mountain. . . . This grotto is called by the local population the troll-cave or troll-parlor. Trolls lived here, among them one named Hagen, possibly Hakon.

Once some brave men decided to investigate the cave. One of them had a rope tied around his waist and he crawled in, after he had asked the others to haul him out if he stayed too long. He proceeded through the grotto, at times on foot, at times on hands and knees. At last he came to a large iron door which was carefully barred from within, so that he couldn't open it. When he pounded on the door there was a low murmuring from within. However, the men believed he had stayed too long and began to haul him out, so he didn't have time to carry out any more careful investigation concerning the mysterious door. And since then no one has tried to penetrate the secret, either.

[IFGH 3714. From Anna Lou. Andersson, born 1841. Printed in Donald Floyd, *Attitudes toward Nature in Swedish Folklore* (Dissertation, University of California, Berkeley, 1976), p. 362.]

Swedish folk tradition is full of such accounts of attempted investigations of the unknown parts of the local environment, usually mountains and rock formations. Since the trolls were thought to live there, this was dangerous business, and it is no wonder his companions feared for his safety and pulled the man out. In general, such investigations seem to have had the effect of reinforcing the folk beliefs concerning the local environment. To a man who accepts the trolls as a part of everyday life, any reasonably flat stone may look very much like a door if it is located deep within a mysterious grotto, and the murmurings of the wind may sound rather like trolls making small talk about the rattling at the door.

For several more such tales in Swedish and translation, see Floyd, op. cit.

2. *Sounding at Vassdal*

I HAVE heard my father, who was born in 1837, say that there was supposed to have been a *sjörå* in the waters of Vassdal. He also said that in places the water was so deep that no one had been able to sound it. One man tried it but almost immediately heard a voice saying: "Cut the line and hurry away from here. Otherwise you'll all too soon have a chance to come down here for a look at the bottom and see if you can find it then." The man was terrified and rushed from the spot. Tradition has it that no one has ever been able to determine how deep the water is, and people also say that the ice never freezes solidly enough to support a man's weight over the deepest places.

[Orust, Bohuslän. VFA 1973: 1,2. Collected in 1932 by Olof J. Larsson from Hilmer Niklasson, born on the island in 1872. Printed in C. M. Bergstrand, *Gammalt från Orust* (Göteborg, 1962), p. 14.]

A variant of the preceding legend, this one is from a seagoing island community. It is interesting to note that the informant, sixty years old when he reported this item, seems to take a neutral stance toward its authenticity. His father apparently believed the account of the failed attempt at sounding and was willing to accept it as explanation for the unknown depths in the water, but the informant himself is rather reticent and prefers to appeal to tradition. This is exactly how the dissolution of popular traditions has occurred.

3. Delsbo's Churchbell

A

THERE is also an age-old tradition relating how a great bell was taken from here, some say on account of the Lübeck debt; according to the tales of others it was to be hung in Stockholm because of its beautiful tone. It is supposed to have happened thus, that when the bell had been transported some miles from here onto the frozen surface of a large lake, Bergviken, between Säderstadh (Segerstad) and Skogh, the ice gave way and the bell sank. But at the desire of those present to get such a valuable object up again, and the promise that they would return it to its original location, it was retrieved. After the bell had been retrieved and placed on the sledge, following orders the men continued their way south, at which point the bell, as if by force, left the sledge again and plunged through the ice, it not being possible to bring it up, neither that time nor afterward, when the Parish sent a man there; soon after beginning his work he departed this life, and inasmuch as no one has subsequently been found who would undertake that job for possible payment, and lack of means has kept the required cost from being raised, the bell therefore still remains in the same spot.

[Delsbo, Hälsingland. Reported by rural dean J. Phragmenius in 1684, in MS KB Sign. F. I. 9. Printed in Arvid Enqvist, "Två folksägner från Hälsingland i äldre och nyare uppteckningar," *Fmft*, 17 (1930), 127–128.]

B

THEY have an old tradition here that Delsbo Parish possesses a churchbell weighing eighteen *skeppund* [ten *skeppund* equal one *skeplast* ("ship's cargo"); the unit was abolished in 1855: see Hellquist, *Svensk etymologisk ordbok*, s.v.] lying sunk in Bergviken, in the eastern rural deanery of southern Hälsingland. It is said to have come there through the following reason and event, namely that for its matchless tone it was accounted far too good to serve peasants and for that reason should be transported overland in winter to the Royal Residence in Stockholm, there to be hung and enjoyed, and thus during the conveying over Bergviken, at Lynäs Point, apparently came to sink down to the place where it still remains. The high regard for this bell by the parishioners perhaps may be ascribed to the fact that Brother Vincentius, the Greyfriar (who accompanied the Archbishop Johannes Magnus when he visited here), had baptized and christened it. For it is hard to believe that the pleasing tone of the bell could be the only reason for its removal, since it, along with other churchbells in the kingdom, can for the sake of the Lübeck debt have taken the plunge. And the basis of this tradition is strengthened by the extent to which all those dwelling around Bergviken in Segerstad, Hanebo, Skog, and Söder-Ala parishes certify that the bell belonging to Delsbo parish is sunk off Lynäs Point, and they relate that 80 or 100 years ago a man from Delsbo (said to have been Olof Dyrikson, a coppersmith in Ala), with the aid of several others, had got the bell up over the gunwale just out of the water, whence unfortunately it slipped from his tongs and in its fall toppled down to a greater depth. What efforts the Parish at the gracious consent of his majesty, granted April 7, 1737, already has undertaken to secure the return of this bell, may be seen in the church accounts (for 1750–51 in church ledger no. 7), and what may in future, with God's blessing, be accomplished, only time will tell.

[Reported by rural dean Lenæus in *Delsboa Illustrata* (1764), pp. 174 ff., printed in Enqvist, pp. 128–129.]

C

In former times Delsbo had a churchbell, the like of which was not to be found in all Hälsingland. Once when the king was up in the tract he heard it ring and he became so attracted to the bell that he immediately ordered it transported to Stockholm, since it was much too good to be out in the countryside. He would send another less good one there. Naturally no one dared to disobey the order, but when they were to drive over Bergviken with it, the ice broke and it sank irretrievably to the bottom. Whether horse and men went with it, no one knows, but there the bell rests to this very day.

[Collected by Pehr Johnsson from J. Svensson, printed in "Folksägner från Hälsingland," *FmFt*, 6 (1919); reprinted in Enqvist, p. 127.]

A clear example of how a local legend can be retained largely unchanged for well over two centuries. Although it is possible that Lenæus could have got his account from a manuscript of Phragmenius, and that J. Svensson might have read *Delsboa Illustrata*, Enqvist, who assembled these variants in "Två folksägner från Hälsingland i äldre och nyare uppteckningar," *FmFt* 17 (1930), 123–130, accepts that they are related solely by oral tradition. The historical explanation alluded to in *A* and *B* is in all probability correct; after obtaining the throne in the early 1520s, Gustav Vasa relied heavily on *silverhjälper* ("silver aids," in effect anything portable and valuable) from the Swedish Church in order to repay his massive debt to Lübeck for its support against Kristian II. Thus the sinking of the bell in the early sixteenth century was still attributed to a valid historical cause as late as during the mid-eighteenth century. By the time the legend was recorded from oral tradition during the early years of this century, however, the historical motivation was lost to the personal motivation of the king's passion for the bell's tone, already present in the earlier variants. Retrieval of the bell and its subsequent loss at the breach of the promise in *A* is a motif found in similar tales; Enqvist cites a legend recorded in Skåne in 1690 which contains a bell lost under exactly the same circumstances when a promise *in pius usus* of four oxen is rescinded.

In a relatively recent variant from Björkling, Uppland, a lost churchbell is said to have fallen into the hands of a *sjörå*. Efforts to retrieve it fail when a prohibition of silence is broken; one of the hands notices a hen staggering by under a load of hay. "How far do you expect to get with that?," he asks without thinking. "You will get no further with the bell than I with the hay," she answers, and with that the lines part and the bell sinks back into the river (Elias Grip, "Skuttunge- ock Björklingemål: Folksägner," *SvLm*, 18:3 [1899], 75). Thus an originally historical event has been completely reformulated by the fantasy of tradition.

4. *The Man Who Drowned in a Washbasin*

I BELIEVE that whatever a man has to go through, he has to go through. It is decided in advance.

In Bäcksedasjön a cry was once heard, "The hour is come, but not the man." The people from Bråtåkra were there on the beach. A while later a man came by and asked the way to Drakulla. He wanted to cross the lake. People said, "You mustn't go over the lake. Stay here tonight."

"I can't," he said.

"You mustn't go over the lake under any circumstances—if you do you'll drown."

They got him inside and he agreed to stay. They warmed a room specially for him and took up a stone tray with the wash basin on it at night. The next morning, when they came up, he lay face down on the tray and was dead. There was nothing to do about it. He was to drown in water no matter what. The hour had come.

[Alseda, Småland. From the soldier Karl Snygg. Printed in Matts Magni Granström, "Soldaten Karl Snyggs levnadshistoria," *SvLm*, B30 (1933), 75–76.]

The legend of the river claiming its due (Christiansen ML 4050) is one of the most widespread in Western Europe; its attestations reach back to the beginning of the thirteenth century. Although some scholars have attempted to tie the story in with regular sacrifice in watercourses, the informant's claim of unavoidable fate is far more sensible for modern variants and indeed is quite regular in Scandinavia. The epic formula, "The hour has come, but not the man," regularly accompanies the story in a variety of European languages and cultures. See Robert Wildhaber, " 'Die Stunde ist da, aber der Mann nicht': ein europäisches Sagenmotiv," *Rheinisches Jahrbuch für Volkskunde*, 9 (1958), 23–58.

5. *Twelve Children on a Platter*

WHATEVER a person has to go through, he has to go through. She found out about that, that girl who wouldn't get married before she was fifty, in order to avoid bearing children. She got twelve at once. That was because she would have had that many if she had married and got what she was supposed to get. All twelve looked dead, but they put them on a platter and put the platter in the oven. And when it was good and hot, one of them came to life and began to move. And that child lived and grew to be full grown, they say.

[VFF 694:45. Klintberg no. 4. Collected in Högsäter, Dalsland, from a woman born in 1871 in Hallingdal, Norway.]

This popular tale has been collected from throughout Scandinavia. The role of fate, of course, is that the number of a woman's children was predetermined, but it is clear that the legend has a strong didactic purpose. In an agrarian society with a relatively high death rate, where many children were needed to work the land and perform household duties, the unnatural behavior of the woman in the legend would be socially undesirable. It seems likely, too, that the twelve children are to be interpreted as a kind of punishment for the woman, which would increase the didactic power of the story. In a similar story, a married couple agree that each will turn his back on the other for nine years. After eighteen years of childless marriage, the man dies, and the woman reproaches him: "You are the reason I am haunted by nine headless children" (*SvLm*, 8:3, pp. 163–164). Still other tales attribute infertility to pacts with the devil.

The rather odd motif of warming the twelve children in the oven may reflect the influence of folk belief and narratives about changelings (see Introduction, p. 12, and story no. 26). The result of this "baking" is the resolution of a bizarre situation, twelve children on a platter, to a normal situation of one healthy child. The parallel of the threat to roast a changeling should be obvious, particularly since in many such changeling stories it is at the moment that the changeling is placed on a platter prior to roasting that the troll mother returns with the human child.

6. The Piece of Straw

ONCE an old woman with second sight came to a certain place. The family there had a young boy, and when she saw him she said, "That's a nice boy, but he will kill a man."

After that they were all afraid, but the boy grew up and was extremely gentle. But once someone came and wanted to fight with him, and no matter how he defended himself, the other would never leave him in peace. Then someone suggested, "Hit him with a piece of straw." He did, and the other fell down dead.

You see, it couldn't be any other way, he had to kill someone.

[IFGH 2601:29. Klintberg no. 3. Helmer Olsson, *Folkliv och folkdikt i Vättle härad under 1800 talet*, p. 139. Collected in 1930 in Stora Lundby, Västergötland, from a woman born there in 1847.]

This story is not widely distributed in Sweden and is for the most part limited to Götaland. It is of interest for two reasons. First, as Helmer Olsson has demonstrated (*Folkliv och folkdikt i Vättle härad under 1800-talet*, SKGAAF, 12 [Uppsala, 1945], p. 30), it has apparently given rise to a now extinct custom in southwest Sweden, in which the victim of drawn-out death throes was struck with a piece of straw to make the struggle end, a practice which shows the belief people had in these legends. Second, the story repeats a motif famous from Old Norse literature. One thinks first of the death of Baldr, the fairest of the gods, as told in Snorri Sturluson's *Edda* and other sources. After disquieting dreams, Baldr was made proof against all things, living and dead, by oaths they gave to Frigg, his mother and chief of the goddesses. Thereafter the other gods threw all manner of weapons at him in sport until the jealous Loki tricked Frigg into revealing the one object that had not sworn the oath. This was the tender mistletoe, which Loki thrust into the hands of the blind Höðr, Baldr's brother. Baldr fell dead when the mistletoe struck. A similar story is recounted in the romantic *Gautreks saga.* A group of becalmed warriors draw lots to determine who shall be sacrificed to restore the wind. When the lot falls to the king, Víkarr, preparations are made for a false sacrifice. A noose of gut is tied around his neck and one of the warriors brandishes a reed. At the crucial moment the gut becomes rope and the reed a spear, and the sacrifice is carried out after all.

Another important attestation of this widespread motif is the story in the Finnish *Kalevala* of the death of Lemminkäinen, who was killed by a reed hurled by a blind shepherd.

7. *Retribution*

A

THE wife of a sergeant was so vain that she scorned her oldest child, a daughter, because the girl showed some interest in housekeeping and persistent hard work. One day the mother blurted: "I wish instead I had given birth to a lamb—at least then I would have the wool." Her last child was a stillborn monstrosity, half lamb, half human.

B

NEAR the church at Bro there are a couple of unusual stones. Two women were disputing with the church about a piece of land that had been given to it. When the time came to decide the case on the spot of the disputed land, the women put dirt from their own fields into their shoes and swore oaths that they were standing on their own earth. But no sooner had the false oath passed their lips than their bodies were turned into the two stones which still stand by the church. And, people say, the crime was that much worse because one of the women was pregnant, as can clearly be seen from one of the stones.

[*A* was collected by Eva Wigström in Östra Göinge, Skåne; *B* by Wigström in Gotland. Both are printed in her "Folktro och sägner från skilda landskap (Folkdiktning, 3:e samlingen)," *SvLm*, 8:3 (1898–1914), 158–159.]

Tales of this nature are inordinately popular throughout Sweden and all Western Europe. *A* should be compared to the preceding "Twelve Children on a Platter," since it also involves an explanation for an unusual birth. Presumably the lamb-like qualities of the stillborn infant were discovered through retrospective activation of the folk belief concerning improper statements: once made, they were likely to come true. The most common subject for such improper statements is the devil, mere mention of whom was sufficient to summon him. See story no. 71, "The Cardplayers and the Devil," for an example.

B demonstrates another popular subject for inexorable punishments, false oaths. This particular story has been localized and has acquired a basically etiological thrust, but its didactic purpose is abundantly clear. In the earliest legal system in Sweden, as represented by the late medieval provincial laws, oaths were one of the primary legal mechanisms, and it is possible that stories of retribution for false oaths may date from that era.

8. *Folk Beliefs about Portents*

When a person is out walking, an invisible spirit goes before him over the earth and another accompanies him under the earth. If the one going under the earth meets or knocks up against one of the dwellers of the underworld, the person gets sick. The one who is going on invisible in front of the man portends his arrival in a place. My father always used to take hold of the door-latch in a certain way which made the lock click. We children always heard that click a while before he would arrive. People say about me that there is a knocking noise at the window before I arrive.

When the cows bellow, stick out their tongues, and lay their heads to one side, it means they see something unpleasant in front of a man, in other words the invisible spirit. If someone is to die, the spirit makes it known. It is perceived by sensing the smell of a corpse. Or in addition the boards which are to be used for a coffin may rattle and shake. That means that a coffin will soon be nailed together. "There have been ten corpses in this house in thirty years, but I've only heard it once," my mother used to say.

• • •

One of my neighbors, Ola Berntsson from Kålund, Mölnefossa, an eighty-two year old carpenter who makes coffins, used to get such warnings frequently. Here is the story in his own words:

Once when I was asleep at night, I woke up and sensed the smell of a corpse. "If it's a ghost, go away, I'm trying to sleep," I said. Then I fell asleep, but shortly thereafter I woke up because someone was pounding on the door. It was a messenger from Skedet, come to tell me that Skesse-Petter's mother was dead and that I was to make a coffin for her.

Another time I was off in Fjällebro. In the evening, when I had finished my work, I heard someone take my plane and pound the bench with it. Then I said, "I have to go home. Harness the horses and give me a lift."

"You can't be in such a hurry," they said. "You can certainly spend the night here."

"No, I've got to get home, I can tell," I said. And when I arrived home, there was a message there that I was to make a coffin for someone. And if I hadn't brought that plane back with me from Fjällebro, I couldn't have made the coffin.

One evening I went past Skåre Nabb. Just before I came to the barn at Skåre I heard a terrible crashing noise. It sounded as if the whole gutter had fallen off the barn. And then it sounded as if a whole series of people were riding on the road. I went off to the side of the road and said: "Can't a person walk here without being troubled by you all?" I thought they were going to ride over me. And I was frightened, as you can imagine. I went home and went to sleep in the barn, and I didn't tell anyone about it before I had slept on it.

• • •

This story was told by Kristian from Sältebo: Once Hans from Sältebo was out walking, when he saw a vision, a funeral procession of ghostly figures going to the church at Klövedal. He recognized all but one of the marchers.

Hans was the skipper of a barge. And not much later he had to anchor in the Halmstad Bay during a storm. But the barge broke loose and was driven aground. Hans was so frightened and overcome that he died. When his funeral was on its way to

Klövedal churchyard, it matched his vision perfectly. All the people he had seen were marching in the procession. And the only one he hadn't been able to recognize was himself, lying in the coffin. He had had a vision of his own funeral.

[All three of the tales above were told by Olaus Olsson, born ca. 1852, to Vilhelm Cederschiöld during the 1920s or earlier and printed in "Ur Olaus Olssons sägensamling," *FmFt*, 19 (1932), 100–102. Olsson was a farmer from Bohuslän who had wandered much about the area and himself become a repository for much folk tradition.]

The three sections illustrate three different aspects of folk belief about portents. The first introduces the notion of guardian spirits, who figure prominently in such beliefs. It will probably never be possible to sort out the Christian and pagan elements of this belief; the doctrine of good angels and bad was widespread in church lore from the Middle Ages onward and would have been familiar to all churchgoers in rural Scandinavia. On the other hand, Scandinavian mythology tells of fetches very much like the guardian spirits of modern folk belief. Spirits called *dísir* were venerated in cult and were thought to control the fate of an entire family, and an individual could be attended by a fetch (Old Norse *fylgja*) who personified his fate and might be glimpsed in crucial moments, particularly by those with second sight. Both spirits are reminiscent of the Roman *genii* and *lares* and of several beings of Mediterranean cultures as well. But as these beliefs are found throughout the world, they are perhaps best regarded as universals of the human imagination.

Another major aspect of belief illustrated here is passive observation of omens, typified by the story of the carpenter Ola Berntsson. Here two ideas are combined, one that almost everything has a meaning if only one knows how to find it, the other that important events will be portended by unusual occurrences. The most striking such occurrence is the sort of thing found in the third portion of the text, where a person has a vision of his own death. These are surely the most dramatic sorts of portents and are often recounted in a vividly realistic fashion. Although visions were ordinarily restricted to those with second sight, a common exception was a vision of one's own death.

9. Portent from the Nissar

LAST year (1883) I spent a lot of time with people from the area of Simrishamn and the fishing hamlets along the beach there. In the little village of Vik, I made the acquaintance of a woman who had had many remarkable visions.

One night she was at a neighbor's house sitting up with a sick person. At dawn she saw a whole flock of *nissar* out on the road, and she had such a strong feeling that they had a message for her that she leapt up from her coffee and breakfast, just to rush home to find out what was going on there.

She was not mistaken, for her husband had carried off their sons in a fit of drunkenness.

[Skåne. Collected by Eva Wigström in 1884 from "the henwife," one of Wigström's regular informants. Printed in Wigström, "Folktro och sägner från skilda landskap (Folkdiktning, 3:e samlingen)," *SvLm*, 8:3 (1898–1914), 143.]

Compare the preceding stories. Here the "spirits" have been identified as *nissar* who apparently revealed themselves to the woman as an omen. This supernatural experience is probably at least in part to be traced to the woman's fatigue and her anxiety over the sick patient, as well as the interest dominance of the drinking husband, with whom she had apparently been at odds over the sons. However, she was one of those persons blessed with second sight, to whom such visions regularly came. Perhaps that is why she was granted this one, which, despite its considerable domestic significance, was of somewhat less importance than a vision of death and destruction.

10. Plague Omens

CONTAGIOUS diseases have their own portents, as is known from the time the plague went around here in this area. The plague showed itself in the form of a man and a woman, he with a shovel, she with a broom. When he entered a house and shoveled, some might survive there. But if she came after and swept with the broom, then every person died, and just to be sure she would touch every single person in the house with her broom.

One night this couple entered a house in which a man, a woman, and their only child were in bed. When the wife saw that the woman with the broom was along, she took the child and stuffed it down between her and her husband. The plague touched first him, then her. In fear that the broom might also touch her child, the wife cried out: "In the name of Jesus, troll, there are no more to take here." The plague believed her: the parents died, but the child survived and inherited the entire depopulated village.

[Göinge, Skåne. Informant not stated. Collected by Eva Wigström and printed in her "Folktro och sägner från skilda landskap (Folkdiktning, 3:e samlingen)," *SvLm*, 8:3 (1898–1914), 13–14.]

The text is composed of two parts, a belief utterance and a short legend. The story is, in effect, a multiform of ML 7085, where a boatman who has ferried the plague-hag across a river is granted an easy death after guessing her identity. Compared to days of suffering, this represents a kind of victory over the plague, parallel to the saving of the child, even though both parents are claimed in the above variant. In both cases there has been a reinterpretation of the narrative rules, which ordinarily would call for a complete victory over the otherworldly being (in this variant even addressed by the woman as "troll"). Given the actual historical ravagings of the plague, a complete victory was impossible, and so the tradition settles for a partial victory. See John Lindow, "Personification and Narrative Structure in Scandinavian Plague Legends," *Arv*, 29–30 (1973–74), 83–92.

11. *Buried Alive to Stop the Plague*

DURING the great plague many people died in this parish. Whole villages died out. The plague was stopped in a village called Grevamåla. It was done by burying alive a pair of living children.

No one knew to whom these children belonged. Their parents had died of plague, and they were wandering from farm to farm begging food. They were a little boy and girl. In Grevamåla they were each given a sandwich and then asked to go down into a hole which had just been dug. Engrossed in their sandwiches, the children went down in the hole without any sense of danger. As soon as the children were in the hole, the villagers began to fill it up, shoveling dirt over them. The boy began to cry and said: "Why are you throwing dirt on this good sandwich of mine?" When the children had been buried alive in that fashion, a voice was heard, saying: "Henceforth as long as the earth shall stand there shall be a cripple on the farm at Grevamåla." And there has been a cripple there ever since, I have been assured.

[Linneryd, Småland. LUF 5393: 2–3. Printed in C. H. Tillhagen, "Sägner och folktro kring pesten," *Fataburen*, 1967, p. 223.]

This terrifying story describes the most desperate means employed to attempt to curb the course of plague and other epidemics. The story is common to south and southwest Sweden and has been collected all over Denmark. In actual practice the burial of animals was common in folk medicine down to fairly modern times, and most folklorists now seem inclined to accept the reality behind this story. At least one attested case from the plague in 1603 in Denmark has been documented (Folke Ström, *The Sacral Origin of the Germanic Death Penalties* [Stockholm, 1942], p. 205), and others seem likely.

The reasoning behind the burial is not fully clear. The informants often mention sacrifice, but since the legend has not been collected until relatively recently, their witness is suspect, and this explanation has been rejected in the fullest treatment of the problem, by Hans-Egil Hauge, *Levande begravd eller bränd i nordisk folkmedicin* (Stockholm, 1965). Tillhagen (op. cit.) regards the victim as neither an innocent party nor a portent of the plague, but rather a demon personifying the disease itself. By burying the plague demon one would trap the plague below ground, since it could not leave the demon's body until she (the demon is female in some two-thirds of the attestations) had died.

12. *Plague Victims Dig Their Own Graves*

THE great plague or Black Death was particularly fierce in Vånga. The ones who got the disease had a cross on their fists, but whether it was black or red I don't know. They also sneezed in a funny way. Then the others said, "Bless you." The ones who were sneezing started to dig their own graves and would sit on the edge. After they had sneezed a third time, they would tumble into the grave, and then the survivors would cover them over.

[Vånga, Östergötland. NM EU 552, p. 40. Collected by Gustav E. Olsson from Anders Hansson in Boberg, Vånga parish, Östergötland. Printed in Klintberg, p. 252, no. 359.]

Sneezing is, of course, not a symptom of plague. As I. Reichborn-Kjennerud (*Vor gamle trolldomsmedisin* [Oslo, 1940], 3: 92) has pointed out, it was a portent of impending death and hence was appropriate for the first symptom of plague in popular imagination. The point of digging one's own grave was to be certain that one would be buried in hallowed ground, and there is evidence that plague victims took themselves off to the graveyard at the first sign of the disease; see C. M. Tillhagen, "Sägner och folktro kring pesten," *Fataburen*, 1967, p. 225.

13. *The Survivors*

WHEN the Black Death was going around, the cause of it was that a strange animal was wandering around the countryside. No one had ever seen it before. Wherever that animal went people turned black, fell down, and died.

There were only two survivors, and they lived far to the south. They were a boy and girl, both unmarried. They were supposed to go up on a mountain and yell and shout. Then one answered the other, and so there was a place called Rophult and one called Svarhult. So goes the story in Sörbygden.

[Collected from Johanness Zachariasson by David Arill in Kåröd, Sanne, Bohuslän and printed in his "Folksägner från Sanne," *FmFt*, 5 (1918), 126.]

The story of the two survivors, whose marriage or cohabitation (some informants point out the difference) repopulates a district, is ML 7095. It has been found in most of Europe, not least in Scandinavia. This particular variant shows an unusual presumed cause of the epidemic and an interesting interpretation of the nature of the "black" death. The story of the survivors here has been assimilated to two local place names, Rophult ("Shout-wood") and Svarhult ("Answer-wood"), in an etiological folk etymology.

14. An Old Troll Is Tricked Into Revealing His Treasure

ONCE there were lights shining at night at a place near Nordre Bäck. There was, of course, a treasure buried there, and many people tried to get their hands on it. When a person sees a troll-light shining out in the country, he should walk straight toward the light and keep his eyes on it constantly, without blinking. A farmer from Tyft was going to try to do that out there near Nordre Bäck. But just as he was jumping over the ditch, he blinked. And at that very moment the light disappeared. But not far away lived another farmer, and he was more clever. He took a big kettle and filled it with old horseshoes and other metal junk. Then he took it out to Nordre Bäck and buried it near the place where the light was shining. He built a fire and fixed it so that the light was shining above his kettle. Then the troll was jealous and so curious that he just had to leave his hiding place and see what the farmer had in his kettle. He crept there and looked, but when he saw what was in the kettle he snorted and said, "Ugh—that's nothing to shine a light over! Come with me and you'll see something different." The farmer went along with him, and the old troll showed him a big kettle full of gold and silver coins. Then the farmer saw his chance and threw a drawn knife down into the kettle. In that way he got power over the treasure and was able to take it home with him. He was rich for the rest of his days.

[Häller, Klovedals sn., Bohuslän. VFF 464A: 146. Collected by Olaus Olsson from Hans i Heller. Printed in Klintberg, p. 266, no. 391.]

In this tale the fantasy of untold wealth through the discovery of treasure is linked with the common story pattern of an encounter between a human and a nature-being. In this case the nature-being is a gullible troll, hardly one who inspires awe or fear, and this alone suggests that the tale shares some aspects of the wonder-tale. Structurally, the tale includes a failed test followed by the hero's passing the test, the test itself involving adherence to an apparent item of folk belief. The failed test resembles a memorate telling of an unsuccessful try to acquire the riches of the trolls, conjured up in a vision or supernatural experience. The second test, however, is more purely epic, involving a clever hero who dupes a troll, and perhaps it should be compared to the tales of the stupid ogre in international wonder-tales.

15. Tokarsberget's Treasure

NEAR the city of Borås is the mountain Tokarsberget, about which the following legend is told:

Once upon a time there was an impoverished crofter. He had a son who often went up on the mountain to gather brushwood and heather, which he later sold in the city in order to provide his parents with an ever so small amount of money. When early one morning, as usual, he went out to pick heather, he saw on a stone slab in the glow of the rising sun, a large silver chest, full of gold and jewels. . . . Oh, how gladly the boy would have taken some pieces of gold to help out his family with, but next to the treasure lay a large dragon who was snoring so loudly that the boy ran home terrified to tell his father what he had seen. The father, who initially assumed that the boy, in exhaustion, had gone to sleep on the mountain and dreamt of the chest and the dragon, nevertheless finally set off with his son to the spot. But by then both the chest and the dragon had vanished without a trace.

[Västergötland. Printed in Hilder Werner, *Westergötlands fornminnen* (Stockholm, 1868), p. 66, and with English translation in Floyd, p. 391.]

Here the motif of buried treasure has been drawn into an obvious description of a supernatural experience. Under stress of poverty and fatigue, a boy dreams of the means to escape. Under the influence or interest dominance of his family's poverty, the boy does not encounter nature-beings, but rather he has a vision of silver and gold. The dragon, ordinarily found in wonder-tales only, is linked in folk belief with buried treasure and so is probably not anomalous. In this case it serves as the explanation for the failure of the boy to obtain the treasure, an obvious necessity if the text is to be interpreted as the description of a supernatural experience.

The slightly "folksy" or quaint aspects of the style, which I have attempted to retain in English, are doubtless to be ascribed to Hilder Werner, the author of the nineteenth-century book in which the text was printed.

The Other World

16. The Giant from Klasahall

LAKE MIE, on the border between Blekinge and Småland, was owned down into modern time by a giant known as old man Klasa. Only one farmer, Sven from the farm Midingstorp, had the giant's permission to fish for the bream in the lake. No one else ever succeeded in catching a single fish there. Sven had to make compensation, however. Every winter his wife had to brew Christmas beer for the giant, using seven bushels of malt. She protested, but Sven wouldn't budge in this matter.

Once, on the day before Christmas, the wife sent her serving-girl down into the cellar to pour some beer for them to drink that morning. "Since we've brewed so much beer, we can afford to have some before evening," she said. The girl went down into the cellar, but she found all the kegs empty, down to the last one.

Old man Klasa used to borrow Sven's silver pitcher when he expected a visit from his brother. This giant lived on that part of the globe where the sun never shines, and which is therefore called "the deepest darkness." When he saw Sven's silver pitcher, he was astonished and said: "You're pretty well off! You're so thick with Christians you can drink out of their pitcher. I'm glad I have a chance to join in." Nevertheless, he advised old man Klasa to move while all was still going well, for it could never last.

Once, however, a fisherman named Jäppa expressed a desire to see old man Klasa, and one night his wish was granted. He saw the giant sitting headless in a boat, using his arms as oars, and he was going so fast the bow wave was surging high up the prow.

Old man Klasa had taken his brother's advice to heart, and one fair night some other fishermen saw a long procession driving across the water. They understood at once that it was the giant moving out of the area. He left the power over the lake to whoever would take it.

[Karlshamn, Blekinge. Collected by Eva Wigström in 1883 and printed in her "Folktro och sägner från skilda landskap (Folkdiktning, 3:e samlingen)," *SvLm*, 8:3 (1898–1914), 37–38.]

Giants are primarily involved in stories emphasizing their supernatural strength or size, frequently in relation to the local environment. They do not tend to be individualized and localized unless there is a prominent mountain or ridge in which they may be thought to reside. Klasahall is just such a formation, and so the old man is made its resident. Once he has been localized into the area, he can take over many of the functions which might otherwise have been assigned to more common nature-beings. One would expect the fishing in the lake to be controlled by the *sjörå* or *näck*, and the vision of the headless boatsman perhaps should have been identified as a *gast*. Regarding this text see further C. W. von Sydow, "Jättarna i mytologi och folktro," *FmFt*, 6 (1919), 82–83. The giants' childish delight at the trappings of Christianity (except the ringing of the church-bells), however, and their decision to leave the area because they cannot abide the changing times, are typical features of belief in giants.

17. A Toy for the Giant

ONCE a giant and his daughter—they lived, in fact, in the mountain at Haxered—were out for a walk. The giant sat down to rest on a stone, but his daughter went on to have a look around. Almost immediately she returned with something in her apron. "What a nice toy!," she said, and she was very happy. And so the old man had to have a look, and he saw immediately that it was a farmer with his oxen and plow. "Take them back where you found them, for those are the people who will come after us," he said. The girl was not very pleased at that, but she did what he said anyway.

[Rolfstorp, Halland. IFGH 1824, p. 15. Collected by G. Johansson in 1929 from an informant born in 1860. Printed in Helmer Olsson, "Sägnen om jätteleksaken," *FmFt*, 22 (1935), 36–37.]

This international tale-type, AT 701 and ML 5015, "The Giant's Toy," has been intensively studied by Valerie Höttges, *Die Sage vom Riesenspielzeug* (Jena, 1931), and *Typenverzeichnis der deutschen Riesen- und riesischen Teufelssagen*, FFC, 122 (Helsinki, 1937), pp. 172 ff. According to her findings, the tale is most widely spread in Germany and Sweden and is likely to have originated during the tenth century in North Germany and spread thence into Scandinavia on a path to the northeast. Her dating has been challenged by Waldemar Liungman, who places the origin of the tale during the later sixteenth century ("Jätteleksaken," *FmFt*, 18 [1931], 83–90). In any case, the earliest attestation is no older than 1595, from North Germany.

This is one of the few giant legends in which the giants are presented as enormous creatures, but of course without the great difference in stature between giants and humans the story could not exist. The statement of the giant father, that men are to follow the giants, is a genuine element of folk belief: the giants were once more populous, but now they have died out, leaving behind only a few ruins and other physical aspects of the landscape.

The tale was popular with romantic poets in Germany. In 1817, Friedrich Rückert composed a little poem in ballad style, "Die Riesen und die Zwerge," which recounted it. The poem was translated into Swedish, and a text from Dalsland, preserved in VFA, is printed in Olsson, op. cit., p. 38.

18. Save It for Tomorrow

NOT far from Askedal there lived long ago a giant who was terribly friendly with his neighbor, Old Man Askedal. The old man got invited to a meal every day. But then there came a day when the old fellow just didn't have time to go, so he advised the giant that if he had more food than he could take care of that day, he should save it for the next. To this the giant replied, "That's really good advice, and you should have told me sooner, then you'd never have been invited." After that day it never occurred to the giant to invite Old Askedal to a meal.

[Näs, Värmland. IFGH 791:11. Recounted in 1926 by Sven Andersson, Takene, S.Ny., born 1846. Printed in Nilsson/Bergstrand, *Värmlandsnäs* 3:92.]

This legend is widely spread in southwest Sweden, displaying many variants, most of which lead up to the same punch line. Since the giants died out long ago, one could afford to make fun of their greed and stupidity, and hence they are the most popular characters in this legend. Trolls and occasionally the devil are also met with.

19. The Giant Who Moved

HERE in Gällstad there was a soldier named Ranke. He was in the war in Denmark. And when the war was over, he set off for home. Then he came to a forest, and a fire was burning there. He went up to the fire and there sat a giant who was warming himself. The giant struck up a conversation with the soldier and found out he was from Gällstad. Then the giant said that he had lived in the nearby Nyckla mountains, but when they built the church in Gällstad he couldn't stay there any longer, since he couldn't stand to hear the churchbells.

Then he said, "I'll help you get home." He took a belt and put it on the soldier, and that belt would somehow move him, so that he would find the right way back. And when he got home he was to go to the daughter of the farmer at Attarp and leave the belt with her.

And then the giant said that he had left two dogs behind in the Nyckla mountains, and he asked the soldier to let them out. And then he could take as much money as was there, but he mustn't say a word, for then the mound would close up.

However, on the way back the soldier had to relieve himself, and so he undid his trousers. He took off the belt and fastened it around a tree, but it got up on the ground and moved off.

Later he came to the Nyckla mountains and let the giant's dogs loose. And he carried out a pile of money. But then someone came and started chatting with him, and he forgot that he was supposed to keep silent. But while he was talking the mound closed up, and he couldn't find any way in. But he had taken out enough to do nicely for the rest of his life.

[Kind, Västergötland. Recounted in 1933 by Lovisa Gustavsson, Gällstad, born there in 1849. Printed in Bergstrand, *Gammalt från Kind* 3, pp. 64–65.]

This story is found throughout southwest Sweden, usually tied to the specific town of the informant. The move because of churchbells is sometimes used to illustrate giants' fear of Christianity. Most variants of the tale also include the motif of the magic belt, the favor for the giant back home, and the monetary reward. Others include a "gift" for the woman back home, frequently a chest, through which the giant hopes to gain revenge—usually in vain when the human(s) involved set off the revenge too soon.

An interesting variant is printed in Swahn, *Blekingebilder*, pp. 252–255. Here the troll has moved to Africa, where he saves a Swedish sailor from cannibals. He sends the man back to Blekinge to release his dog. The narrator anticipates two problems and provides solutions: the dog will ignore the man because of its joy in freedom, and the key will magically direct the sailor to its lock. Ultimately he fails to recover any treasure because he instinctively recites the Lord's Prayer at the terrifying sight of the hellhound.

Nordic folklorists refer to the legend as "The Giant on the Island." After the investigation by the Danish folklorist H. F. Feilberg in his classic *Bjærgtagen,* Danmarks Folkeminder, 5 (Copenhagen, 1910), pp. 82–84, most now agree that the non-Scandinavian attestations of the revenge-gift tale are to be traced to the ancient Hellenic tradition of the cloak of Nessos, sent by Deianeira to Herakles, who was tormented and finally killed by it. Johan Kalén, however, in "Hämndegåvan: några ord om en sägentyp," *FmFt,* 22 (1935), 107–120, has argued that the point of the Scandinavian variants is primarily the message home. The revenge motif occurs, according to his statistics, only in approximately one-fourth of the attestations of "The Giant on the Island" in Scandinavia.

20. The Big Boulder North of Torstuna Church

In pagan times when churches were being built, there was a giant who was helping with Torstun Church and another with Östrund Church. Now it happened that the giants had a falling out over who had finished his church first, for you see they both finished on the same day, nearly at the same hour, and now they both claimed to have finished first, of course. But as they quarreled over it, the Östrund giant became extremely angry and took a huge stone and threw it at Torstun Church. But the stone didn't make it the whole way; instead it landed on Härleberget (a nearby mountain), and there it stands today, right opposite our church. And to this very day marks are visible on the stone from the giant's fingers and thumb. The stone stands all by itself on the flat mountain, so it's obvious it was thrown there. But Torstun Church—why, it stayed there, since the giant couldn't knock it down.

[Torstuna, Uppland. Collected by Alfr. Thorén, between 1870 and 1890, from Mother Thorén, reported by Lasse Collén. ULMA 26:3, p. 15. Printed in Lundell et al., *SvLm,* 3:2 (1881–1946), 207.]

A typical *jättekast* in explanation of a major feature of the landscape. Noteworthy is the idea that the giants helped build churches; cf. ML 7065 "The Building of the Church."

Identification of marks on various stones and rocks as the imprints of giants is a frequently encountered etiological motif. It is often thought to have taken place "at the time when the rocks were soft." For another variant, cf. Linné, *Lapplandsresa år 1732* (Stockholm, 1965), p. 25.

21. *It's a Long Way to Gamla Uppsala*

SPEAKING of trolls and the like, I recall they say that near Svista at Prästberget there had come a giant with a whole boulder (Prästberget) on his back. He was on his way to Gamla Uppsala Church in order to destroy it. At Svista he met a shoemaker with a load of old shoes on his back.

"How far is it to Gamla Uppsala?," the giant asked.

"It's unbelievably far," the shoemaker is supposed to have said. "I'm just coming from there now, and remember, I wore out these shoes along the way."

Well, then the giant thought it wasn't worthwhile to carry that big stone such a long way. He threw it into the field, and it's still there.

[Skuttunge sn., Bälinge hd., Uppland. Collected by Elias Grip in 1896 from the mother of Jan Pär. Printed in Grip, "Skuttungeock Björklingemål: Folksägner," *SvLm*, 18:3 (1899), 7.]

An interesting variation on the *jättekast*. Here the motif has been recast into a legend displaying the characteristics of most narrative legends. A villain (the giant) threatens an area with devastation (destruction of the most important Christian symbol in the parish). The threat is countered by the actions of the hero (the unnamed shoemaker), who tricks the giant in a multiform of battle and thus saves the community from disaster.

The story has affinities with various fictional folktales, particularly the Tales of the Stupid Ogre. The hero's identity is unspecified, and it seems from the tone of the story, from the very first line, that the informant was unwilling to vouch for its veracity.

In a parallel story from Skåne, the giant Finn is said to have set out with a bag full of gravel to bury the cathedral at Lund. As he strode toward the church the gravel ran out of a hole in the sack. This was the origin of Brusabrink in Linderöd, Skåne, and the discarded sack became a nearby pine-covered slope. See William Lengertz, *Sägner och historier från Gärds,* p. 122. Many other variants are also attested.

22. *A Giant Builds a Church (The Finn Legend)*

My mother used to say that in the parish was a parson who wanted to get a church built. He was out walking one evening when he met an old man, who agreed to build the church; but for his wages he was to have either the parson himself or the sun and the moon, as long as the parson could not figure out his name before the work was finished. But the parson discovered what the old man's name was. When the church was very nearly finished, the parson was out and he walked by a mountain. Then he could hear how a woman was singing inside the mountain:

Tomorrow Skalle will come home
With the sun and moon or the parson, too.

When the parson arrived at the church, the old man was putting up the cross on the tower. "Put the cross up straight, Skalle!," the parson called out to him. Then the old man threw himself down and tried to land on the parson and kill him, but he landed on the ground and killed himself.

[Kind, Västergötland. Linus Karlsson, born in Holsljunga in 1865. Printed in Bergstrand, *Gammalt från Kind,* 3:62.]

Swedish folklorists usually refer to legends of this type as the Finn-legend, because in South Sweden many of the variants describe the construction of the cathedral at Lund for St. Laurentius by a giant named Finn. It is ML 7065, "Building a Church. The Name of the Masterbuilder," and is found throughout Scandinavia and along its periphery in Finland and Germany. In Sweden the tale has a center of distribution in the southwest and is also found in the north. It is closely related to the account in Snorri Sturluson's *Edda* of the construction of Asgard, the stronghold of the gods, by a giant aided by a horse with supernatural powers. According to his agreement with the gods, he is to receive Freyja, the fairest of the goddesses, as well as the sun and the moon, if he completes his work during the allotted time. He fails, of course, but only in the nick of time: Loki, whose counsel led to the striking of the bargain, changes himself into a mare and lures away the giant's mighty horse. The giant is subsequently killed and the gods get their stronghold. Certain Irish saints' legends and heroic tales are thought to have provided the sources of this Old Norse myth. Its popular counterpart was presumably our legend, and most scholars feel it got the element of guessing the masterbuilder's name from the international wonder-tale of Titeliture (Rumpelstilzchen, Tom-Tit-Tot), AT 500, "The Name of the Helper." At any rate, it seems to have settled first on the church in Trondheim, Norway, with St. Olof as the patron building the church, and spread thence to other areas. Some scholars divide the variants into groups, based on the giant's name; Skalle, the name of the giant in our variant, is said to typify a Trondheim or northern group, but this has been challenged. Dividing the attestations of this legend into groups appears, indeed, a rather misconceived task, since what is most striking about it is its homogeneity. The only real variety is in the name of the giant, who is called, besides Finn and Skalle, also Tvester and a few other names. The contractor for the construction is a local patron saint, if one is available; otherwise generally an unnamed parson, as here.

Perhaps because it is associated with the cathedral in the university town of Lund, the Finn-legend has been scrutinized closely. Among the more important works are the following. By C. W. von Sydow are the standard works, now somewhat outmoded, including "Studier i Finnsägnen och besläktade byggmästarsägner," *Fataburen*, 1907, pp. 65–78, 119–218, and 1908, pp. 19–27, and "Iriskt inflytande på nordisk guda- och hjältesaga," *Vetenskapssocieteten i Lund, Årsbok*, 1920, pp. 26–61. Generally following von Sydow, Mai Fossenius pinpoints the spread of the legend outward from Trondheim during the fourteenth century, in "Sägnerna om trollen Finn och Skalle som byggmästare," *Folkkultur*, 3 (1943), 5–144. This is the most complete discussion of the distribution of the Swedish variants. More critical stances are taken by Jöran Sahlgren, "Sägnerna om trollen Finn och

Skalle och deras kyrkobyggande," *Saga och Sed,* 1940, pp. 1–50, and 1941, pp. 115–154 (which attacks von Sydow and stresses the value of older recordings), and Waldemar Liungman, "Finnsägenproblemet," *FmFt,* 29 (1942), 86–113, 138–154 (which denies Celtic influence and assigns origins to Denmark). The European context is treated by Inger M. Boberg, *Baumeistersagen,* FFC, 151 (Helsinki, 1955).

23. The Old Man from Håberg

On a farm in Jörlanda parish they had a child who was to be christened. The farm hand was supposed to go around inviting people to the christening. The farmer wanted to invite the old man from Håberg, for if he is invited he gives a sumptuous christening gift. But they did not want him to come to the festivities, for he is so dreadful to look at, and he eats much more than any Christian. Well, the farm hand entered the old man's cave, conveyed the farmer's greetings, and invited him to the christening. The giant thanked him happily. Then he asked: "But isn't it customary to give a christening present?"

"Yes indeed, it certainly is." The lad was asked to accompany the giant into the mountain and hold open a large sack. And the giant poured in a large scoopful of gold and silver coins. "Have you ever seen anyone give more?"

"That I have," said the lad. Then the giant added another scoop.

"Have you ever seen anyone give more than *that*?"

"Some give more, some less," said the boy. With that the giant added a third scoop, and then the sack was so heavy the boy could hardly carry it.

"Well, I've never seen anyone give more than this," he said.

"Now," said the giant, "tell me who is coming to the party."

"Well," said the lad, "many great people will be there. St. Peter is coming, and so is the Drumbeater."

"Ah, so the Drumbeater [thunder] is coming. Well, in that case I can't make it, since I can't stand the sight of him. He hit me in the leg the other day and I'm still limping."

[Sibräcka, Bohuslän. Collected by Vilhelm Cederschiöld from Olaus Olsson, who had it from Herman Nilsson, seventy-two years old at the time. Printed in Cederschiöld, "Ur Olaus Olssons sägensamling," *FmFt*, 19 (1932), 103.]

This wonder-tale, AT 1165, "The Troll and the Christening," was extremely popular in Sweden, where it is ordinarily associated with the rock formation called Hoberg on Gotland, a thirty-seven metre tall outcrop of limestone on the south tip of the island. Attestations of the tale reach back into the eighteenth century in Sweden, and it was the subject of a widely distributed broadside which was dramatized at the Royal Theatre in Stockholm in 1836. Many of the subsequent recordings of the tale, including perhaps the one printed here, seem to have been influenced by the broadside. See Waldemar Liungman, *Sveriges samtliga folksagor* (Djursholm, 1952), 3:327.

The folk belief behind the tale is that lightning seeks out trolls and giants, perhaps a reflection of the giant-slaying of Thor in Old Norse mythology. Many informants have told collectors that the reason the giants or trolls are no longer populous is the accuracy and efficiency of the lightning strokes.

24. Trolls Take Over the Farm

THERE was a farmer in Millesvik who could never get peace from the trolls on Christmas Eve. As the night wore on, they always came and made their mischief in the sitting room. The man was beside himself every Christmas, since he was afraid that in the end they would take him too. But then he was informed by a wise old woman that he should put the bible over one door and the hymnal over the other, and on the chimney he should make a cross. This he did, and the trolls couldn't get in; but they made a huge racket outside and on the roof. And so he did the same thing afterwards every Christmas as long as he lived.

[Näs, Värmland. IFGH 1523-1. Recounted by Anders Fröjdendahl in 1929. Printed in Nilsson/Bergstrand, *Värmlandsnäs*, 3:107.]

A more straightforward story than the fanciful "Bear Trainer and the Trolls," which follows. In this story the traditional symbols of Christianity are used to ward off the trolls. The forces of the other world were particularly dangerous during the time around great holidays (see Introduction, p. 17), and this kind of occupation is frequently attested in Scandinavian folk tradition. In Norway the supernatural beings are likely to be the dead; in Sweden the trolls are more common.

25. The Bear Trainer and the Trolls

THE trolls came to Lycke and wanted to borrow something to drink every Christmas. They brought copper buckles and copper yokes from their plows to carry it away in. One Christmas when they arrived, there was an animal tamer there who had taken lodgings for the night, and he had a little bear with him. He had gone to lie down on top of part of the oven, and he had the bear with him. Now when the trolls came and stood on the floor demanding their drinks, the animal trainer pushed down his bear onto the floor, and the trolls were terrified and fled.

The next year, one of the trolls came up and asked the people who lived there if they still had their big, fierce cat. "Now she's much worse," they said, "now she has seven kittens." After that the trolls never again dared show their faces in Lycke.

[Hemsjö, Västergötland. IFGH 2879: 28–29. Collected by Helmer Olsson in 1932 from Frida Svensson, from Finndalen, born in 1871 in Hemsjö. Printed in Klintberg, p. 130, no. 113.]

Folklorists will recognize this as an international tale type, AT 1161 "The Bear Trainer and His Bear," which is widely represented in Scandinavia and is also found in Germany, Scotland, the Baltic, and some Slavic-speaking areas. Christiansen has designated it ML 6015 in his catalogue of Norwegian migratory legends. Indeed, the most well-known variant is Norwegian —namely, "Kjetta på Dovre" from Asbjørnsen and Moe, which has acquired an extensive bibliography; it has also been associated with the Peer Gynt of folk tradition. Bruno Schier, "Die

Sage vom Schrätel und Wasserbären," *Mitteldeutsche Blätter für Volkskunde,* 10 (1935), 164–180, thinks the legend originated in southern Scandinavia and was spread to the east and south by the migration of the East Germanic tribes during the period of Germanic migrations, which began more than two millenia ago. Although this hypothesis is unlikely for a number of reasons, it is true that the tale is attested as early as 1217 in the verse of Heinrich von Freiburg (see Lutz Röhrich, *Erzählungen des späten Mittelalters und ihr Weiterleben in Literatur und Volksdichtung bis zur Gegenwart,* 1 [Bern, 1962], pp. 235–243; Heinrich von Freiburg's poem and fifteen other early variants are found on pp. 11–26). For a list of the Swedish variants, see Waldemar Liungman, *Sveriges samtliga folksagor* (Djursholm, 1952), 3: 506–509. The Norwegian variants are studied in Reidar Th. Christiansen, "Kjætten på Dovre," *Videnskapsselskapets skrifter, II. hist.-filos. kl.,* 6 (Oslo, 1922), and "The Dead and the Living," *Studia Norvegica,* 1:2 (1946), 72 ff; and in Knut Liestøl, "Kjetta på Dovre," *Maal og minne,* 1933, pp. 24–48.

In comparison with the preceding tale it is clear that although the stories are structurally very similar they are worlds apart in tone and purpose. "The Bear Trainer and the Trolls" is a purely entertaining story. Firmly anchored as it is in folk belief, the tone, and particularly the characteristic statement to the trolls that the "cat" has had kittens, belong to the realm of the wondertale. In contrast, "Trolls Take Over the Farm" might well have been told as a memorate.

26. *Beating the Changeling*

Britta-Stina in Toknejala told how a troll had come to a certain place around here and left a changeling for a human infant. She took the child and put her own in its place. But then a wise old lady came by, and she advised them to beat the changeling three Thursday nights in a row. On the third Thursday night the troll came in. "I haven't been as mean to your child as you have been to mine," she said. And so she left the human child and took back her own.

[Näs, Värmland. IFGH 5324:25. Collector and informant not stated. Printed in Nilsson/Bergstrand, *Värmlandsnäs,* 3:105.]

The classic changeling story in its barest essentials. Note the magic value of consecutive Thursday evenings, also found in story no. 55. A version of the changeling story as short as this one makes it clear that much of the value of the story is the didactic statement by the troll mother regarding mistreatment of children. This statement is not often omitted.

27. The Changeling Speaks on the Way to Baptism

WITHOUT her knowing it, a woman had her child exchanged by the trolls before she had a chance to make it Christian (i.e., by baptism). Well, she sent for a godmother who was to take the child to church and other godparents and made preparations for the celebration as best she could. Now when the godmother came riding to church with the baby in her lap on the way to the baptism, there was a little troll-child sitting on a rock by the side of the road. As they rode by, the troll-child said:

"Kille Kopp, where are you going?"

The changeling, who lay on the woman's knee, replied: "I am off to the church to become a Christian." But when the woman heard the little baby on her knee begin to talk, she knew something was wrong. She was frightened and turned home. And when she got home she explained everything and told them the child must be a changeling. Then they all decided that the best course was to fire up the oven and burn the troll-baby. Well, they fired up the oven and when the coals were as red as could be they put the child in a pan and pretended they were about to throw him in. But at that moment the troll-woman came in, snatched up the baby, and threw the human child down in a heap.

[Värend, Småland. Collected by G. O. Hyltén-Cavallius from "Halta-Marita" in June, 1843. Printed in *Wärend och Wirdarne* 2:317 and Hyltén-Cavallius, "Folksägner från Värend," ed. Nils-Arvid Bringéus, *Kronobergsboken,* 1968, p. 88.]

In this more clearly fabulous changeling tale, the troll-child gives himself away without any encouragement from his human family. His only odd behavior is to speak at an absurdly early age, but otherwise he does not seem to have been much of a problem. After the recognition the tried-and-true method of threatening the changeling with bodily harm effects an exchange. Since the story omits the intolerable behavior of the changeling and the didactic comment of the troll-mother at the moment of the re-exchange, one can assume that the tale was intended more solely for entertainment than certain other changeling stories.

As it happens, the story is not strongly rooted in Nordic tradition. It is attested in Central and South Sweden and in Denmark but is rare in North Sweden and Norway. This distribution accords well with the obvious German origin of the tale. The epic moment is the exchange between the two troll-children in a formula which is tolerably constant throughout most of the attestations. The name of the changeling, *Kille Kopp*, reflects German dialect *Kielkropf* ("changeling, aborted fetus, etc."), and there are even variants attested in Denmark in which the two trolls speak Low German to each other (J. S. Møller, *Moder og barn i dansk folkeoverlevering*, Danmarks Folkeminder, 48 [Copenhagen, 1940], p. 259). A standard monograph is Gisela Piaschewski, *Der Wechselbalg: ein Beitrag zum Aberglauben der nordeuropäischen Völker*, Deutschkundliche Arbeiten, A, 5 (Breslau, 1935).

The changeling is of course delighted to be on his way to church for baptism, since joining the Christian community will assure him of eternal salvation, otherwise unknown to members of the other world. See story 50, "The Näck Longs for Salvation."

28. *Changing a Housewife*

A MAN was supposed to leave on a journey in the morning. His wife was named Sara, and she had just had a child. And when he was riding off and had just reached the pear tree, he heard someone chopping on a piece of wood. And he stopped, and he heard people saying:

"Sara's breasts are like this, Sara's arms are like this, Sara's legs are like this." When he heard people talking like that as they were chopping wood, he turned back. When he came home, he met them in the entry hall with Sara, and they had put the wooden figure in the bed in place of the human.

She had not yet formally re-entered the church.

That farm still exists.

[Falsterbo, Skytts härad, Skåne. LAF 382. Collected by Emil Sommarin in 1897. Printed in Ingemar Ingars, ed., "Texter från Skåne," part 2 of J. A. Lundell et al., "Sagor, sägner, legender . . . ," *SvLm*, 3:3 (1945), 41.]

An unusual story in which the otherworlders seem to be attempting to carry out a changing on a grown woman rather than an infant, a variation of *bergtagning*. Substitution of the wood figure is reminiscent of the ability in Nordic folk tradition of witches to transpose common items, frequently of wood, into their shape when they are off to attend a black mass. Typically they are found out when a knife stuck into the woman turns up the following day in the wood object; cf. Christiansen ML 3055 and story no. 79.

The important point of the story is that the woman has not yet undergone formal re-entry into the church after childbirth (*kyrktagning*) and hence is vulnerable, rather like a new-born child. See Introduction, pp. 12–13.

The pear tree mentioned in the story has been the subject of a number of folk traditions. See Nicolovius, *Folklifvet i Skytts härad*, 3rd ed., p. 116.

29. Communion Wine in the Troll Food

ONCE there were three boys who had been out partying and didn't come home until Sunday morning. As they passed by a mountain they saw a beautiful girl washing herself in front of the mountainside. She asked who they were, and they responded that they were musicians. "Then you shall play at my wedding," she said.

"Yes," they said, "if we're invited, we'll do it." But later, when they had sobered up, they regretted what they had done and went to talk with the parson. He told them that a promise was a promise, and they had to keep it. He gave them communion before they left, however, with a little extra communion wine which they were to put into the trolls' food; but they were not to eat or drink if the trolls offered them anything.

They did what the parson had told them—and when the trolls tasted the wine in the food, they went crazy, and there was such a brawl that all the trolls killed each other.

But up on the oven sat an old hag. "I have outlived seven oak forests," she said, "but I've never seen such a wild bashing of heads."

[Rolfstrop, Halland. IFGH 3634:6–7. Klintberg p. 132, no. 116. Collected in 1935 from Maurits Bengtsson, born 1864.]

According to Klintberg's note, the tale is distributed from Blekinge to Dalarna and was particularly common in Östergötland. It is an interesting story in several respects. The boys have broken two unspoken rules: by partying late they have apparently missed church service (cf. the Hårga-dance); and they have made a promise to a supernatural being. Ordinarily one would expect them to be taught a severe lesson, but in the more traditionalized legends the humans always triumph over the otherworlders, and so the boys are saved. The parson assumes the role of the "clever" adviser, and his advice turns on the tacit assumption throughout this tradition that Christianity is anathema to the non-Christian inhabiters of the other world. So it is here, and one should contrast the wild brawl the inverted Eucharist inspires in the trolls with the solemn ceremony of the Christian community.

The final remark of the old hag on the oven, typical of troll talk (cf. the musings of changelings when confronted with inverted or bizarre household practices), ends the story with a rather light touch.

30. Bergtagen

There was a serving-girl from Våla who was tending cows up on Lansberg. Once she noticed a charcoal-black cow in among her flock. Then she took out her knife and threw it over that cow, so that it had to stay there, for you see, it was the trolls that owned it, of course. And later, in the evening when she sat milking that very cow, the troll-hag came into the barn and asked why the girl had taken her cow. And then the girl asked her to take it back. But she didn't want it, and instead she said: "You'll pay for this on your day of honor."

Then the girl burst into tears and begged her to be merciful and not harm her. But it didn't do any good. Then the troll-hag went away.

And when a year or so had passed, the time had come for the girl to marry. And then on her wedding day she remembered what the troll-hag had said, and so she took every care not to go out. But at one point it became impossible for her to stay inside, and then she was taken by the trolls. And while they were carrying her off, the wedding guests shouted to her: "Kick back, Annika!" And she kicked back, as hard as she could, but it was too late for her to be able to defend herself from the trolls by any means. They still didn't have any power over her gold crown, however, and that very day there came a goat up to the wedding party and placed the crown on a stairway. It also had a napkin with it which it was able to spread out under the crown, and then it went away.

Afterwards they sometimes saw that girl wandering among the mountains, but they were never able to get her back.

[Norberg, Västmanland. ULMA 93:37:3. Reported by Erik Andersson (Brate) in 1878, informant not stated. Printed in J. A. Lundell et al., "Sagor, sägner, legender, äventyr och skildringar av folkets levnadssätt på landsmål," *SvLm*, 3:2 (1881–1946), 221–222.]

Here the *bergtagning* has been motivated by the girl's theft of the troll cow. Throwing her knife over it broke the trolls' power over it because, presumably, of the iron or steel in the knife. Although one expects theft of anything from the trolls to lead to trouble, it should be noted that there is a vast number of memorates telling of the acquisition of cows from the other world in just this manner, in which the cow simply joins the protagonist's herd and the protagonist suffers no ill effects from the otherworldly beings.

A pair of traditions seems to be involved in the timing of the *bergtagning*. Marriageable men and women are extremely vulnerable to the trolls until the vows are exchanged (see Introduction, p. 14); this has formed the subject of a number of migratory legends, ML 5090–6005 and related tales, and has also affected the conception of certain beings, such as the *näck* in ballads. In this story, however, arranging the kidnapping for the very day of the girl's wedding seems to be little more than an act of vicious revenge on the part of the trolls. A second tradition which may also have been at work, however, is that of the *vättabröllop* or fairy wedding. In these tales a girl witnesses a fairy wedding and inadvertently does something to interrupt or spoil the ceremony. Later at her own wedding the same thing happens to the girl. Traditions of this nature may well have contributed to the seizing on her wedding day of the girl who took the trolls' cow.

Return of the crown seems to symbolize continued viability of the marriage sacrament despite loss of the bride in this one case.

31. The Silver Mountain

AT SILVERBERGET in the vicinity of Södra Vi is the croft Rotebäcken. A five-year-old boy was kidnapped by the trolls (*bergtagen*) when he was at the household well in the garden. A giant who lived in the mountain came to the well, took the boy under his arm, and carried him to his dwelling in the mountain. But the churchbells have a power no trolls can manage. When the boy was questioned, he answered that it gleamed inside there. And from that comes the name Silverberget (the Silver Mountain).

[Södra Vi, Sevede härad, Småland. Collected from K. Edvin Isaksson, born in 1895, and printed in Elis Åström, *Folktro och folkliv i Östergötland* (SKGAAF, no. 39, 1962), p. 24; also printed with English translation in Floyd, p. 386.]

Here *bergtagning* has been employed in an etiological legend (origin-tale) explaining a local place name. The *bergtagning* itself, since it was not of principal interest in the story, has been reduced to paradigmatic format. A member of the other world comes to our world and steals away a boy. This is relatively rare in the annals of *bergtagning*, which usually occurs far from human habitation. As is usual in most of the traditionalized legends, the victim is rescued from the trolls, in this case by the ringing of the churchbells, a common motif in narrative with real practical value (see Introduction, p. 34).

32. Stealing for the Trolls

It happened long ago in Skatelöf parish that a girl disappeared so completely that no one knew what had become of her, wherever she was. After they had searched far and wide for her and turned up nothing, the only explanation was that she had been kidnapped by the trolls. And in fact she had been. For the girl had been taken into the mountain by the mountain trolls, and there she had to perform every sort of service for them, like it or not, and the worst was doubtless when they sat her down to "milk the perch." But from time to time the trolls ordered her to go to town to steal grain and food and anything else she could lay her hands on. But when they sent her to the farms they always put a hat on her which made her invisible.

It happened one day that she came to Gunnarslöf's mill near Högnalöf to steal grain. But she fared no better there than a lamb among the wolves, for just as she was dragging away a heavy sack of flour, the miller without knowing it bumped into her so that the hat fell off. Then the miller could immediately see what was going on, and he took her home to her parents. There she told much about the trolls and *tomtar* and all their behavior, and about all the riches inside the mountain and above all in

Kungshögen near Ingelstad and in Lindeberg near Kalfsvik. But every now and then her mind seemed to wander, and from that time on she was twisted and bent; the cause of this was that she had had to carry so many heavy loads for the trolls.

[Värend, Småland. Collected by G. Hyltén-Cavallius in 1839 from a fisherman at Åsnen. Printed in *Wärend och Wirdarne,* 1:12 ff. and N. A. Bringéus, ed., "Folksägner från Värend, upptecknade av Gunnar Olof Hyltén-Cavallius," *Kronobergsboken,* 1968, p. 87.]

In this story of *bergtagning* the problem of the return has been solved by incorporating the motif of the hat of invisibility (MI F451.3.3.8), so popular in medieval narrative. In Scandinavian legends this motif is generally found in short accounts of the adventures of someone who has somehow briefly got hold of one. A rare but distinct pattern has been discerned by Christiansen (ML 6050, "The Fairy Hat"), in which a man wears such a hat to a wedding, where he learns that a number of the guests are trolls with the same kind of hat; this story is also found in southern Sweden.

The hat of invisibility in the story printed here would, of course, provide a seemly explanation for the appearance of the long-lost girl caught lugging off a sack of the miller's flour. The same might be said of her tales about the inside of the mountain, and one wonders whether her disappearance might have been voluntary. Her mental and physical deformity after the *bergtagning* are traditional, but perhaps she hurt her back slinking off with heavy sacks of the miller's flour, and perhaps her mind wandered because she often wished she were somewhere else. At any rate, we are now dealing with a migratory legend. No one seems to know who she was, and the tale is set in the distant past.

33. The Pan Legend

At another farm where they also were doing their brewing, there came in a little man with a kettle, and he helped himself to the best wort for himself without anybody noticing it. And there was also a man who was on his way to that farm, and along the way he met someone who said to him: "When you get to that farm, tell Vurtesniken to hurry home, for Ållermore is dying."

Then you should have seen that miserable old man get moving! He ran out the door as fast as he could and left his kettle behind.

[N. Ving, V. Valle härad, Västergötland. ULMA 111:348. Collected in 1900 by Hj. Alner, informant not stated. Printed in Inger M. Boberg, *Sagnet om den store Pans død*, SKGAAF, 2 (Copenhagen, 1934), p. 73.]

The classical Pan legend, Christiansen ML 6070A, "Fairies Send a Message," is found throughout Scandinavia and Western Europe. The legend is called the Pan legend because of the similarity, first pointed out by Felix Liebrecht in 1856, of the European tales with Plutarch's account of the message of the death of the Great Pan ("De defectu oraculorum," *Moralia*, 3:17). The account, which is ascribed to a certain Epitherses, tells of a voice requesting a passenger on a merchant ship to report, when the ship reached Palodes, that the Great Pan was dead. When the ship was becalmed off Palodes, the man complied with the request, and a great wailing was heard from the shore. Although Pan is not named in the European variants, the similarity is striking, particularly as the dead being is sometimes said to have been a king of the spirits.

In Norway and Sweden the legend has frequently, as here, been expanded to include the motif of theft of beer; a second popular motif is identification of the dead troll as the beer thief's child, who is said to have fallen into the fire. In many variants the kettle or bucket left behind is still said to be on hand and is cited as authority for the legend.

The form of the legend printed here is typical of Southwest Sweden (Halland, Småland, Västergötland, and Dalsland). Boberg (pp. 71 ff.) regards it as a contamination with a second and rather minor group of legends detailing the activities of beer-stealing *vättar*. Since a principal version of the Pan legend in Scandinavia includes beer-stealing, this was a natural crossing. It is certainly true that the supernatural beer thief in our variant is no common troll, for his name, Vurtesniken, means "covetous of wort."

Archer Taylor, *Northern Parallels to the Death of Pan*, Washington University Studies, 10 (Seattle, 1922), has shown that the basis of the story is likely to be wind or other sounds of nature interpreted by a lonely traveler as some sort of message from the other world. Indeed, many of the Swedish variants stress the human protagonist's ignorance of whom the message is intended for. Taylor's hypothesis takes in all sorts of messages from the other world, but the epic basis of this group of legends is precisely that someone has died, presumably because that is the most important kind of message one can send.

34. A Message for the Cat

A FARMER was walking alongside the mountain Klockberget. He was wearing white gloves. He saw a large white cat sitting on the top of a ledge. The cat howled: "Per with the white gloves, tell Katte-Kurr that Katte-Murr is dead." The farmer's cat was named Katte-Kurr, and when it heard what the man had to say, it said: "You could have told me sooner," leapt at the man and bit him fatally, and then vanished out the window.

[Angered, Västergötland. IFGH 1620, recorded by Sigurd Dahllöf. Printed in Joh. Kalén, "En typ av Pansägnen i västsvenska uppteckningar," *FmFt*, 23 (1936), 91–92.]

The Pan legend with feline characters, Christiansen 6070B, "King of the Cats," is prevalent in England and frequent in most of Western Europe. About one-fifth of the Danish Pan variants fall into this category, but the type is quite limited in Norway and Sweden; in the latter the center of distribution seems to have been Götaland. Most of these stories end with an expression of joy and subsequent departure of the cat, either because she has now become king of the cats (whence the tag of Christiansen's archetype), or because her enemy has died.

Boberg (*Sagnet om den store Pans død*, pp. 66–101) was unable to locate any Swedish or Norwegian variants of the Pan legend which ended with the motif, familiar in Denmark and elsewhere, of the killing of the messenger. Clearly this text belies her findings.

35. *Ljungby Horn and Pipe*

THERE was a hill in Ljungby where the trolls lived. The coachman at the estate was daring enough to ride there. When he got there, the top of the hill was elevated and they were dancing under it. He rode there on a stallion. Then one of them came out and offered him something to drink. He took the horn and pipe and rode off. But he happened to spill a few drops onto the horse and it burned the skin right off. He rode across the plowed furrows, but the trolls had to run along parallel to them. He got into the barn and they followed him in, but they couldn't do anything to him because of the kicking and fighting of his stallion. But then along came his girlfriend with a lantern, and that was his undoing. Horse and man, they both died.

However, the trolls did not get back the horn and pipe, which are still there. They said that if they got them back, Ljungby would be the richest of all estates, but otherwise it would be the most impoverished and would burn down three times. And that it has done. But the trolls have disappeared.

[Hagestad, Skåne. Collected by Sigfrid Svensson in 1922 and printed in Svensson, "Folksägner om de underjordiska upptecknade i södra Skåne," *FmFt,* 9 (1922), 125.]

The internationally popular tale of the "Drinking Cup of the Fairies," Christiansen ML 6045, in Sweden is centered in the southern and central portions of the country and does not seem to have reached Norrland. Most of the variants from Skåne have been localized to Ljungby, as in the story printed here, with the result that among Swedish folklorists "Ljungby Horn and Pipe" has become a tag for all variants of the migratory legend.

Early attestations abound: the story is found in England in a twelfth-century note by William of Newbury, and is represented in a church painting from the late sixteenth century in Våxtorp, Småland (see Tobias Norlind, *Studier i svensk folklore* [Stockholm, 1911], pp. 61–78). Many variants end happily (cf. story no. 36), and a specifically South Swedish oikotype (regional version) has assimilated the *vantevän* or "glove-friend," whose advice leads the hero to safety (see Klintberg, p. 137 for an example). Our other variant, no. 36, shows why the coachman rode across the plowed furrows: he formed a rudimentary cross which was proof against the trolls.

Many of these stories include some verse, as in our other variant. Quite often, however, the verse is spoken not by the trolls, as there, but rather by a clever person, friendly troll, or some other donor figure, and includes the advice which saves the hero.

The dispersal of the trolls is quite often linked with their loss of the drinking cup, which thus seems to have been a kind of talisman for them. Apparently it was central to their gatherings, primarily, one assumes, for dancing and making merry, and without it they have lost their sense of community; as some variants end, "after that they never got together any more."

36. Retrieving the Cup

A STORY is told about the church at Bro, to the effect that it had had a golden cup, used for communion, which the small underground people took from one of the clergymen and ran off with to a rock outcrop in Bro parish.

The holy vessel was in their power for quite some time. But then along came a lad. First he plowed crossing furrows in the ground around the outcrop. Next he cut the tail and mane off his horse, and then he rode one night up to where the *vättar* lived in the outcrop. They emerged and in welcome offered him a drink out of a horn. But he disdainfully poured the contents out behind his horse. Then they came out with a silver beaker, to which the lad showed no more respect than he had to the horn; he refused to drink from it. And so at last the golden cup was produced. The lad snatched the holy altar vessel and rode off straight for Bro church, the *vättar* in hot pursuit. But they had to make a detour around every point where the furrows crossed, and that gave him a good head start. Nevertheless, the fastest had soon almost caught up with the back of his horse, and those who were puffing and panting behind cried out:

"Grab the door-pull—seize the twine!" But the ones in front called back regretfully:

"There's no door-pull here, no twine to seize," as they reached for the horse's tail and mane.

At last the boy escaped by flinging himself off the horse and over the churchyard wall, the cup in hand. But the *vättar* tore apart the charger.

[Gotland. Collected by Eva Wigström and printed in her "Folktro och sägner från skilda landskap (Folkdiktning, 3:e samlingen)," *SvLm* 8:3 (1898–1914), 88–89.]

This is another variant of story no. 35, "Ljungby Horn," Christiansen ML 6045, "The Drinking Cup of the Fairies." Our two variants demonstrate that the cast of otherworldly characters easily fluctuates in migratory legends and that the boundary between *vättar* and trolls, who in Sweden predominate in this legend, is quite fuzzy.*

What distinguishes this variant is primarily the human provenance of the communion cup, stolen by the *vättar.* More frequent is the notion, as in "Ljungby Horn," that the cup or horn was of fairy origin. The lad in our story is thus out on something of a quest, an elaboration which is perhaps echoed in the epic triad of the drinking vessels offered him by the *vättar.* The questing nature of this little story is aided by the resolute way in which he prepares his escape in advance, with evident foresight. In many other variants of the legend the hero's escape is a breathless, last-minute affair pulled off only at the advice of some onlooker; or, as in our other variant, the hero may fall victim to the trolls. Here the horse seems to die a substitute death, another epic trait, although one might also regard the horse's fate as a parallel to the nearly universal motif in the Swedish form of this legend that the troll drink which the hero sloshes out singes the horse where it grazes him.

---

*Indeed the original of the story does not refer to *vättar*, the term being for the most part limited to the southern provinces, but rather to "the underground people," which I have retained in the first paragraph, and "the small ones," for which I have regularly substituted *vättar* as a fitting and less awkward designation. I have also rendered *stenrös* "rock outcrop" instead of a perhaps more accurate "pile of stones," since the latter does not grant an adequate impression of what a *stenrös* on Gotland really looks like.

37. Encounters with the Skogsrå

A

THERE was a very old woman, Kajsa—she would easily be 140 years old if she were still alive. She had worked as a serving-girl at Längnum, and she used to say they had such large tracts they used for pasturage there. And once the man went out to look for the horses. He looked and he looked, but he didn't find them. And at last he came to the end of the mountain, Galgeberg, in Främmesta, and there stood a truly beautiful girl, combing her hair, but from behind she was hollowed out, like a trough for kneading bread. And she told him where the horses were. That was a *skogsrå.*

[Fridhem, Västergötland. IFGH 1143, p. 3. Reported in 1927 by August Andersson, born in Fridhem in 1858. Printed in Granberg, *Skogsrået,* p. 88.]

B

ONE of my aunts worked as a shepherd, and the *skogsrå,* or Talle-Maja, as they call her, played tricks with her eyesight so that she couldn't find her sheep. My aunt turned her sweater inside out and recited the Lord's Prayer, and then the *skogsrå* lost her power and was turned into a stump, from which could be heard noises like the whinnying of a frightened foal.

[Stavnäs, Värmland, IFGH 2674, pp. 3 ff. Recorded in 1931 from Albert Carlsson, born in Stavnäs in 1854. Printed in Granberg, *Skogsrået,* p. 91.]

C

Two hunters went out hunting one night in the forest near Gissume pond. One of the hunters was an old drunkard, Anders Andersson, and the other was named Oskar Fagerdal. According to Oskar, when they arrived at the pond they saw a beautiful woman walking in the forest. She went up to Anders Andersson's rifle and blew into the barrel, but she ignored Oskar's rifle. When the beautiful woman turned around, Oskar noticed that from behind she looked like a hollowed-out oak tree. Oskar went home right then, but the other hunted and had a good catch.

[Ringarum, Östergötland. LUF 1496, p. 20. Reported in 1925 by Anders Pettersson, born in 1856. Printed in Granberg, *Skogsrået*, p. 120.]

D

Albert E. from Kramptorget, Heds parish, had a charcoal kiln in the vicinity of a lake people call Lorttjärn. One evening he set off for home, and although he was familiar with the area, he just couldn't find his way at all. He became so confused that he was just going in circles. From eight at night until two in the morning he wandered around, then he realized he was dealing with the *skogsrå*, and he did what others had done—and to good purpose—in such circumstances. He took off his coat, rolled it up, and put it on the ground near the roots of a spruce tree. Then he stretched out on the ground, with his head on the coat, but only for a few minutes. When he got up he saw clearly where he was and went straight home.

[Hed, Västmanland. ULMA 3686, p. 16. Reported in 1930 by Albert Eriksson, born in 1866. Printed in Granberg, *Skogsrået*, p. 144.]

These memorates give a rather good image of folk belief concerning the *skogsrå* as it was retained earlier in this century. The informants agree that the *skogsrå* had the form of a beautiful woman when viewed from in front; from behind she looks like a hollow tree trunk. Other common notions are that she is frequently combing her hair, or, on the negative side, that she had a tail. The first three memorates stress her rule over nature and animals, a reflection of the idea that when things go wrong, as when domestic animals are nowhere to be found, the supernatural powers are generally at fault. The positive possibilities of the *skogsrå* have to do with her ability to grant good luck to hunters, frequently, as in *C*, made concrete by her blowing on the rifle of her favorite. That her favorite in this story happens to be a drunkard no doubt reflects negative attitudes toward the *skogsrå* and perhaps also toward those whose hunting success might be traced to her. *B* and particularly *D* deal with the *skogsrå*'s most dangerous ability, to confuse and lead astray. *B* is an example of confusing, one which takes the unusual turn of the *skogsrå*'s transformation into a treestump. This is related to her appearance from behind, one which folk belief held to be more essential to her being. The story told in *D* is one of the most common of *skogsrå* memorates, the story of someone lost in the woods because of the *skogsrå*. The most striking feature of the story is that the *skogsrå* herself never appears. Losing one's way in familiar territory was naturally attributed to the *skogsrå*, and actually catching sight of her was unnecessary to confirm her role. The informant (Albert E. in the story is surely identical to the Albert Eriksson who reported the encounter) used a tried-and-true method, stretching out for a rest near a spruce tree, to break the *skogsrå*'s spell. What he was doing, of course, was what anyone lost in the woods is always instructed to do: stay calm, relax, and think through the situation rationally. After reducing his anxiety, he saw signs he had previously missed and easily found his way home again (perhaps, too, the sun came up, if the incident took place in summer). Although certain of the methods attested for breaking the *skogsrå*'s power in these cases evidently succeeded by calming down the worried victim, the most frequently encountered method seems to be that of *B*, reversing a garment. This cannot have had much of a practical value, except perhaps briefly to take the victim's mind off his predicament, and its origin is unclear. Perhaps it is best regarded as a magic act similar to the choice of a spruce in *D* and not, say, a pine.

A very complete discussion of beliefs concerning the *skogsrå* is found in Granberg, *Skogsrået*, pp. 73–169.

38. The Rå Helps a Charcoal-Burner

The story is told from Linde parish that a lad was out in the forest to burn charcoal and it was in the Hartzsberg Forest. Whenever there was something wrong with the charcoal stacks they would let him know by pounding on the door, and so he could sleep in peace until it was finished. One evening a nice-looking woman came into his hut and spoke with him. She said she had just arrived in the vicinity and was on her way to Stripa but couldn't find the way there. She was cheerful and nice, and he liked her well enough for her to stay there with him and clean house for him and help him with the charcoal stacks. And she stayed for three years and had three children by him, and the youngest of all was a girl, and they called her Snorvipa. But he had had to promise her that when he had been away and was returning to the hut, he would first pound on a pine tree she pointed out to him, and he was to strike three times. But then once he forgot, and when he came up to the stack, he could see her as she really was. She was using her nose as a hook and was tearing out charcoal with her claws, and dousing the fire with her backside, which she would dip in a bucket. He was terribly frightened, for he realized that he had been living with a *rå*. He said nothing to her, however, but turned around and went to an old Lapp and told him what was going on. The Lapp advised: "Get a sledge and take her and the children out to Råsvaln, but you sit on the horse and ride. Put in the saddle-pins so loosely that you can get them out with your heels, and don't have any real knots about you, tie everything with slip-knots. When you get out to the middle of the lake, you must ride away from them, but don't turn around until you get to Gullsmedshytta."

Now the charcoal burner went back and knocked on the pine as usual, and now she was a good-looking woman. He had at this point the sledge and horse with him. He told her they were going for a ride and put her and the children in the sledge, but as for himself he mounted the horse. When they got to the middle of the lake seven white wolves came out on the ice. When she saw that and realized what he was going to do, she begged on behalf of herself and the children and said: "If you don't have mercy for me or the others, at least have mercy for little Snorvipa. And if you do what you intend to, I will call on my brother in Hartzberg (a mountain), my sister in Ringhälla (a rock formation), and my cousin in Stripa (a mountain)," but her man rode away, he did. Then she started to scream for help. Then they started to shoot at him from all three mountains, and it thundered like cannons and the shells hit the ice behind him, and the ice was glassy. But he got away, for he had all his knots tied in slip-knots, but the wolves ate up her and the children.

[Hed, Västmanland. ULMA 4008, pp. 1 ff. Collected in 1932 by Ellen Lagergren from August Blomkvist, born ca. 1857, who had heard the tale as a child from an old man from Linde. Printed in Granberg, *Skogsrået*, pp. 174–175.]

The legend of the *skogsrå* who helps the charcoal-burner at his work is found for the most part in central Sweden and was particularly popular in Bergslagen. The simplest tales simply recount the aid of the *rå*; she departs when her identity is disclosed. In more complex variants, like the one here, the man has to carry out some action, typically riding out onto wolf-infested ice, in order to rid himself of the *rå*. In many cases that incident makes up the kernel of the story and the motif of aid in charcoal-burning is not present.

Our story contains many typical elements of story tradition: secret identity of a spouse, troll beauty that is literally only skin deep, advice from a "clever" person, interdictions, and a confrontation with the forces of the other world leading to a satisfactory resolution of the danger.

39. Tibast and Vändelrot

THERE was a man. He was married. Once he was out looking for some cattle. On the way he met the *skogsrå*. He couldn't withstand the temptation, and he was with her every evening after that. Although it just got to be too much for him and it got to be more than he could stand. But he couldn't hold out against her anyway. He had never seen her from behind, however. At last he became so limp that he could hardly walk. Then one time, however, he asked her what he should do, and he got around her by asking her what he should do about a little bull he said he had, who was such a problem: he never did anything but mount the cows and would never let up, so that he was completely wiped out. Then she answered that *tibast*, she said, and *vändelrot*, would be good. Then he got some *tibast* and *vändelrot* and fastened it to himself, and he couldn't leave things at that but went to meet her that evening, too. But when he came *that* way she said:

Tibast and vändelrot is sure,
Fie on me for telling the cure.

And then she turned around, so that he could see her back, and so she disappeared.

[Länglot, Öland. LUF 1271, p. 1. Collected in 1928 from Johan Olsson. Printed in Granberg, *Skogsrået*, pp. 183–184.]

A very typical variant of the Tibast-legend. In two basic forms the legend is distributed throughout Scandinavia, including Swedish-speaking areas of Finland. This version, from Öland, is typical of the so-called Southern form of the legend, which involves a male human and a female otherworlder. The Northern form, found in North Sweden, Norway, and western Finland, reverses the roles: a girl alone at a shieling suffers the erotic attentions of a male otherworlder. As was best demonstrated in the classic study of Gunnar Granberg, *Skogsrået*, from which our examples have been chosen, the distribution of the Northern and Southern variants corresponds to socio-economic conditions. Southern and central Sweden are covered by vast forests, in which it was typical for men to spend long periods of time alone burning charcoal. Northern Sweden and Norway are more mountainous, on the other hand, and there it is young girls who spend much of the summer alone at the shielings. Cf. Christiansen no. 6000, "Tricking the Fairy Suitor." Related is no. 6005, "The Interrupted Fairy Wedding."

As we see from the next story, the herbs used could vary. Besides *tibast* (daphne mezereum) and *vändelrot* (valeriana officinalis), which are the most widely distributed, in certain areas locally popular medicinal herbs like polypodium vulgare or orchic maculata are found. See Granberg, *Skogsrået*, Maps 22, 23, 24, for a picture of the distribution of the means and the epic formulas used in this legend.

In our story, the importance of seeing the *skogsrå*'s back refers, of course, to her tail. She loses her power when her victim catches sight of it.

40. *Garlic and Tar (Tibastsägnen)*

They could call the *skogsrå* Talle-Maja. There was a man who had met her in the forest and he had intercourse with her during the nights. This was particularly bad for his wife, for as soon as it was evening the *skogsrå* would come, and then he had to go. There was no power that could hold him back then. But one evening the wife went out and met her before she had reached the window. Then she asked the *skogsrå* what she should do about a bull who never came home at night. "Well," the *skogsrå* answered, "you should give him garlic and tar and grass from the north side of the chimney."

She did as the *skogsrå* had said and gave her husband this mixture, and after that he always was able to stay at home. The next time they met, the *skogsrå* said to the wife: "Had I believed this of you, you would never have gotten *that* piece of advice."

[Kila, Värmland. IFGH 1331, p. 7. Collected by Ragnar Nilsson in 1931 from the crofter Sven Andersson, born 1840. Printed in Granberg, *Skogsrået*, p. 183; Nilsson/Bergstrand, *Värmlandsnäs*, 3: 58–59; Klintberg, no. 18.]

This form of the Tibast-legend is characteristic of West Sweden. The protective power of garlic is widely known and calls for no comment. Some scholars believe that the legend is secondary and originated to explain protective customs involving the use of garlic and similar plants or herbs (Klintberg, p. 294; Granberg, *Skogsrået*, pp. 183–202).

The name Talle-Maja, which probably means "Pine-Maja" (the second component being an ordinary woman's name), is characteristic in particular of Värmland. Compare story 37B.

41. *Shooting the Skogsrå*

There was a man who had spent a great deal of time with a *skogsrå* but had grown tired of her. He just didn't know how to get rid of her. Then he asked her what he should do to be able to shoot everything. "Sometimes when I'm out hunting birds," he said, "there are some birds it's impossible to hit. What should I do about that?"

"Well," said the *skogsrå*, "you must take bulbs and roots and grass from the north side of the chimney and mix it in with gunpowder. Then you can hit things you otherwise can't shoot." Then she started to think of herself and said to him: "You wouldn't shoot me, would you?"

"Yes, I would," he said, and so he did.

[Tösse, Dalsland. IFGH 1004, p. 1. Collected from A. F. Gustafsson, born ca. 1860. Printed in Granberg, *Skogsrået*, p. 199.]

This story is clearly closely related to the Tibast-legend, of which it may represent a secondary development. This kind of tale is in general limited to southern Sweden, although it is ultimately related to a broad cycle of legends dealing with the elimination of supernatural beings. In this particular legend other special ammunition includes communion wafers, silver, wedding rings, and the like. Since the central moment is the unwitting aid of the *skogsrå*, sometimes the special ammunition or loading is excluded. A related set of legends involves killing the *skogsrå* by striking or stabbing her in the one vulnerable spot, which she has been tricked into revealing; thus these legends remind one of heroes like Achilles and Siegfrid. (Granberg, *Skogsrået*, pp. 198–202.)

---

42. A Rude Awakening

In the vicinity of Övedskloster there is a little sandstone outcropping usually called Fruali. Many, many years ago a Mistress Lia [Liafru, obviously formed from the name of the ridge] is said to have lived there. She was a dazzling woman who managed to lure many a young man to his doom. A story is told by the old folks in the neighborhood that a farm hand named Tule once got lost in that area. After a while he met a woman and asked her if she knew of some place where he might spend the night. "Yes," she said, "come with me and you will certainly get lodgings for the night." He thanked her and followed her to a little rock in the ridge. In the rock was a door through which they went in. "You can sleep in that bed," the woman said and pointed to a bed along one of the walls. Tule started to undress, and in so doing he happened to drop his pocket knife on the covers. He thought he heard a splashing noise, as if the knife had fallen into some water, but he was so tired that he didn't pay any attention to it. Instead he sat on the bed and said: "It certainly was fortunate, by God, that I got a roof over my head tonight."

When he said that, he sank down into a pool of water, with drops splashing up around him. He found himself sitting in a pool in the middle of the forest.

Tule had encountered Mistress Lia, and he could be thankful he had mentioned the name of God, for otherwise things wouldn't have turned out well.

[Övedskloster, Skåne. LUF 128, p. 1. Collected in 1922–23. Printed in Granberg, *Skogsrået*, p. 205.]

This tale, limited to the southern-most provinces of Skåne, Halland, and Blekinge, repeats the widespread motif that appearances are deceiving in the other world. What is specific to these South Swedish stories is that the hero, usually male, escapes from an erotic encounter in the other world by naming God or by some similar action and ends up in a swamp or puddle. The variant printed here is tied to a specific *rå*, the lady from *Froalid* or *Fruali*, a ridge situated directly East of Övedskloster; a number of closely related variants have been collected about her. All the action, however, is essentially a multiform of a number of legends and memorates concerning encounters between members of our world and the other world. (Granberg, *Skogsrået*, pp. 205–209.)

43. *Tricking a Christian*

An old smith has said that when he was young and had a fiancée, they used to arrange to meet in a barn in a meadow outside of town. One evening when he came there for a rendezvous, his fiancée had already arrived. That night she seemed particularly gay and absolutely insisted on having her arms around him, and after a time he responded in kind. After a while, though, she let out a hoarse laugh and said: "It was fun to trick someone of Christian blood."

The man got a grip on himself immediately, however, and responded: "It was fun to sleep with a devil for once."

It was the *skogsnuva,* who first had led his fiancée astray in a different direction and then had taken on her appearance and gone to the rendezvous in the barn.

[V. Torsås, Småland. IFGH 2449, p. 2. Collected in 1931. Printed in Granberg, *Skogsrået,* p. 244.]

According to Granberg (pp. 244–245), this story is limited to Sweden, where it shows a sporadic and rather diffuse distribution through the eastern part of the country from Skåne to Hälsingland. The point of the story is the verbal exchange between the male hero and the otherworlder, most often the *skogsrå.* It is evident that the encounter ends in a victory for the man, enabling him to avoid unpleasant consequences from his contact with the otherworlder. The legend is therefore closely related to the Tibast-legend, "Shooting the Skogsrå," and so forth.

44. *Oden Was a Sunday Hunter*

If one is outside at night on great holidays, one can hear Oden's hunt. It moves high in the air and follows the forest. It goes faster than a bird can fly. But it is actually three dogs barking. Two of them have low voices and the third a high voice.

There was a man named Oden. He was a sharpshooter and went hunting on Sundays. His punishment was to hunt *skogsrån* until the end of the world. Many of the old people here had heard the hunt on Ķroppefjäll. I particularly remember one old man who claimed that he had heard the hunt one New Year's Eve when he was on his way to a dance.

[Gunnarsnäs, Dalsland. IFGH 5244:25. Collected in 1947 by Ragnar Nilsson from David Jansson, born in 1861 in Gunnarsnäs. Printed in

C. M. Bergstrand, *Dalslandssägner* (Göteborg, 1951), no. 1, p. 9, and in Klintberg, no. 8, p. 82.]

This short text is almost paradigmatic of the beliefs in Oden's hunt in more recent Swedish folklore. The hunt "moves high in the air and follows the forest," surely an indication of the accepted feeling among folklorists that the background in reality of the folk belief, that which triggers legends of this sort, was the noise of flocks of birds or the wind in the treetops. The noise is traditionally explained, as here, as three hunting dogs barking as they join in the chase. The name Oden apparently is a descendant from the Old Norse Óðinn, the chief of the gods in Scandinavian mythology, but the large amount of work that has been done on this problem has still not satisfied every scholar that this derivation is correct, and it remains unclear. However, it is quite apparent that in modern tradition "King Oden" has nothing to do with the head of the Scandinavian mythic pantheon. The text printed here is typical: it calls him a man and ascribes his wild hunt to a breach of the sabbath with a punishment which meets the crime. The hunt has, according to the informant, been heard on Kroppefjäll, a local mountain where the wind presumably blew more fiercely than on the surrounding plains, and one man heard it on New Year's Eve—as an important holiday, a time when many spirits would be abroad.

Some of the more important works on Oden's hunt are Karl Meisen, *Die Sagen vom wütenden Heer und wilden Jäger*, Volkskundliche Quellen, 1 (Münster, 1935), which puts it in a European context, and Hilding Celander, "Oskoreien och besläktade föreställningar i äldre och nyare nordisk tradition," *Saga och Sed*, 1943, pp. 71–175, a complete account of the traditions in Scandinavia.

45. The Woman Was Tied Behind the Horse by Her Braids

My grandfather told me that once there was a woman living in Bodsjö who was out looking for her cows. It was night during a violent lightning storm.

Then a woman went running by, and asked her not to tell anyone they had met. Right after her came a man on horseback who asked if she had seen a woman; she said she had not. Then he rode on, but after a while he came back, and the woman was tied behind the horse by her braids.

And as he rode by he told the woman who was out looking for her cows that if she had answered him honestly she could have avoided seeing that.

[Brunflo, Jämtland. NM HA, Övernat. väsen, 3, Odens jakt. Collected in 1925 by Ella Ohlson (Odstedt) from Mathilda Rigner, born in 1868. Printed in Klintberg, no. 12, p. 83.]

The only migratory legend associated with the wild hunt is ML 5060, "The Fairy Hunter," of which this text is a variant. The earliest attestation is from the Cistercian monk Heliand de Froidmont (1156–1229), retained in a copy by Vincenz de Beauvais. It tells of a charcoal-burner who one night sees a naked woman being pursued by a soldier on a black horse. The rider catches her, runs her through with his spear, and throws her into the fire. After having the vision for several nights in succession, the charcoal-burner reports it to the local count, and the two of them set off one night, fortified by communion, to try to make sense out of it. When the woman and hunter appear, the count challenges them to speak, and the hunter explains that he and the woman are spirits and paying for an earthly sin: she was his lover, and she murdered her husband. Their punishment is this eternal hunt, in which the devil joins as the black horse. Already this medieval exemplum contains the basic kernel of the legend in recent tradition; the hunter is male, the quarry female, and the observers of the supernatural event are human, and we may note that the hunt in the preceding story is motivated by a sin, a breach of the sabbath. In approximately this form the legend has been collected in North Germany and the three continental Scandinavian lands, and related stories are found in the rest of Germany and in Ireland. In Scandinavia the story is most strongly represented in Sweden, particularly the south. In most of the south and southwest the wild hunter is identified as Oden and his quarry as a *skogsrå*. In other areas other identifications are made: the hunter has been identified as Dietrich von Bern in some of the medieval German variants, and in Denmark he may be King Valdemar, for example. This suggests that the South Swedish identifications are secondary additions to the legend. Our text lacks them, since it stems from an area where conceptions of Oden's hunt are unknown, as Klintberg notes (p. 292), but reference to the earliest attestation of the tale shows that this is a very old and perhaps original form.

On the European and Scandinavian distribution of the legend, its regional oikotypes, and similar matters, see Lutz Röhrich, "Die Frauenjagdsage," *Laographia*, 22 (1965), 408–423; Röhrich, *Erzählungen des späten Mittelalters und ihr Weiterleben in Literatur und Volksdichtung bis zur Gegenwart: Sagen, Märchen, Exempel und Schwänke*, 2 (Bern und München, 1967), 5–52 (texts, including Vincenz de Beauvais) and 393–407, with literature.

46. The Näck's Reel

But to hear the *näck* play his fiddle, let me tell you, that is really something. They say his bowing is better than Spingepelle-August [a local fiddler?], and that it is so beautiful it can make you weep to hear it. Much more beautiful than when Kalle from Stuva plays on the concertina. You see, the *näck* can play a reel, and a person who heard it couldn't stop dancing, even if he were sitting in the stocks at Bellö Church. If a man can learn to play that, he doesn't need to be able to play anything else. These days there aren't many who know it, but when my mother was a serving-girl for Pär Ola at Krånglebo, there was a farm hand there who could play the *näck*'s reel, and so well that both barrels and benches were dancing in the parlor. But he was fed up with the skill himself and didn't much care to play it, for he easily could see there was something not quite right about it. You see, he had learned it from the *näck* himself by going down to the lake three Thursday nights in a row, before the sun's rays ran over the tops of the pines, and playing for the *näck*, and after that he knew how to play it.

When there was a party here in the village one time and that farm hand was supposed to play for them, they wanted him to play the *näck*'s reel, because, you see, it is so easy to dance to. He didn't want to play it for them, for he knew well how it would turn out, but they were set on it and finally he had to give in. But then, let me tell you, there was dancing like never before. Girls and boys, old women and men, they all had to get up and dance, every last one, until they were panting like bull-frogs, and barrels and chairs and cupboards and benches were dancing wildly, and even the cat, who had been lying against the wall, had to join in, and no one could stop, but bit by bit it got worse and worse, until at last someone came in and took the fiddle away from him, but it didn't do any good, since he could play on his arm just as well, and they danced on. But then they took away his bow, and at last it stopped. But then they had had their fill of dancing, and they asked him never again to strike up the *näck*'s reel.

[S. Vedbo, Småland. ULMA 92:43, p. 169. From A. G. Svensson in 1875. Printed in J. A. Lundell et al., "Sagor, sägner, legender . . . ," *SvLm*, 3:2 (1881), 331–332.]

The *näck* is best known for his role in ballads, where he combines fatal erotic attraction with musical virtuosity. The latter quality has entered legendary tradition, and a number of tales attribute great musical skill to the teaching of the *näck*. (See Maja Bergstrand, "Näcken som musikaliskt väsen," *FmFt*, 23 [1936], 14–31). Carrying out some action on consecutive Thursday nights, as in the tale printed here, is common, and is, of course, typical in general of magic formulae.

There has been obvious crossing between this tale and other dances in which the devil rather than the *näck* or one of his music students plays. (See stories nos. 68–70). Such crossing probably does not indicate great evil on the part of the *näck*—though he could be dangerous, as the following tales indicate. Rather it would appear that any music and dancing held potential danger, particularly if the dancing got out of hand, and so the migratory material was applied to any musical being. However, the crossing has gone so far that in certain parishes of Ångermanland, for example, the devil himself was said to teach fiddlers to play in mills (Ella Ohlson, "Naturväsen i ångermanländsk folktro: en översikt," *FmFt*, 20 (1933), 74); and in one part of Värmland an informant stated that some people thought that a horse who led people astray in the forest was the *näck,* while others thought it was Satan himself (Nilsson/Bergstrand, *Värmlandsnäs,* 3:31). Other similarities are noted in Maja Bergstrand, op. cit.

47. The Näck Pulls the Plow

LILL-OLE from Lotorp plowed with the *näck* a whole day long. He had gone down to fetch the horses. They were grazing down near the river. And there was a horse there he didn't recognize, although it looked just like the others. And he took it and yoked it before the plow, and when the horse had got the steel bit in its mouth, it had to pull the plow. And it pulled the plow the whole day. But late in the evening when Lill-Ole put the horse out to pasture he learned what kind of horse that was, for it rushed off down to the river the instant it was released.

[Risinge, Östergötland. Collected in 1912 by Sven Rothman from a certain Hagenberg, born 1834. Printed in Rothman, *Östgötska folkminnen,* SKGAAF, 8 (Uppsala, 1941), p. 70.]

This tale has been collected throughout central and particularly southern Sweden. In the few cases where the *bäckahäst* or *näck* in horse form is not used for plowing, some other agrarian activity is substituted. This may indicate that the tale had a certain function of wish fulfillment in areas or times when a farm seemed undermanned, an assumption strengthened by the variants in which it is reported that the horse could do without food or rest.

In certain of the variants the farmer attains power over the supernatural horse simply by putting the bridle on him, but the use of steel or iron, which according to folk belief could always stop the supernatural forces, is more common and better motivated.

A related group of stories, said to have entered Sweden from Germany, where it is most widely distributed, tells of the service of the merman for a time as a farm hand. For his wages he demands only a tool, often a scythe, and the power of the tool from the Christian community enables him to rule over his fellow beings of the other world.

The oldest Scandinavian variant is from *Landnámabók*, the Old Icelandic Book of Settlements. A man harnesses a horse he has never seen before which has run up from a nearby lake. The horse works well during the day but becomes increasingly restless as evening approaches. After sunset it breaks its harness and plunges back in the lake. It was never seen again. (Jakob Benediktsson, ed., *Landnámabók*, Íslenzk Fornrit, 1 [Reykjavík, 1968], 1:120.)

48. *Riding the Bäckahäst*

ONE beautiful winter evening eight boys were out playing on the frozen surface of a brook. And suddenly there stood a white horse, apparently quite meek, right next to them on the ice. One of the boys was daring, and he crept up on the horse's back and called to the others to do the same. For they were going for a ride! One after the other the boys mounted the horse, and there was still room. But when the eighth got up he glimpsed all the others on the horse in front of him, and he couldn't help saying: "Jesus Christ, what a long horse!" And in the same moment all eight boys stood in a row on the ice and the horse had vanished. But it was just as well that boy happened to mention the name of Jesus; otherwise the horse would have ridden down into the brook with them. That bunch cannot, you see, stand the name of the Savior.

[Skårby, Ljunits härad, Skåne. Collected in 1916 by Theodore Tufvesson from an unnamed informant and printed in Tufvesson, "Bäckahästen i svensk folktro," *FmFt*, 3 (1916), 170.]

The point of the story is the length of the horse, emphasized here by the unrealistically large number of riders. In other variants the horse is actually said to grow longer as the riders mount. The epic formula which saves the children generally rhymes in the original language: "Jussu *kors*, sickjed et lant *hors*" in the imitated dialect in the text translated here. In certain areas where the *näck* is prominent a variation is found: the last child complains, "I can't get [reach, stretch] up," but with imperfect childish pronunciation says *jag näcker inte upp* instead of *jag räcker inte upp* or something similar. The effect of hearing his name is similar to that of hearing the name of Jesus.

For the most part the riders are children, but many variants tell of the ride of a single adult. The rider is almost without exception saved, but sometimes the mechanism of escape is omitted and the rider is simply deposited on the ground.

The tale of the ride on the *bäckahäst* or *näck* in horse form is found throughout Sweden. In a few variants from Halland, Västergötland, and Ångermanland, the escape is lacking and the tale ends tragically with the drowning of the rider(s). The center of the tradition is thought to be Skåne, since that is the center of distribution of the term *bäckahäst*. In central Sweden the water horse is the *näck* and in North Sweden the *sjörå*. See Brita Egardt, "De svenska vattenhästsägnerna och deras ursprung," *Folkkultur*, 4 (1944), 119–166.

49. The Strömkarl at Garphytte

A FEW kilometers west of the village Garphytte is a saw works next to a stream from the lake Aspen. In the beginning of the nineteenth century there was a *strömkarl* who made his home there. The number of people who caught sight of him was not small, but for most of those who wanted to see him he never showed himself. This *strömkarl* was especially good at fiddle playing. It is said that whoever heard him play went into such a state of ecstasy that almost everything else was forgotten. The bells of heaven must sound exactly like that!

In appearance the *strömkarl* was small and unpretentious and was always seen wearing red clothes. He was peaceful toward all and never got in anyone's way. At the saw works he was seen only at such times as timber was ordinarily cut—that is, spring and early summer.

A number of people learned from him how to play the fiddle. The only payment he asked for his trouble was a piece of horsemeat, for he loved horsemeat. Once in the 1840s a man named Strand, whose trade was horse-skinning, wanted to learn how to play. One Saturday evening he went to the saw works to look him up. It was just after sunset. Strand sat down on the saw and waited for the old man to reveal himself. Sure enough, the little man, all dressed in red, quickly appeared before him, tuned his fiddle, and then Strand's. Strand then took up a piece of horsemeat to placate the *strömkarl* with and gave it to him in payment for his effort:

"Here you are, old fellow!"

The *strömkarl* greedily received the piece of meat, bowed, and appeared to be thankful. To Strand's great astonishment, however, he immediately vanished.

Nevertheless, Strand had now learned to tune the fiddle, and he became very skilled at it, but—he never learned how to play. He came several more times to the saw works at Garphytte on the same errand, but the *strömkarl* never again revealed himself to Strand. Those who know about such things were of the opinion that the cause was that he had been too stingy toward his teacher with the horsemeat.

[Linde, Västmanland. From Erik Bore, collected in the late nineteenth century and first printed in *Bergslagernas tidning*, June 3, 1893, in a slightly reworked form. The text printed here is taken from Bore, "Sägner och händelser upptecknade i Västmanland," *SvLm*, B31 (1934), 50–51. Some non-essential material has been omitted from the translation.]

The term *strömkarl* might be rendered "water man" and is a neutral referent for the *näck*. This particular one seems rather like a *tomte*; perhaps his association with water attracted the migratory legend to him. See Jöran Sahlgren, "Strömkarlen spelar (Nordiska ortnamn i språklig och saklig belysning, 10)" *Namn och Bygd*, 23 (1935), 42–55.

The tale is a widespread migratory legend, collected from all areas of Norway (Christiansen ML 4090) and quite popular in western Sweden. In many variants the stingy portion of meat is replaced by a bone from which the meat has been gnawed, and sometimes a verse formula is exchanged between the water-sprite and the human, to the effect that the payment is enough only for learning how to tune, not for learning how to play. This gives the story a humorous cast suitable for a migratory legend.

50. The Näck Longs for Salvation

ONE evening a boy from Gylltorp was on his way home from a day's work at the manor. When he came down to the river, he saw the *näck* sitting on a stone out in the water, playing his fiddle and singing:

On Judgement Day, on Judgement Day,
Then shall God's Grace be mine.
On Judgement Day, on Judgement Day,
Then shall God's Grace be mine.

Then the boy shouted back, "You'll never get God's grace—you're too ugly for that!" When the *näck* heard that, he became so terribly disconsolate that he started to shriek so loudly that it could be heard far away.

When the boy got home his father was standing out in front of the farm, and he asked what was going on down by the river. When the boy had explained what it was, his father told him, "Go down to the river and say to the *näck*, 'My father has read more than I have, and he says you will get the grace of God.' "

The boy ran down and said it. Then there was an end to the wailing, and the *näck* began instead to play his fiddle, ever so beautifully, and with that he sank down into the water.

[Hällestad, Östergötland. NM EU 546:15. Collected in 1922 by Gustav E. Olsson from Adolf Johansson in Ränninge, Hällestads sn. Klintberg no. 50, p. 100.]

As Christiansen ML 5050, "The Fairies' Prospect of Salvation," demonstrates, this tale is but one of a series in which a supernatural being hopes for the grace of God. The pattern of such stories is largely consistent: merriment or singing of the otherworlders is interrupted by a human who dashes their hopes for salvation. He relents, however, either upon reconsideration, the advice of someone more in position to know, or through some token. At that the otherworlders cease their wailing and rejoice. The motif of the flowering staff and others similar to the Tannhäuser story are sometimes used as the portent boding forgiveness for the otherworlders.

Dag Strömbäck has shown that the inclusion of the *näck* in these stories is due to the folk belief, noted as early as 1741 by Linnaeus and printed in his *Öländska och gotländska resa*, 1775, that the *näck* is one of the fallen angels who were cast out of heaven with Lucifer.

The best-known variant of the tale in Sweden is the ballad "Necken," printed in the famous ballad collection of E. G. Geijer and A. A. Afzelius, *Svenska folkvisor*, 1814–16 (see Introduction, p. 20). The material has become even more widely known through the beautiful poem "Necken" by the romantic poet Erik Johan Stagnelius, which however focuses on the tragic moment when the *näck* learns of his doom. The reversal is omitted, and the poem ends with the melancholy note that the *näck* never again played by the silvery brook.

The earliest attestation of the tale seems to be in a Danish book of devotions from 1509, where the supernatural being is a "spirit" under the earth, the one who calls his prospect of salvation into question a young priest, and the one who restores the prospect of salvation a bishop. The "spirit" plays a simple stringed instrument called a *hackbräde* (literally, a "chopping block"). See Dag Strömbäck, "Näcken och förlossningen," *Varbergs Museums Årsbok*, 1963, pp. 77–85; reprinted in Strömbäck's *Folklore och filologi*, SKGAAF, 48 (Uppsala, 1970), pp. 115–122.

It would appear that the key in attracting various supernatural beings to this story is the element of music. In the archetype postulated for the Norwegian tales by Christiansen, the human overhears the fairies "singing, making music and dancing" (Christiansen, p. 89). Thus the *näck* would be strongly attracted to this story, and, judging from the printed material, it appears that he is more popular in Sweden than other figures.

---

51. The Mill Spirit

It was Autumn, and people had harvested the grain, done the threshing, and were at their busiest grinding flour in their mills. There was an old man, tight-fisted and greedy, in his mill watching over the work. But he didn't grant himself a moment's rest; the mill was going full force both day and night.

One evening it was rainy, bleak, and coal-black outside, but the mill was going just as much, of course; and when much of the night had passed, the man put some more wood on the fire and put on porridge. The porridge was very nearly ready, and the man was holding onto the pot, when he heard something outside the door. "What in Heaven's name is that," the man thought to himself, "that dares to be out in this terrible weather?" But at that moment the door flew open and in walked a little fellow; but he was an odd one, and he didn't give any kind of normal greeting. The fire was rather low, so the old man couldn't see too clearly, either. But before he knew it, the fellow walked up to the old man and stuck his nose practically in the old man's eye and asked this:

"Have you ever seen a nose as long as this, old boy?"

But immediately the old man grabbed the pot of porridge and threw it all in the other's face and said:

"Have you ever felt such hot porridge, old boy?"

And the one who took off was the strange visitor, out the door with the old man at his heels. The man stopped at the door but the other rushed off, wailing and carrying on at the top of his lungs.

[Hälsingland. Collected by Johan Nordlander, informant not stated. Printed in Richard Bergström and Nordlander, "Sagor, sägner ock visor," *SvLm*, 5:2 (1885), 64–65.]

Compare story no. 78, "Old Erik in the Mill." Tales of this nature have been collected from throughout Sweden and have been associated with all kinds of environments and supernatural beings. Among the most popular, however, are the *kvarngubbar* (literally, "old men of the mill"), who are characteristic of northern Sweden in particular. They are reminiscent of both the *näck*, in that they inhabit watercourses, and the *tomte* or *gårdsrå*, in that they are associated with human habitation and industry.

The story is ultimately a variant of the exceedingly popular structure, common to most forms of folk narrative, in which a hero outwits a supernatural being or adversary in a contest of words or wisdom. The form is common in the mythological poems in the *Poetic Edda* (e.g., *Vafþrúðnismál, Alvíssmál*), in various ballads, and in many folktales. The fact that the exchange in prose narratives frequently is couched in verse might indicate the poetic primacy of such stories but is hardly a necessary hypothesis; see Ronald Grambo, "Verse in Legends: Some Remarks on a Neglected Area of Folklore," *Fabula*, 11 (1969), 48–65.

52. The Sjörå Warns of an Impending Storm

ON NOVEMBER 6, 1866, a large number of herring fishermen from Aspö were lost at sea and sixty children were fatherless. The men had gone out at two in the afternoon and the weather was beautiful. During the evening a storm blew up. One of the fishermen saw a hand stick up above the crests of the waves and point out the way home. Then he said to the others: "Pull up the lines, we must go home now." The others laughed and said no. "Yes," he said, "we must get back ashore. I have seen the warning three times."

With that he sailed home, but all the others perished.

But he himself was lost in a storm at sea a few years ago.

[Aspö, Blekinge. Collected in 1915 by William Andersson from Johann Nilsson, a church caretaker from Hasslö, born in 1853. Printed in Andersson, "Folktro från Blekinge skärgård," *FmFt*, 7 (1920), 122.]

The notion that the *sjörå* warns of impending bad weather is a widely spread one in Scandinavia. Perhaps the tale might have been used to explain a lone survival from a devastating storm? At any rate, the scorn of the others is a frequent motif in such tales, nearly as frequent as their death. The story is a variant of ML 4055, the following tale. The guiding hand seems to be based on the *vantevän* legend (cf. the next two stories).

53. Helping the Sjörå (Vantevännen)

ONE stormy and cold evening on Lake Vänern, the *sjörå* emerged from the water next to a boat, stretched out her hands, and complained: "I'm so cold, I'm so cold!" The skipper threw her a pair of gloves, which she immediately put on. All at once she cried out: "Steer for the east side of the lake, my glove-friend." The skipper did so and thereby avoided a heavy storm.

[Näs, Värmland. IFGH 4857:22. Collected in 1943 by Sigurd Dahllöf from a story "originally told by" Captain John Eriksson, from Kila. Printed in Nilsson /Bergstrand, *Värmlandsnäs*, 3:43.]

An almost paradigmatic version of the popular *vantevän* (literally, "glove-friend") legend, told in coastal areas throughout Northern Europe. This legend is more openly didactic than others, like the preceding story, in which the sea spirit openly volunteers help. Here she (in many cases he) is first in need of help, and the generous gesture of the human leads to a valuable reward. This also clarifies the motivation of the otherworldly being.

In Sweden the story was noted as early as the sixteenth century by Olaus Magnus and printed in his *Historia de gentibus septentrionalis* (1555), II:23.

As the variation in Christiansen's ML 4055 makes clear, the point of the story is the aid to the sea spirit, which could take many different forms, including food, money, or other kindnesses. The *vantevän* motif, however, is perhaps most popular. Often the aid of the *sjörå* is given in verse, as "*Det sjuder i tallen,/skramlar i hallen,/far iland, vantevän*" ("The wind is shrieking/rocks are creaking,/go ashore my glove-friend"), or *far i land, vanteman./I natt blir många änkor och faderlösa barn* ("make for land, mitten-man, tonight many wives and children will lose their man").

54. *The Sjörå in Helgasjön*

A CROFTER in Kronoberg was rowing home one evening over the Lake Helgasjön. When he had reached the middle of the lake, his boat stopped and he could move neither forward nor backward. At the same time he noticed that the boat was slowly beginning to be drawn down deeper and deeper into the water, until finally the rail was even with the water's surface. As he now began to look around he noticed that a hand had seized each side of the boat and was pressing it down. There was no time to gather his thoughts, but the crofter in fear grabbed an axe and swung it on both sides at the rails, and so quickly that all ten of the troll's fingers fell down into the boat. At that instant the boat was freed, but in the lake there was a terrible din and there grew up such a storm that the crofter only made it back to the village at the risk of his very life. Some time later the *sjörå*'s corpse washed up on the shore of the lake.

[Värend, Småland. From a written account by Gustaf Bonde Classon dated March 3, 1752, sent to the Royal Scientific Academy around that time and later acquired by the English antiquarian George Stephens (see Introduction). Stephens sent it to Hyltén-Cavallius, from whose papers it was edited by Nils-Arvid Bringéus, "Folksägner från Värend, upptecknade av Gunnar Olof Hyltén-Cavallius," *Kronobergsboken*, 1968, p. 69; see also p. 118.]

According to the rest of Classon's account, the veracity of the tale was assured by the existence around 1700 of a rib and thumb of the *sjörå*'s carcass. The thumb was sent with the written account to the Royal Scientific Academy in 1752, but Hyltén-Cavallius's notes report that it was said to have been lost when that organization moved to new quarters. It seems likely that the legend may have served in part to clarify those bizarre relics, since otherworldly beings do not ordinarily have corpses. At any rate, the tale is a variation on a traditional theme. The threat of the otherworldly being (even called a *troll* once in the manuscript) is met by a quick action of the hero, who emerges more or less unscathed. In a sense, too, this story is the opposite of the preceding story, in that mistreatment of the *sjörå*, however deserved, brings about a storm which threatens the protagonist's life. That only the *sjörå*'s hands are sighted is surely due to the tradition of the *vantevän* legend.

55. "Binding" and Driving Off a Sjörå

IN THE old days if someone wanted to have particularly good luck at fishing, he had to "bind" or drive off the *sjörå*. The method was for the fisherman to go alone to the churchyard on a Thursday night and take away some consecrated earth in a bag or wooden container. The next Thursday night he would take his fishing gear and the consecrated earth with him and go down to the pond or lake where the fishing was to take place. He would sprinkle out the dirt in a thin ribbon all around the pond, being careful to leave no openings anywhere in the ribbon of dirt, except one. There he would stand and cast out his line. Immediately the *sjörå* would be visible above the water, knowing that she was being driven off. First she would go all around the pond to see if the ribbon of dirt was incomplete at any point, which would have given her a way out. After she found that the whole ribbon was intact, she would use every possible trick and conjure up all sorts of visions to try to get the fisherman to leave his post. The idea now was to stay put until the *sjörå* decided it was time to negotiate.

Then she would ask: "What do you want?"

The fisherman was supposed to answer: "Fish."

The *sjörå* would say: "Large or small?"

The fisherman: "Both large and small."

Then she would ask what body of water the fisherman wished to "send" her to, and he was to answer with the name of a lake or pond. [One more question and answer sequence has been omitted here, because it was forgotten by the collector.]

At this point the fisherman would step aside and the *sjörå* would fly off amid a lot of noise. After that the fisherman could get as much fish as he wanted from the pond.

[Lekvattnet, Värmland, VFF 287:2. Collected by a certain Fritiofson from Mattias Nordlund and printed in H. Fernholm, "Fiskelycka: Studier över valda delar av fiskets folklore," *Folkkultur*, 3 (1943), 274–275.]

A belief in "binding" a *sjörå* or *näck* was spread throughout the land and was activated for most activities having to do with water, primary among them being swimming and fishing. For swimming one might "bind" the *näck* with a piece of steel, a bible, a cross, or the like, but for fishing certain other customs were more prevalent. The most common involved the use of consecrated earth, as in this tale, sometimes placed in the shoes while one walked around the lake, sometimes placed in a bag which was then set on fire, but most often sprinkled in a ring around the lake. Other magic aids for fishing were the heads of seals, cats, and, from a presumably inland northern area, beavers. In general, the heads of animals were used in the north, and consecrated earth was used in the central and southern regions; one part of Västergötland substituted seed for the consecrated earth. Similar customs and tales are found in Denmark and Norway as well, the best-known probably being the two attestations in Asbjørnsen's *Huldreæventyr* (1:138–139, 2:271–274). For a complete discussion, including a map of the Swedish distribution, see Fernström, "Fiskelycka," *Folkkultur*, 3 (1943), 273–283. Similar rituals involving sprinkling a ring of consecrated earth to enable one to take possession of a piece of land have been recorded from many areas. See J. Ejdestam, "Omfärd vid besittningstagande av jordegendom," *SvLm*, 69 (1946), 86–114.

56. *A Handout for the Merman*

THREE or four years ago a real merman floated ashore in the fishing village at Gislöv. A rich farmer's son and a farm hand were there down at the beach to fetch sand, when the merman was thrown up on the beach. He was white in front but scaly in back and was naked except for a belt around his waist. He asked for a few shillings for a drink, but the farmer's son said no. "No good shall come to you," the merman said then. On which the farm hand gave him six *öre*, and also a lift, as he had asked, out beyond the sand bank. There the merman dove into the sea, and the water was boiling around him.

From that time the farmer's son was slow and somewhat odd, but for the farm hand everything has turned out his way.

[Skanörs Ljung, Skåne. Collected by Eva Wigström from "the old lady," one of Wigström's regular informants, probably in the late 1880s, and printed in her "Folktro och sägner från skilda landskap (Folkdiktning, 3:e samlingen)," *SvLm*, 8:3 (1898–1914), 126.]

In a footnote to this tale Wigström writes that she had heard it in three different places before it was revealed that the "merman" was actually a man who used to row about in a sealskin boat. It is therefore a good example of how specific variants may originate, and how unusual events may enter narrative tradition. The story itself is a common one, whose point was both to demonstrate the value of respecting the beings of the other world and not crossing their wishes and to take the rich farmer's son—and by extension his whole class—down a peg or two. It is somewhat reminiscent of ML 5080, "Food from the Fairies," which also contrasts the consequences of respect and disrespect for the beings of the other world.

57. *Håvålen*

SEVERAL miles off Tjörn is a fishing bank known as Håvålen. One summer morning the farmer from Grinneröd and his sons were fishing there. They caught a lot, and on one of the hooks a little boy was caught. Some people say that he had a bundle of hay under his arm, since he was just on his way to his father's barn to feed the cattle. The farmer immediately realized that they had caught one of the sea people. He was all for setting the boy free, in view of the danger of irritating them. But his sons were set on taking the boy back, and the father let them decide. And so they sailed home and the sea boy grew up at Grinneröd. They called him Håvålen.

He grew up big and strong and had unbelievable success at fishing. But he would not eat just any kind of fish. Rays and wolf fish he wouldn't touch. "Back home we throw them on the garbage heap," he would say. At last Håvålen got himself a woman, married, and had several children. When he grew old and felt that death was at hand, he ordered his sons to get their boat and take him out to the part of the sea where he had been found. When they arrived there, he said: "Now you are to throw me in the water and sail home as quickly as possible. But don't turn around to look for me." His sons did as they were told. But when they were approaching land, the youngest turned around to have a look. He saw Håvålen sitting there, rocking on top of the waves, with the fishes jumping all around him. But instantly a fierce storm blew up, and they were barely able to get ashore.

It is believed that there still are descendants of Håvålen in Tjörn. They are distinguished by dark eyes, brown hair the color of seaweed, and ugly faces, but they are generous people and successful fishermen.

[Tjörn, Bohuslän. First printed in *Bohuslänska folkminnen utg. av Västsvenska Folkeminnes Föreningen* (Uddevala, 1922), pp. 67–68. Reprinted in C. W. von Sydow, "Scyld Scefing," *Namn och Bygd,* 12 (1924), 92; and H. Fernholm, "Fiskelycka," *Folkkultur,* 3 (1943), 249–250.]

A variant, with a rather literary air, of a legend widely known in Bohuslän. It is attested at least as early as the late eighteenth century (von Sydow, "Scyld Scefing," p. 93), and seems to have been used to explain the physical appearance and success at fishing of a real family from Bohuslän. It answers to Christiansen ML 5090, "Married to a Fairy Woman," which, however, usually has a somewhat more elaborate structure. The bundle of hay the boy was carrying when fished up demonstrates that the undersea people, like their counterparts on or under the land, lead lives very much like those of the tradition-bearers. They have barns and cattle, and sometimes on a rather large scale, as is demonstrated by story no. 58, "The Blind Sea Captain."

Many, if not most, of the variants of the Håvålen story are simpler than the one printed here. Some explain the source of Håvålen's success at fishing by a quasi-magical rite he passes along to his descendants. Almost all agree that he returned to the sea to die; the storm which ends our variant is probably an elaboration borrowed from traditions where sea people call up storms against misbehaving humans.

58. The Blind Sea Captain

In the mid-eighteenth century Captain M. Pettersson sailed from Gothenburg to Spain for a cargo of salt. He skippered a large brig belonging to some merchants from that city. He filled his hold with salt and was returning homeward with a favorable wind and high hopes of soon returning for a new load of the same cargo.

When they had sailed a good distance out to sea, the vessel suddenly stopped, as if some invisible power had grabbed it. That no reef or other hindrance had slowed its progress was obvious, since it didn't give a start, as ships do when they hit something, but rather it just stopped quietly and stood quite motionless. The Captain and all the others on board became quite puzzled over this unexpected event and looked in dismay at each other, not knowing what was going on.

Just as they were sunk deepest in meditation about this mishap, there stood an old man before them, who began to address them in the following manner:

"Fear not, Captain. No harm shall befall you, as long as you comply with my demand. I know that you have a cargo of salt aboard your ship. I wish to buy it all, or at least the greater part of it. You will be well paid for it."

The Captain objected that neither salt nor ship was his property, but rather both belonged to certain merchants in Sweden, and he thus had no right to sell a cargo which was not his. The old man looked angrily at the Captain and said:

"It certainly does not matter whether you sell the salt to me or to someone else, since you will be properly paid for it. Whatever you ask per barrel, you will get; and make no mistake, you will never budge from this spot until you comply with my wish."

The captain was visibly disconcerted by this unusual buyer and no longer dared refuse him.

"Where shall I unload the salt?," asked the captain, looking around with obvious anxiety.

"Throw it down here!," said the old man and pointed with his right hand directly over the side next to the ship.

"How many barrels do you want?," said the captain, gazing uncertainly at the old man.

"I'll be quick to tell you when it's enough," he said, "if only you will start unloading immediately."

At once they began to carry out the old man's order, and everyone worked calmly and in silence. When they had unloaded perhaps several hundred barrels, the old man ordered them to stop.

"That will do. I am satisfied now, although I could have used it all," the man said. "But which of you lads wants to go along with me to get the payment? No harm will befall you."

They all stood in silence and looked at each other. The captain would have preferred to sail off without the payment, since he was beginning to have doubts about the outcome. At last, one of the sailors stepped forward and said he was willing to go along.

"Where do I go?," the sailor asked with a somewhat anxious tone of voice.

"Jump after me and don't be afraid," said the old man. And immediately both he and the sailor disappeared into the calm sea.

"Now it's finished for both the sailor and the old man," said the captain in a dubious tone of voice. "I doubt we'll ever see anything more of them."

"We should be calm, captain, and await the outcome," said one of the crew.

At the same moment that the sailor jumped into the ocean he found himself standing next to the old man on the mound of salt, which proved to be lying on a large green field where several hundred cattle were grazing.

"Do you see all these cattle?," the old man asked and pointed out over the field with his hand.

"I see them quite well," said the sailor, looking attentively.

"Well," said the old man, "Don't you think I need salt, since I intend to slaughter all these cattle?"

"Yes, certainly a lot of salt would be needed," said the sailor as he accompanied the man to a large building, where they entered a magnificent room filled with beautiful furniture of all sorts.

"Sit down, my friend," said the old man, while he went up to a large desk which stood under a window. Here he pulled out a large drawer which seemed to be full of money.

"Come here and get the payment for the salt. And here is a little extra for you, since you were not afraid," said the old man.

The sailor received the money with thanks and put it carefully in his pocket. At that moment there entered through the door from another room a beautiful girl, followed by an older woman who seemed to be the lady of the house.

"Go get a glass of wine for this man," the old man said to the younger woman, who immediately left without a word and after a few moments returned with a large glass in her hand, which she offered him.

"Drink," said the old man. "There is no need to be afraid."

But the sailor still refused to take the glass for fear of the dangerous consequences which might accompany this drink. But the old man renewed his request, assuring the sailor he would suffer no ill effects. Now he no longer dared refuse, because he was more afraid of the old man's threats. He received the glass with shaking hand and commended himself to God's protection and drank off the wine, which tasted excellent.

Now he wished to be on the ship and wished he might come safely up.

"Come with me back to the salt mound," said the old man, "then you will come up quickly."

And at the same moment that they came to the salt mound, the sailor stood on the deck. They were all completely dumbfounded when they saw the sailor and when he told them about what had happened where he had been. He gave the captain the payment for the salt, and immediately the ship began to move again and seemed to sail off even faster, until it made harbor safely in Gothenburg.

The captain continued sailing for several years and often passed the same way, but he never heard anything more.

Some years later the captain settled in Sandsjö parish in Småland, probably tired out from his many years at sea.

At the market in Sandsjö one time he saw the same old man who had bought the salt from him on the Spanish Sea. He went up to the man and greeted him in a friendly way:

"Hello, old fellow, I enjoyed our dealings together. Are *you* up here in Småland?"

The old man looked at him sharply and said:

"Can you really see me?"

"Yes, of course I can," said Captain Pettersson.

"Well, since you couldn't keep your mouth shut when you saw me, you'll never see the daylight on this earth again."

And at that moment the captain became totally blind.

A certain widow, the wife of a doctor, who is still alive—born at Fröderyd—spoke when she was a child with that same Captain Pettersson, who told this story as the true cause of his blindness. He was then old and spoke often of this event.

[Aringsås, Småland. Recorded before 1845 by Sven Söderström. Printed in Gunnar Olof Hyltén-Cavallius and George Stephens, *Svenska sagor*, ed. Jöran Sahlgren, 3 (Stockholm, 1965), 71–74.]

This tale demonstrates that the scholar's firm distinction between wonder-tale and legend often breaks down in actual tradition. The material is that of a popular legend, told throughout Sweden, regarding the purchase of some ship's cargo by a sea-creature, sometimes male, sometimes female. Also from the realm of the legend is the motif of the blindness of an apparently real person who lived in a real place in Sweden. A great many stories of encounters with nature-beings result in a permanent change for the worse in the human, quite often insanity or maiming, laconically reported in tradition with the words "he was never the same since."

However, the apparatus of the first encounter with the *sjörå*, at sea, is full of the wondrous. The other world under the sea is certainly more reminiscent of the wonder-tale than of legends. The narrator seems to revel in detail, and it appears that he has added certain blind motifs. The beautiful daughter functions as no more than a servant, and the drink of troll-wine leads nowhere. One has the impression that vague notions of the other world have been fleshed out with detail from the wonder-tales; the last portion of story no. 81, "The Witch at Tådås," contains some of the same blind motifs and gives a similar impression. Like the farm hand in that story, the sailor who accompanies the *sjörå* to his undersea world looks much like the hero of a wonder-tale; but he vanishes from the tale when his usefulness ends. Perhaps the elements of the wonder-tale should be ascribed to the recorder of the tale, Sven Söderström, who intended it for inclusion in the wonder-tale collection of Hyltén-Cavallius and Stephens.

59. Encounters with Tomtar

A

We also have the *goanisse* (good *nisse, tomte*) here in our district. An older man from down in Simris was just saying that during his youth one of the farmers there had a *nisse*. The man who was telling me this saw the *nisse* one morning busy cleaning out that farmer's barn. The *nisse*'s wheelbarrow was so wide that he had to hold his arms out straight from his sides in order to push it.

It could be seen in more than one way who the farmer's helper was. If you walked through the village grain field when the grain was ripe, you could see how all the grain flew from his neighbors' patches into his. And when the others harvested they only had straw to put in their barns. It was the same with the liquor. It was drawn from the other farmers to the distillery where the *nisse* was in charge, and you could practically smell it going by in the air. But all the neighbors had to make do with the dregs after the mashing. (Skåne).

B

On the estate Rydsgård in Södra Villie parish, Ljunits härad, there were—and probably still are—three *tomtar*. My neighbor, old mother Svensson, worked there for several years as a washerwoman. She and two other serving-girls went down one evening to take the skiff out for a row. But when they came to the water, they saw three small boys standing there, and no matter how much they tried, the three girls were unable to untie the skiff, until finally they went home without having had their boat ride.

The next day they told the woman in charge of the washhouse what had happened. She answered: "Don't pay any attention to that, those were my boys. I talk nicely to them and they carry my water and firewood." Then the other girls understood that it had been the estate's *tomtar* they had seen. (Skåne).

C

In this area the *tomtenissar* are thought to be good creatures. In my youth I worked as a serving-girl for a lady on Öland, and one day I was supposed to scrub the kitchen shelf. At that time I saw with my very own eyes a *tomte* come climbing down from that shelf, with his arms around his little bed.

If *tomtenissar* are to feel at home in a house, every nook and cranny must be kept clean. And on all the great holidays food should be put out for them. (Öland).

D

In Kil someone once heard the *tomtar* threshing in a neighbor's barn. One night he saw the neighbor, wearing a shirt and leather coat, stick his head into the barn door and holler three times.

After a while he heard the *tomtar* begin threshing. Besides, this neighbor always did well. (Närke).

[*A*, *B*, and *C* were collected by Eva Wigström from various regular informants; *D* was collected by Dr. A. G. Nyblin. All four are printed in Wigström, "Folktro och sägner från skilda landskap (Folkdiktning, 3: samlingen)," *SvLm*, 8:3 (1898–1914), *A* p. 140, *B* p. 141, *C* p. 138, *D* p. 140.]

This group of memorates is typical of encounters with the *tomte* or *nisse*. Note that the size may vary from quite small (*C*) to the size of small boys (*B*). The *tomtar* take on various kinds of farm and household work: they clean out the barn, help carry things, do the threshing, and so forth. All these activities are common in *tomte* stories, as is the rather suspicious aid provided by the *nisse* in the second paragraph of *A*. The *tomte* in *C* is not said to have done much for the household, but belief that he liked an absolutely clean house, even in every nook and cranny, would have provided an incentive for zealous housework.

60. *The Tomte Carries a Single Straw*

People say that at a place down near Bryna, there was a little *tomte* walking along helping to carry things. And he had only a piece of straw when he arrived. Then the farmer said to him: "That isn't much of a load."

The *tomte* answered: "A long road makes a load heavy. And after I have taken away as much as I have brought here, you will be a poor man," he said angrily.

And the farmer did become a poor man, after all.

Tomtar usually live on a place, and the people give them porridge Christmas Eve. And it is obvious they eat up the porridge, since the bowl is always empty in the morning. So it must all be true.

[Angerdshestra, Mo härad, Småland. Collected by Bärnhard Karlgren from Nils Svensson, born in 1816, and printed in Karlgren, "Folksägner från Tveta ock Mo härader," *SvLm*, B2 (1908), 45.]

This is one of the most popular Scandinavian and German legends of household spirits (see H. F. Feilberg, *Nissens historie,* Danmarks Folkeminder, 18 [Copenhagen, 1918], pp. 50 ff.), and has been awarded an ML type number by Christiansen: ML 7005, "The Heavy Burden." In some of these legends, the burden is actually heavier than it appears, but more frequent by far in Sweden (and Norway) is the notion, as in the tale above, that a single straw is a perfectly suitable load for a *tomte.* The point of the story is not the size of the burden or the amount of help provided by the *tomte,* but rather the need to respect him. Disrespect usually, as here and in story no. 63, "The Missing Butter," below, causes the *tomte* to leave a household, thus drastically changing the occupants' luck for the worse. In some variants the *tomte* moves in with a neighbor who knows better how to respect him, and the neighbor's prosperity is compared with the poverty of the man who insulted the *tomte* for the small load he was carrying.

An interesting feature of the story printed here is the proverb uttered by the *tomte,* "A long road makes a heavy load" (*Vägens längd gör bördan tung*), which probably had didactic value. It indicates a more fundamental "meaning" of this legend: one should always respect the honest efforts of others.

The tale ends with a belief utterance, including a frequent kind of "proof" attesting the existence of the otherworldly beings. It seems to have survived from medieval times, where it could be used to prove the existence of pagan gods. In Scandinavia the most famous example is surely the idol whose god had been regularly consuming offers of food. When St. Olaf overturned the idol, all manner of well-fed rodents, snakes, and other pests crawled out. (See chapter 113 of *Óláfs saga helga,* in Bjarni Aðalbjarnarson, ed., *Heimskringla 2,* Íslenzk fornrit, 27 [Reykjavík, 1945], pp. 188–190).

61. *New Clothes for the Tomte*

THERE was a *tomte* who would carry flour and pour it into a vat for a certain farmer. The farmer could see that the *tomte* was shabby and dressed in rags. He said: "Since you come and carry flour for me, it would make sense for me to get you some nicer clothes." He had a coat sewn for the *tomte* and left it hanging on the flour bin. But after that the *tomte* did not come with any more flour.

The farmer met him and asked: "How is it that you no longer bring me any flour?"

"The little dandy doesn't want to get flour all over himself," said the *tomte*.

[Kind, Västergötland. IFGH 3104:19. Collected in 1933 by C. M. Bergstrand from Anton Svensson, who lived in Ljungsarp. Printed in Bergstrand, *Gammalt från Kind*, 3:93.]

Variants of this story have been popular all over Western Europe; see Feilberg, *Nissens historie*, pp. 86 ff., and *Handwörterbuch des deutschen Aberglaubens*, s.v. "Ausgelohnt." The idea that the *tomte* has been carrying flour, which he is afraid will dirty his clothing, is particularly characteristic of the Swedish variants; elsewhere in Europe ordinary farm and household duties of all sorts are found.

The popularity of the story is probably due primarily to its value as entertainment, but perhaps also it served to restrain true believers from showering lavish gifts on the household spirits, whose proper due was a bowl of porridge and a measure of respect; see stories nos. 60 and 63. Doubtless the story also could be pressed into service as an exemplum against pride.

62. *The Tomte Learns to Rest*

THERE was a farmer who was out with his *tomte*, and each one took a load of grain from someone else's land. On the way home the farmer put down his load and panted for breath. "If I'd known there was such a thing as panting, I would have taken as much as there is at Källunge," said the *tomte*.

[Frillesås, Halland. IFGH 3791, p. 18. Printed in Helmer Olsson, "Tomten i halländsk folktro," *FmFt*, 24 (1937), 113. Collector and informant not stated.]

This legend is said to be an oikotype limited to Northern Halland. However, similar motifs are recorded of giants elsewhere. Compare, for example, story no. 18, "Save It for Tomorrow." The story of the *tomte* who learns to rest is essentially a joke, but it also helps explain all the energy and hard work attributed to the *tomtar.* Ultimately the tale appears to be related to the preceding story. It seems that behind the *tomte*'s astonishing capacity for work there lurked a touch of sloth just waiting to be exposed, either by fancy clothes or the discovery of rest. Since the otherworldly beings are projections of ourselves, this is not to be wondered at.

63. The Missing Butter

THERE was a farm around here where they had a *tomte.* Porridge was left out for him on Christmas Eve. But when he arrived there was no butter. The butter was under the porridge, but the *tomte* did not see it. He was so outraged he went out to the barn and killed the best cow they had. After he had killed the cow he ate up the porridge, and when he discovered the butter he was beside himself. But he knew that at Skårby they had a cow which was exactly like the one he had killed.

He had a busy Christmas Eve. He took the dead cow and dragged it to Skårby and led home the living one. And it all worked out well. But in summer, when the weather had turned warm, then, as everyone knows, cows eat grass. That cow wanted to cross the river and eat the grass back at Skårby. But then the *tomte* had to stand in the river and make waves so that the cow could not get back to Skårby for grazing.

[Älvsåker, Halland. IFGH 937:40 ff. Printed in Helmer Olsson, "Tomten in halländsk folktro," *FmFt,* 24 (1937), 116. Collector and informant not stated.]

This extremely popular tale from throughout Scandinavia is thought to have originated in Denmark and thence spread to the North (Feilberg, *Nissens historie,* pp. 61 ff.). The Swedish variants are similar to those discussed by Christiansen for Norway (ML 7010, "Revenge for Being Teased"). Sometimes the butter has been deliberately covered, and in other cases the person, usually a servant girl, sent out with the bowl of porridge or other food for the *tomte* either eats it herself or soils the bowl. The revenge in these latter cases quite often takes the form of the girl's being danced to death by a mockingly singing *tomte.*

The point of the stories where the cow is killed and replaced, however, seems to be the dilemma caused by the *tomte*'s overreaction to the missing butter and his subsequent excessive act of remorse, ordinarily at the expense of a neighboring farm. In a group of variants limited to southern Sweden, for example, the *tomte* ruins a batch of bread and promptly steals freshly baked bread from some neighbors (Klintberg, "När tomten skulle baka bröd," p. 82). The primary value of such stories was surely entertainment, but they must also have underlined the need to respect the *tomte,* as in "The Tomte Carries a Single Piece of Straw" (story no. 60). Like that story, the "butter" legend illustrates the extremes of the *tomte*'s behavior and its effect on human prosperity. The two stories are thus closely related.

64. *The Tomte's Favorite Horse*

A FARMER came home drunk one evening. He had two horses, and one was always sleek and well-fed, the other always bony. He had been out riding the thin one then. When he came into the stall, the fat one kicked at him, and so he decided to lash it. At that moment the *tomte* told him to leave Pålle [the sleek horse] alone, and then he hit the farmer so hard it knocked him out. He lay there until he was discovered next morning, for no one knew he had come home. After that he never again dared go alone into the stall when it was dark. And Pålle was always fat and the other horse always thin.

[Kåröd, Sanne, Bohuslän. Collected by David Arill from Johannes Zachariasson and printed in Arill, "Folksägner från Sanne," *FmFt,* 5 (1918), 122.]

Judging from the legends, quite often folk belief ascribed the health or infirmity of household animals to the whims of the household spirits. Legends tell of the extra rations the *tomte* would bring for his favorite, or his mistreatment of a farmer who sold a beloved horse or cow, and sickly animals were said to have been beaten by an outraged or annoyed *tomte.* Such belief is merely a specialization of the general belief that the prosperity of a farm or household had a lot to do with its treatment of the resident spirits and their whims.

Of interest in this story is that it accords so fully with the general outlines of supernatural experiences and memorates (see Introduction, pp. 28–29). Drink has dulled the farmer's senses, and he may also (retrospectively) have felt guilty about his intention to whip the sleek horse. It seems fairly clear that Pålle's kick was right on the mark, at any rate, and the *tomte* presumably only entered the picture the following morning. The *tomte*'s punch is one of the most widely encountered motifs in *tomte* stories; he regularly delivers a box to the ears when someone's behavior is unacceptable, either to him or by community standards. Frequently, of course, his standards and those of the community are identical.

65. *Exorcising the Tomte*

THERE was once an old woman with a son who was studying for the ministry. She was quite well off, for you see she had a *nisse* who lived on the property. But the son disapproved of her having any contact with non-Christian monsters. He wanted to drive away the *nisse.* But the *nisse* did not want to leave. The boy spoke with him and asked, "Why do you need milk and porridge?"

"Well, all the porridge I've got from your mother, I intend to have with me on Judgement Day, so I can prove I've been in her service." (Then the woman would be damned, he thought.) Then the boy read scripture over him, and the *nisse* had to leave.

When he left, the *nisse* said: "Now I will take away from the farm just as much as I brought here in the first place." And he did. The woman fell into total poverty.

[Bohuslän. Collected by Vilhelm Cederschiöld from Olaus Olsson, born around 1852, and printed in "Ur Olaus Olsson's sägensamling," *FmFt*, 19 (1932), 106.]

Legends of this nature owe much to church doctrine that all otherworldly beings are evil, and therefore they contrast with the friendly relationship between household spirits and humans typical of most legends. When an evil spirit is to be exorcised, the prime example is the devil, and details from many exorcism legends have entered *tomte* and *nisse* stories. Although a boy studying for the ministry is the most frequent hero in these stories, one also encounters ordained ministers and an occasional bishop. In more elaborate stories the *tomte* may be forced into a bottle or through a narrow opening or may be driven off in some other way openly borrowed from the legend cycle of conflict between devil and clergy.

The desire of the *tomte* to prove on Judgement Day that he has been in the service of a Christian is a frequently encountered motif in Swedish legends, here interpreted negatively by the informant. Sometimes it seems, however, that the otherworldly being is trying to attain salvation for himself by his service to the Christian community; cf. story no. 50, "The Näck Longs for Salvation," for a story with similar sentiment.

Although this legend presents the *nisse* in a negative light, the old woman's poverty resulting from crossing the household spirit is typical of a great many stories, as we have seen.

66. A Ship's Tomte

THERE was a sailor from Bohuslän who had loaded cargo in Åmål, and the weather turned nasty. They were making for the harbor at Koggen in Dalsland, where there was a lighthouse. The fog came in, and they didn't know their way around the coast. The sailor put the helm to port, but it swung to starboard. Behind the transom, at the stern, was a step near the rudder, and the skipper leaned over the stern and looked down at it. There sat a little old man holding both hands around the rudder post where it ran up into the deck. "Good, now we are out of danger," thought the skipper. He let the old man steer them into the harbor at Koggen. When the boat luffed up and they awoke, they were at the best mooring in the harbor at Koggen.

The weather hadn't been all that overwhelming—that is, there hadn't been a strong storm—but probably the thick fog had caused them to run for shelter.

It was probably a *nisse.*

[Orust, Bohuslän. IFGH 5368:2. Collected by C. M. Bergstrand in 1948 from Karl Johansson, born in Röra (Orust) in 1870. Printed in Bergstrand, *Gammalt från Orust* (Göteborg, 1962), pp. 72–73.]

Just as there are *tomtar* who help farmers in agricultural areas, so in coastal regions *tomtar* and *nissar* inhabit ships and help the crews in need. Additionally, many of the other familiar *tomte* legends may be encountered in nautical contexts. There are legends of *tomtar* who load and unload ships, carry out repairs, and do other kinds of work. A thoughtless or unkind word to the ship's *tomte* leads directly to undesirable results: the mast may carry away, the ship founder, and so forth. Improper behavior is punished at sea just as on land. In short, anywhere there is human habitation and regular human activity, one can expect to find the household spirits. Note that the ship's *tomte* is an essentially friendly creature—he must not be crossed, of course—whereas the *sjörå* is decidedly unfriendly unless propitiated, as in the *vantevän* or "glove-friend" story. The difference is that the ship, like the house, barn, mill, and so forth, is familiar territory, whereas the sea is, like the forest and mountains, *terra incognita.* Despite the basic differences between sea-going and agrarian life, the cast of beings in the other world and their functions remain remarkably constant; making harbor in a thick fog presents the same kind of attraction to the imagination as, for example, getting in hay before rainfall.

The World of Religion

67. The Devil as a Black Dog

A

AT A DANCE at someone's house right here in this parish, I myself, and several others, saw a big black dog with flames coming out of its mouth. It was prowling around, back and forth among the dancers. The fiddler got a glimpse of it too; and he threw down his fiddle and never played again. The dog disappeared through a crack in the window, and we all went home.

[Näs, Värmland. IFGH 884:11. Nilsson/Bergstrand, *Värmlandsnäs,* 3:9. Collected in 1927 by Ragnar Nilsson from Johan Larsson, a shoemaker who lived in Finntorp, Bro, born in 1837.]

B

ON ANOTHER occasion there was a farmer here in this parish who was seated having a meal. He happened to glance under the table, and there lay a big black dog. And the farmer gave it a kick, but then the dog flew at the farmer, took him by the collar, and dragged him off to bed, big as he was. For that was no ordinary dog, but the devil himself. And there he held the man fast, and no one could manage to free him. They called seven parsons to the spot, but none had more success than the next. Finally, however, they sent for Lagergren, and then the dog released his grip and wanted to leave. But the rector wanted to make Satan know he had suffered, and so he drove him out through the keyhole.

[Tveta, Småland. Collected before 1905 by Bärnhard Karlgren from "Madam Sandberg," born early in the nineteenth century (ca. 1810). Printed in Karlgren, "Folksägner från Tveta ock Mo härader," *SvLm,* B2 (1908), 33.]

According to folk belief, Satan could assume virtually any guise he wished, including invisibility, a power he shared with most of the other supernatural beings. Most often he seems to have been in human form, usually that of a well-dressed man. In these cases he is often given away by his tail or hoof. When he adopts non-human guise, the black dog is the most popular. This guise is common to Christian folklore throughout the world; see Barbara Allen Woods, *The Devil in Dog-Form,* University of California Publications in Folklore, 11 (Berkeley, 1959). Legend *A* has the didactic purpose of other dance legends; *B* is a tale of exorcism. Lagergren, in *B,* was once rector of Tofteryd. Exorcism through a tiny hole is a very common motif, here interpreted as a means of making the devil suffer.

68. The Hårga-Dance

In the village of Hårga in Hanebo parish there lived some time ago an evil group of people who would dance in the village on Saturday and Sunday evening, sometimes all through the night into the following day. One night before a great day of prayer they danced until the church bells rang the next morning. At that point a well-dressed man came into the hall where they were dancing and wanted to join in. He was welcome, too. And finally they were dancing the so-called "long dance." They joined hands in a circle and the circle danced right out the door. Now it happened there was a man there whose fiancée was part of the circle, though he was not. He noticed that the well-dressed gentleman dancing with them had horse's hooves for feet. When he saw that, he stood up and tried to pull his fiancée from the long dance, but no matter how he pulled and shoved, he only came away with one of her arms. The line of dancers now continued on its way out over hills and rocks until it came to Långhällan, the top of the mountain Hårgaberget. There they danced until only their skulls were left.

[Järvsö, Hälsingland. ULMA 2093:9. Collected by J. Cardell from a woman born in Hanebo in 1842. Printed in Dag Strömbäck, "Kölbigk och Hårga I," *Arv*, 17 (1961), 38.]

The Hårga-dance is now the most widely known of the localized dance legends in Sweden. It was first noted during 1783 but is presumably considerably older; the legend of the sinning dancers who could not stop is widespread in European medieval literature and was frequently included in collections of exempla. Olav Algot Ericsson was the first to see the connection between this and a similar dance, said to have taken place in the German village of Kölbigk in the early eleventh century. It apparently made its way from the Low German *Seelentrost* into the Old Swedish *Siælinna Thrøst* and thence to oral tradition, which in Hälsingland localized it to the remarkable mountain top near Hårga ("Sägnen om Hårgadansen och dess rötter," *FmFt*, 15 (1928), 92–98). As Dag Strömbäck has shown in a number of papers, however, the legend was very widely distributed throughout medieval Europe ("Den underbara årsdansen," *Arkiv för Nordisk Filologi*, 59 (1944), 111–126, reprinted in his *Folklore och filologi*, SKGAAF, 48 (Uppsala, 1970), 54–69; "Kölbigk och Hårga I," *Arv*, 17 (1961), 1–48).

The legend may be based on an elaboration of a temporary outbreak of "dancing sickness," a kind of collective hysteria documented in the Middle Ages. See J. F. C. Hecker, *Die grossen Volkskrankheiten des Mittelalters* (Berlin, 1865), and A. Martin, "Geschichte der Tanzkrankheit in Deutschland," *Zeitschrift des Vereins für Volkskunde*, 24 (1914), 113–134, both cited in Strömbäck, "Den underbara årsdansen," *Folklore och filologi*, p. 55. According to Strömbäck's findings, the notion of the long dance is important to early variants of the story. One is to imagine the devil leading the dancers off to destruction on the mountain top, rather like the piper of Hamlin or Death in the familiar medieval image used by Ingmar Bergman at the end of his film, *The Seventh Seal*. This enables the legend to be set initially in the town, thereby allowing the narrator to comment on the generally sinful lives of the dancers; in this case the endless dancing is a punishment for riotous living. Other variants place the entire story, like the Dala-dance, atop the mountain, and in that case the punishment is primarily for wild dancing and violation of the sabbath. Ericsson has also suggested that the Hårga-dance legend had an etiological purpose—namely, to explain a ring said by many informants to be found worn into the rock on the top of the mountain at Hårga. This point is questionable at present, since no one has been able to find the ring for years. Strömbäck's search failed to turn it up in 1944, and he therefore doubts whether it ever existed ("Kölbigk och Hårga I," p. 47). Whether it did or not, the primary purpose of the story was always without question that of a moralizing, didactic exemplum.

69. Dancing in Dalarna

There was a village in Dalarna where both young and old used to dance on a mountain, whether it was the right time for dancing or not. Once while they were there dancing, a stranger came with a fiddle under his arm and asked if he might play for them, for he was good at it, he said. This pleased the dancers and they asked him to play.

But when he started to play, it was as if all the dancers had gone mad; they started to dance absolutely uncontrollably. They danced over stones and stumps and holes, all at top speed, but soon they grew tired and wanted to stop. But it was impossible to stop. It just got worse and worse, and it wasn't long before they had worn out the soles of their shoes and were dancing barefoot. They yelled at the fiddler to stop, but he pretended not to hear and just played even faster. Finally they had worn away their legs up to their knees, but they still had to keep dancing; and they couldn't stop even when only their skulls remained, but the skulls leapt and danced with the beat.

But a parson found out about that dancing, and he went to the mountain and ordered the fiddler to stop, and the fiddler had to obey. But the people who went there with the parson said it was the Old Man himself who was playing. He used his tail as a fiddle and played it with a bow.

[Åsele, Lappland. ULMA 884, p. 121. Collected by O. P. Pettersson and printed in his *Sagor från Åsele lappmark*, Svenska sagor och sägner, 9 (1945), 174–175. Reprinted in Klintberg, p. 204 and in Dag Strömbäck, "Kölbigk och Hårga II," *Arv*, 24 (1968), 95.]

The evident similarity between this text and the preceding "Hårga-Dance" requires no comment. It is worth noting, however, that a parson is able to stop the dance, presumably to save what is left of the dancers. Since only their skulls were left hopping about in time to the music, one might wonder about the value of the parson's effort. Other variants clarify it, since in most of them only a few of the dancers have worn away any of their bodies, and usually no higher than their knees. The other variants, too, often identify the parson as "Tillberg," a parson named Thelberg who was in the parish of Fjällsjö, Ångermanland, during the last decade of the eighteenth century.

What separates the Dala-dance, as this legend type is called, from the closely related Hårga-dance is, besides the role of the parson characteristic of the Dala-dance, the geographical location of the two legends. But while the Hårga-dance is a true local legend, perhaps used in part for etiology, the Dala-dance is, rather strangely, centered in Norrland, where it seems to have originated and received its name. Even more strangely, it is virtually unknown in Dalarna, where the one recording of it has turned out to be untrustworthy as a local tradition (see Dag Strömbäck, "Kölbigk och Hårga II," *Arv*, 24 (1968), 95–98). On the other hand, northern Sweden does have localized variants, of which the most well-known is from the village of Hacksäng in Jämtland. It has the structure of the following story.

70. *The Dance at Frisagård*

At the farm Frisagård people decided one evening to organize a dance. On that same day there arrived two journeymen who asked for lodgings for the night. But they were turned down, because of the dance, and so they continued on their way.

Something was very strange, however, about that dance. For once people had started dancing they simply couldn't stop. They thought that those two journeymen must have had something to do with it, and so some others set out in pursuit of them and managed to catch up with them. The journeymen said simply that a little slip of paper was sitting on the door post of the room where they were dancing, and if that slip were removed the dancers could stop whenever they wished. The messengers did what the journeymen had told them. They returned home and indeed found a piece of paper over the door. On it was written: "People will dance here." As soon as they had taken down that piece of paper the dancing stopped, since the dancers inside had just about danced themselves to death.

[Harplinge, Halland. NM EU 21318. Reported by K. A. Karlsson. Printed in Dag Strömbäck, "Kölbigk och Hårga II," *Arv*, 24 (1968), 100.]

Legends of this sort are localized throughout Sweden, and the localization has affected certain details. In northern Sweden, for example, the disappointed guest who plants the piece of paper is likely to be a Lapp who has been turned away from the dance. Elsewhere beggars, students, and other undesirable characters are employed. The main point, however, is that the spurned guest be a stranger to the community. In a rather unusual variant from Ångermanland, for example, he is a foreign "gentleman" traveling at the expense of King Karl Johan (Richard Bergström and Johan Nordlander, "Sagor, sägner och visor," *SvLm*, 5:2 (1885), 87). In that variant it seems that the informant may have meant the foreigner to be the devil, since Rev. Thelberg is summoned, and it is he who finds the paper—guided to it, according to the guess of the informant, by his knowledge of the black book.

71. *The Cardplayers and the Devil*

Some men in Ausås, Södra Åsbo, were lounging in a meadow one Sunday playing cards. One of them was cheating. When his comrades reproached him for it, he started cursing and swore he was playing honestly. But the others shouted back that he was cheating. And then he said the devil could come and take him, body and soul, right where he lay, if he was guilty.

He had hardly got the words out of his mouth before one of his arms shot straight up in the air, his hair stood on end, and his body was lifted a few feet off the ground. In that position he began to move rather quickly forward. One of his comrades threw down the cards, rushed into the stall, grabbed a stallion, threw himself onto its back, galloped after the disappearing liar, and finally managed to get a grip on his thumb, at which point he invoked the name of Jesus and began reciting the Lord's Prayer, until the devil had to let go.

By this time the sinner had fainted, so the fellow had to drape him over the horse and lead him home. There he came to, but he had no idea of what had happened to him. His left thumb had withered away and remained like that as long as he lived. People believed that the devil had been hanging on to that thumb when he dragged the man, but that he probably still hadn't had power over more of the man's body than just that finger. Because of that, he had had to release his grip when he heard the name of God.

[Skanörs Ljung, Skåne. Collected by Eva Wigström from the "old woman," one of her regular informants, and printed in Wigström, "Folktro och sägner från skilda landskap (Folkdiktning, 3:e samlingen)," *SvLm*, 8:3 (1898–1914), 160.]

Dancing and cardplaying are the two most popular subjects depicted in devil legends. The common migratory legend, ML 3015, "The Cardplayers and the Devil," depicts the actual participation of the devil in the game and his subsequent encounter with a clergyman, who succeeds in driving him out through a pinhole in the window. That legend is also found in the more northern areas of Sweden, whereas in the south the devil is more likely to appear as a dog who watches the game from under the table.

The legend printed here is an elaboration of the simple proverb, "Speak of the devil and he is there," set in the context of card playing. The narrator has left no doubt that the game is sinful, since she has set it on a Sunday. Similarly, she has made clear her opinion of the cheater by referring to him as "liar" and "sinner." It is worth noting that the sin of card playing is often intensified by cheating, quite often with the involvement of the devil, in these legends. Presumably such legends could be used to explain someone's good luck at cards. Our legend has didactic overtones, and it may also once have been used to explain a real person's withered thumb, but basically it is entertaining, a variation on the familiar theme of escape from the devil, in this case from his very clutches.

72. The Devil Advises Suicide

THERE was an old man who could never get along with his wife. One day he got out a rope and took it with him into the forest where he intended to hang himself. When he was out on the road, another man joined up with him, who looked like someone from Björud who had recently died. When they had gone a short distance, the stranger said: "Do what you have planned, for it will never get better at home."

"No, God spare me that," the man answered and turned around. He had been walking with the devil, and he knew it full well.

[Näs, Värmland. IFGH 1220:20. Nilsson/Bergstrand, *Värmlandsnäs*, 3: 11–12. Collected in 1928 from Erik Börjesson, born in 1837 in Eskilsäter.]

Common to most genuine devil legends, as opposed to wonder-tales, is the notion that the devil tries to tempt someone into sinful behavior. It is a measure of the psychological realism of these tales, however, that more often than not he only reinforces an idea that has already come to someone, as here. Suicide figures frequently in such stories, no doubt because of the theological doctrine that it is a mortal sin. In keeping with this, another sin often met with in these legends is murder, sometimes infanticide. The epic moment in the legend printed here is the man's resolve not to kill himself, strengthened by his mention of God. The effect of such a mention, as we have seen in many other cases, is to sap the power of a supernatural being. A great many of the variants of this legend end in this or similar fashion, with the human able to resist the devil's temptation by invoking a power against which Satan is powerless.

73. The Girls at the Parsonage Get Help Sewing Crinoline

It was a long time ago; my mother told me about it. It was supposed to have happened in the parsonage at Västanfors. The dean had been away visiting the sick in the parish, and it was Whitsuntide. Some of the girls at the farm were to take their first communion on the holy day, and when the dean came home he walked by the kitchen window and noticed that his serving-girls were sewing crinoline they were going to wear at the communion service. And that was a grave breach of the sabbath. And when he looked more closely he saw that a tailor's apprentice was sitting among them and helping them to sew the crinoline, but he had horns on his forehead and a tail and a horse's hoof for a foot. The girls didn't notice a thing, however, they just went on chatting and giggling.

Then the parson went in to them and threw his cloak over them. *Then* they could see whose society they were in, and they saw that it was Shame himself. And then they were terrified and put off their first communion, since they were unprepared for it, and after that they asked God for forgiveness for their breach of the sabbath.

[Norberg, Västmanland. ULMA 8045:4. Klintberg no. 266, pp. 205–206. Collected by Ellen Lagergren in 1934 from Hilda Nilsson, Norberg, born in 1856 in Söderbark, Dalarna.]

Here is another legend telling of the devil's role in sin. The gravity of the breach of sabbath is increased by the sanctity of the holiday, which would have improved the didactic value of the story. However, the great holidays were the times when the supernatural beings were out in strongest force, which may provide additional motivation for the timing of the story. Important, too, is the status of the girls. They are just on the border of formal entry into the church by taking their first communion. Initiates at this stage of an important rite of passage would be particularly vulnerable, since they are in a category of unclear status. See Victor Turner, *Dramas, Fields, and Metaphors: Symbolic Action in Human Society* (Ithaca, N.Y., 1974), for a recent anthropological restatement of this problem.

The foremost didactic message of the legend, of course, is that the girls are paying more attention to their finery than to the religious significance of the upcoming communion service. Considering the lack of opportunities for young girls to dress up in this culture, their attitude must not have been uncommon, and so the legend points out the religious aspects and hints at the consequences of this sort of pride.

74. *Giving the Devil a Ride*

AT SUNDSHULT they used to row people across the sound. One evening there was a terrible hue and cry from the other side. A boatman rowed across to fetch the traveler. A large, heavy man got into the skiff.

"Where are you from?," the boatman asked.

"Both near and far, but tonight I am on my way to Rastad to make an inventory," the other answered.

"What is your name?"

"It is said in so many different ways that I cannot tell you."

They landed. "Where is Rastad?," asked the devil, for that is who it was. He was told. Sinful people lived there. That night both of them were hanged. Perhaps he did it.

[Naverstad, Bohuslän. IFGH 5012, pp. 2–3. Collected in 1945 by C. M. Bergstrand from Anders Thulin, born in 1866 in Naverstad. Printed in Bergstrand, *Bohuslänska sägner* (Göteborg, 1947), p. 5, and in Klintberg, no. 60, p. 203.]

An unusually imaginative variant of the common tale of giving the devil a ride. In most variants the ride is in a carriage on land; rowing the devil across a watercourse reminds one of the ferrying of the troll-hag (cf. ML 7085), but would of course be expected in areas situated near water. Giants and trolls sometimes enter into stories of this kind, too, which range from very short memorates to the more lengthy, fanciful tale printed here. The combination of any strange traveler and a suicide or murder in a district would no doubt quickly lead to realization of this legend.

The inventory referred to was usually carried out after death for probate purposes and hence is ironically portentous; the soon-to-be dead had presumably made a pact with the devil.

75. *The Devil as the Fourth Wheel*

During the seventeenth century there was a parson here named Sten Mattsson. He had attended the school of black arts abroad and had properly studied the black books, with the result that he could do with the devil whatever he wanted. Once it was Sten Mattsson's turn to deliver the sermon at Assizes in Hammenhög, and there he preached a sermon sharply attacking the devil. Well, the devil was certain to watch out for a chance to get his own licks in. During the evening when the parson was on his way home and had just gotten half way between Hammenhög and Vranarp, the boy driving thought the horses were having trouble with the cart. "Get down and look," the parson said. The boy got down, but, no, he couldn't see a thing. Then Sten Mattsson himself got down from the cart and pulled the harness off one of the horses, and when he looked through the harness he could see that the devil and a number of smaller demons were riding along, sitting on the rear axle. But Sten Mattsson knew what to do. He ordered the boy to remove one of the wheels from the axle, and then the devil had to lift the axle and carry it. "Off we go," the parson said to the coachman, "and don't worry about holding down the speed." And indeed off they went, at a gallop, to Simris. But the devil must really have been in a hurry that time, since he had to run alongside holding up the axle. And he had to stand in front of the parsonage all night long holding it up, but then in the morning Sten Mattsson came outside and set him free. And when the devil set off on his way, he tore the roof off a row of farm buildings.

[Simris, Skåne. LAF 318. Reported by Per Larsson in 1898; printed in Ingemars Ingers, ed., "Texter från Skåne," part 2 of Lundell et al., "Sagor, sägner, legender . . . ," *SvLm*, 3:3 (1945), 12–13.]

The story is known throughout Europe and is one of the most popular devil legends in Sweden: Christiansen ML 3010,

"Making the Devil Carry the Cart." Sten Mattsson, rector of Simris from 1649–1689, is just one of the many clergymen to whom this legend has been individualized. Many variants, however, do not mention a specific parson but speak rather of "a parson" or "a certain clergyman," as one would expect in a migratory legend.

The reference to the devil's haste ("But the devil must really have been in a hurry that time . . .") alludes to variants of another very popular legend, the previous story, in which the devil asks someone for a ride somewhere because, he explains, he is in a hurry. After giving Satan a lift, the man who was driving learns that there has been a death or suicide at the devil's destination.

76. Outwitting the Devil

A SKIPPER had signed on Old Shame as mate. He was to do all the work without pay, but in exchange he was to have the skipper's soul. The skipper could escape this fate if he could give the devil a job he couldn't carry out. In the end the skipper was worried and wanted to get rid of his mate, since both the skipper and the boat were getting on in years. He tried having the mate cast anchor with his bare hands, but he stuck in the hawsehole instead of going to the bottom. Then in Vänersborg harbor the skipper put the pump through the bottom of the boat and ordered the devil to pump the boat dry. He pumped and pumped, until fish were coming up. But when Old Shame discovered he was outwitted, he wept tears of rage, gathered up his things, and went ashore. He shook his fist at the skipper and said: "Don't you go out to sea again!"

The skipper, however, signed on a new crew, and light at heart he put out from Vänersborg, but he was lost off Naven.

[Eskilsäter, Värmland. Collected by Sigurd Dahllöf and printed in his "Västsvenska skepparsägner," *FmFt*, 16 (1929), 127.]

Popular tradition records almost as many ways to trick the devil as he finds people who wish to sell their souls to him. This story, AT 1179, reaches a high level of entertainment by employing a false start, the aborted trick with the anchor, and hitting on a relatively uncommon means of tricking Old Shame. We leave the realm of the wonder-tale in the last sentence, however. However light the tone of the tale, violating the devil's interdiction would always lead to disaster.

The story has affinities with AT 810–814 and is closely related to ML 3020, "Inexperienced Use of the Black Book. Ropes of Sand." The central motif is the same, but the framing is different. ML 3020 is not widely attested in Sweden among the countless tales of outwitting the devil.

77. *The Devil in the Church*

Once long ago there was a farmer, much like many others, but this one was a sensible, serious, and God-fearing farmer, you see, and so there was never a Sunday when he was healthy, on his feet, and had a way of getting there that he was not in church listening to the word of God. One Sunday as he sat in his pew listening devoutly and attentively to the parson, just as the parson was reading the gospel the farmer cast down his eyes, and who should he see sitting under the pulpit but the devil himself! And the farmer was shaken, no doubt about it, and was not just a little curious about what the evil one was up to there. And as he looked him over, he noticed that the devil had a piece of parchment balanced on his knees and was writing on it with a quill. And there he was noting down the names of all those who were misbehaving in church.

"That's disgusting, it is," thought the farmer and began to look around in the church, and he saw one person after another doing things he shouldn't have been doing. Some were whispering and grinning at each other, some were shining mirrors at each other, some were drifting off to sleep, and to tell all the things people were doing would be unwise. The farmer felt very sorry for them, but then he reflected that they were not worth his pity, since they were such sinners. "But you won't trick me, you evil tempter," he thought to himself.

Be that as it may, it ended no better than with him staring straight at the devil the entire time without paying the parson or the service any attention at all.

And the devil just kept writing, until at last he had the whole parchment filled up with names. Then he tried to stretch it out in order to make room for more names, but he got nowhere with that, no matter how much he pulled and tugged, and at last he sank his teeth into it and pulled angrily as hard as he could. But at that point the piece of parchment tore, and the devil jerked backwards and his horns hit the pulpit with a crash.

The farmer found that amusing, you can imagine, and he broke into a grin over it. But then the devil added his name to the list.

[Kalmar, Småland. Recorded from memory by Emil Svensén, who heard it first in the 1860s. Printed in Svensén, "Sagor från Emådalen," *SvLm*, 2:7 (1882), 1–2.]

The story of the devil and his parchment in the church, AT 826, "Devil Writes Down Names of Men on Hide in Church," was one of the more popular exempla of the Middle Ages. The earliest attestation is in the *Sermones Vulgares* of Jacques de Vitry, and another thirteenth-century attestation is provided by Vincenz de Beauvais. The story was also popular in medieval church art, a fourteenth-century fresco in the St. Georgskirche, Insel Reichenau, providing the earliest example. In Scandinavia the earliest attestation is probably in the Old Icelandic *Maríu saga*, a compilation of translations from various European sources, usually attributed to a certain Kygri-Björn Hjaltason who died in 1237 or 1238. In Sweden the story is recorded in the so-called *Järteckensbok* or *Book of Miracles*, from around 1385, also translated from various foreign sources, and in *Siælinna Thrøst* ("The Souls' Consolation"), translated from the Low German *Seelentrost* during the first part of the fifteenth century.

In the legendary form typical of the exemplum, the story was told about saints; in Sweden it has been recorded about St. Birgitta, and some of the variants, in Sweden as elsewhere, are told of a man who could walk over water. He loses that power after laughing at the devil in church. Most of the modern variants, however, are humorous and have nothing to do with saints. The humorous qualities of the variant printed here may have been stylistically emphasized in the re-creation, in dialect, by Emil Svensén.

Many medieval texts, including that of Jacques de Vitry, are printed in Lutz Röhrich, *Erzählungen des späten Mittelalters und ihr Weiterleben in Literatur und Volksdichtung bis zur Gegenwart*, 1 (Bern, 1962), 113–123; discussion on pp. 267–274. The distribution of the modern variants is elucidated by Robert Wildhaber, *Das Sündenregister auf dem Kuhhaut*, FFC, 163 (Helsinki, 1955). See also D. Jakobson, "Den onde i kyrkan," *Skånska Folkminnen*, 1926, 91 ff.

78. Old Erik in the Mill

THERE was once a shoemaker who was away stitching up shoes the days before Christmas. He kept up his stitching until Christmas Eve, and around dusk he was ready to go home. But since it was quite a distance to where he lived, when darkness fell he had to enter a mill along the road and stay the night there. Now that particular mill was not so well known in those parts, since rumor had it that Satan himself put up there occasionally. And the shoemaker knew about that, too; but since he knew a bit more than others, he could also arrange matters so that no harm would come to him.

After he had gathered up some wood scraps from beside the wall of the mill, he made a roaring fire, and then he took a cookpot which some miller had left there and put it on the fire and in it he started boiling some cobbler's wax which he had with him. And then he took a piece of paper which he cut into narrow strips and, using the wax, attached together into a ribbon on which he wrote the Lord's Prayer and which he then tied around his waist. Now he went to the bench and lay down, but he left the pan on the fire, so that it would stay hot through.

It was quiet, and the shoemaker went to sleep, he did. But sure enough, around midnight he heard a terrible clamor in the mill-house, so he had to get up and check out what sort of creature was there. And he didn't leave behind the pan of wax, either. When he entered the mill-house, who do you think he saw but Old Erik himself, stepping out of the mill spout, with a body as small as a *tomte* but with an incredibly huge head!

"Have you ever seen such an enormous head on such a little body before?," he asked the shoemaker.

"Have *you* ever tasted such strong soup before?," answered the shoemaker and threw the pan of hot wax right in his face.

Getting scalded like that by a plucky shoemaker could hardly have been pleasant for Old Erik, but you should have seen how he ranted and raved—particularly since he couldn't get at the shoemaker at all because of that paper with the Lord's Prayer he had around his waist.

After a while had passed and the devil, who was scrubbing his face furiously the whole time, had returned to something approaching normal, there came from all sides troll-hags riding brooms and stumps, just as they usually do on their way to Blåkulla. They had large leather sacks on their backs, filled with buttertubs, since they intended to exchange their Christmas presents then. It was not surprising that Old Erik was so intent on staying there, despite all the unpleasantness the shoemaker caused him. When a big mob of them had assembled, they brought in a large earthenware dish and put their gifts in it, each and every one of them. Now, believe me, they certainly were not stingy. The shoemaker had never seen such pats of butter, though he had been all around the parish. They started a eulogy, all together, though the one they were dealing with could otherwise never get enough. But when the troll-hags were about to leave, the shoemaker stationed himself right in the doorway and hacked at them as they went by.

Naturally they did their best to defend themselves, but still each got her share, and they were so furious they would have spat poison at him, if only they could have done him any harm.

After they left it grew quiet, and the shoemaker went back and lay down to sleep until morning. But then when he went home he met the people coming from church, and he saw how it was with the women: they had cuts on their faces, virtually every single one.

[Rättvik, Dalarna. ULMA 90:41:7. From K. Karlsson, during the 1870s. Printed in J. A. Lundell, Manne Eriksson, Gunnar Hedström et al.,

"Sagor, sägner, legender: Äventyr och skildringar av folkets levnadssätt på landsmål," *SvLm*, 3:2 (1881), 126–129.]

A wondrous tale composed of two legend types. The first is that of story no. 51, "The Mill Spirit," but here Satan has been substituted for the troll. The second is story no. 79, "The Easter-Hag Put a Water-Trough in Her Place," here generalized to an entire community. Stylistically it is clear that this tale was recounted by an able narrator, one at home with the wonder-tale. His combining of two legend types indicates the fluidity of actual oral tradition, as opposed to the rigid classification of archivists, and gives a good idea of how entertaining legends could be made in the hands of a skilled storyteller.

79. *The Easter-Hag Put a Water-Trough in Her Place*

THERE was once an old man whose wife was an Easter-hag. He asked a good friend what caused his wife to be so cold on Easter night. "She's at Blåkulla," the friend replied. The old man did not believe him; the friend taught him what to do: he should take a knife and stick it into the thigh of his bedmate. If she didn't say anything *then*, it would be clear that she was off with Old Shame.

The man stuck a knife in her thigh on Easter night and left it there. The old hag didn't say a word. The next day, when the man was watering his horses, he saw the knife embedded in the water-trough. And that was what he had slept with.

[Råggärd, Dalsland. NM EU 49548. Klintberg no. 310, p. 228. Collected in 1929 from Jakob Olsson, who was born in Håbols sn.]

This popular story depends on the ability of the witch to change the appearance of things. It also answers the question of why witches were not missed at home during their all-night revels at Blåkulla (cf. story no. 80, "With Her Godmother to Josefsdal"). A very frequent variation, similar to the incident in story no. 81, "The Witch at Tådås," has a man stab an unknown witch or threatening being in human or non-human form. Later, often at church, he notices that one or more women have stab wounds. In the more extravagant variants the parson's wife and all the women in the town may be wounded, as in the preceding story.

80. *With Her Godmother to Josefsdal*

In the past, parents themselves didn't take their children to be baptized; instead someone else did it for them and stood godfather or godmother. Now there was a real troll-hag here in this parish who stood godmother to an infant. But everyone said that she hadn't taken the child to the priest; but when she went to him and was going to have the child baptized, she took something else instead of the child. It could have been a broom or an old log, since she cast a spell on the priest so that he was baptizing an infant, as far as he could see. The woman wanted to take the child off with her on her witch's journeys.

One evening when she was around nine years old, the girl was sitting in the kitchen, and, truth to tell, she said, "Mama, come here and hold me, for Godmother is here and wants to take me away again, but I don't want to go with her now."

"What's wrong with you, child?," the mother asked, but at that point the child couldn't answer. She sat just as she had been sitting before, but it was as if she had been turned to stone. That meant that the old troll-hag had taken the girl herself with her to Josefsdal and put a spell on something there in the kitchen so that it would look like the girl.

When they woke up the next morning the girl was asleep in her bed as if nothing had happened. But later that day the mother took her aside and asked her what the godmother was up to with her those nights. Then the girl explained all about what went on at Josefsdal. The godmother had a big group of hags with her, and they all rode up there and set up housekeeping; the hags baked bread and scoured the floor and brewed beer and cooked food. The children in the group were allowed to play and have a good time.

But there was one room the children were not permitted to enter. The women went in, and then the children crept up and peered in. There was a man in there, and the girl thought he had been tied up; and when the women came out they had got that salve which they smear on things in order to fly on them.

When the girl's mother had heard this strange story, she took the girl to the parson and had her baptized. The priest sprinkled her with water, and then the godmother lost her power to make the girl go with her.

[Grangärde, Dalarna. ULMA 1878:3.10–12. Klintberg no. 315, pp. 230–231. Collected by Ingegärd Isaksson in 1928 from an informant known only as "Enbacksbo."]

As Klintberg points out in his note (p. 339), the most striking aspect of this legend is the close similarity it bears to testimony describing Blåkulla in witchcraft trials. Although nothing is known of the informant or the circumstances of collecting, it seems most likely that the legend was transmitted in genuine oral tradition for a period of almost two and a half centuries. The description of Josefsdal, said to be in a nearby parish, is sober and straightforward, completely lacking in fanciful details. It is, indeed, characteristic of the testimony of confessing witches that they were unable to evince much imagination in their descriptions of Blåkulla. In our legend, for example, the witches perform normal household duties, the sort one would carry out before a holiday or party: they wash, bake, and brew. The children play contentedly and the whole picture is more one of domestic contentment than frenzied orgy. The point of the meeting seems to be acquisition of the witch's salve, in fantasy and reality the vehicle for the witches' sabbath (see Introduction, pp. 48–49).

81. The Witch at Tådås

Off in Tådås there lived a troll-hag. One day her husband was out harvesting in the fields. The troll-hag prepared some food for him and packed it in a basket. Then she called in the serving-girl and said: "Here is a basket. You are to take food out to the master. But you must not look in the basket." After the girl had gone a short distance she could not control herself any longer. She simply had to see what kind of strange food it was that could not be looked at. She carefully lifted the top of the basket, and then she saw that the basket was filled with toads and horse manure. Once she had looked at the witch's food, the farmer could also see what kind of filth his wife had to offer him. But if the girl had not been curious, then he wouldn't have noticed anything either.

One day the witch at Tådås had a cow die. She bawled and wailed over her cow. Then her *nisse* came up and said: "Don't grieve, I'll get you another cow." He took the dead cow and dragged it off to Säby. There he stole a living cow and put it in the dead one's place in the stall.

The witch in Tådås did a lot of harm, but finally she was caught at last. On a farm in an entirely different district far from Tådås people had started having very bad luck with their cattle. Every Easter one of their cows died. Then they got a new farm hand there and he decided he would try to figure out who was coming to visit their barn every Easter. On the evening of Maundy Thursday he stationed himself behind the door inside the barn with a sharp knife in his fist. For a long time he stood and listened, but he couldn't hear anything. A short while after midnight he heard a whirring in the air and it sounded as if something had come in through the barn door. Immediately he struck out with his knife. There was a scream, and the man saw before him an ugly witch with the knife embedded in her thigh. But before he could gather his thoughts she was gone again.

From that day forth the farm hand was so hoarse he could not say a single word. He just wheezed like a goose. A long time later he learned that seven parishes distant there lived a woman who was known for her witchcraft. But ever since that Maundy Thursday evening when the man had stood watch over the barn she had been sick, and people said she had an ugly wound in her thigh which would not heal. When he had heard that, the man set out and wandered through all seven parishes until he came to Tådås. He recognized the woman easily, and she recognized him. But he was well received, in any case. The witch had several beautiful daughters, and they put before him the best food and drink they had. When he had eaten and drunk his fill, he sat next to the witch and began to write out a message to her. If she would remove the hoarseness from his throat so that he could talk again, he would cure her leg. They agreed to that, but the man had to swear he wouldn't tell a living soul the woman was a witch. The man got back his speech and the woman her health, and with that she left her sickbed.

As the man was walking home he mulled over how he could see to it that the woman got the punishment she deserved for her witchcraft without his having to break his word. The next Sunday he went into the churchyard. When a group of people had assembled there the man fell to his knees before a large tombstone and addressed the stone in a loud, clear voice. He explained to the stone that the woman at Tådås was a witch, and he told it what she had done with the cows. It wasn't long before the sheriff was in Tådås, and the woman had to follow him off to jail. Her serving-girl gave evidence of one crime after another against her. Among other things the woman had taken her to Blåkulla, and the devil and the witch had wanted her to sign a contract, but she had screamed and refused the entire time. That was proof enough, and the woman was convicted and burned on a pyre together with several other witches.

[Sältebo, Bohuslän. Collected by Vilhelm Cederschiöld from Olaus Olsson, who had it from a certain Kristian in Sältebo. Printed in Cederschiöld, "Ur Olaus Olssons sägensamling," *FmFt,* 19 (1932), 118–120.]

In many cases a group of legends such as these must have been drawn together into cycles about people believed to be witches. This little cycle has three parts, all of which have important analogues. The point of the incident with the basket of food is that witches, like other supernatural beings, have the power to change the appearance of things. Food among the trolls in the other world was regularly thought to consist of the most repulsive things imaginable, made to look like gourmet fare, and the *skogsrå* could make a shepherd's flock look like a pile of stones and a familiar forest look utterly foreign. In this world, food that made people sick (perhaps through bacterial growth while it sat in a basket in the hot sun?) might well be identified afterwards as toads and manure in the guise of bread and cheese.

The second legend in the cycle is the familiar fetching of a cow by a *tomte* from a neighboring farm, in migratory legends often encountered as part of ML 7010, "Revenge for Teasing the

Nisse" (see story no. 63, "The Missing Butter"). Here it has been stripped to its essentials and associated with other negative actions of an apparent witch. On the parallel witnessed by this association, see Introduction, p. 50.

The longest tale in the cycle deals with the overcoming of the witch by the farm hand, and here we are near the wonder-tale. The motif of the knife in the thigh has been borrowed from tales like "The Easter-Hag Put a Water-Trough in Her Place," where it attests a woman's identity as a witch; here it serves that purpose but also is a weapon of defense in the short portion of the tale that is reminiscent of the legend type of ridding an area of annual visitors from the other world, AT 1161, ML 6015, and story no. 25, "The Bear Trainer and the Trolls." Talking to "no living soul" is a common sort of humorous motif, but the ending of the tale is chillingly real. The testimony of the serving-girl sounds rather like the record of witchcraft trials of the seventeenth century, as in the preceding story.

82. The Magic Horn

SPEAKING of black magic and so forth, I remember something that happened here in this parish. You see, a witch lived in the village near the church. Her husband had no idea that he was involved with such a troll-hag.

One day—it was just when she was getting ready to fly off—her husband came into the house to get a horn with grease in it to grease the carriage. But he got the wrong horn, of course, for when he smeared it on one wheel, it began to spin around, and when he had greased the entire carriage—all the wheels, I mean—then it flew up into the sky. As for the man, he was scared, for he had never seen anything like *that* before. He rushed in and told the old woman that the carriage he had just greased had flown away. The woman was out the door in a second, as you can imagine, just in time to see the carriage flying over the forest. Then they say she ran around to a large stone in the ground near the corner of the house and slammed against it with a resounding clatter. Well, and then the carriage fell down into a bog. And that is the truth, it is, for I myself have seen the marks in the bog.

[Skuttunge, Uppland. Collected by Elias Grip in 1896 from "mother" Björklund, and printed in Grip, "Skuttunge- ock Björklingemål: Folksägner," *SvLm*, 18:3 (1899), 57; and in Klintberg, no. 311, pp. 228–229.]

The tale, which has been collected in most of central Sweden, is related to the more humorous migratory legend recounted in the following story. It has to do with the use, or rather misuse, of the witch's salve, about which see Introduction, pp. 48–49. Apparently the witch had just mixed up a fresh batch in preparation for her journey to Blåkulla, and that batch is what fell into the hands of her husband. Such a tale may have a background in reality, since the salve might well enter the man's body through the skin of his fingers and cause hallucination, and his concern with his cart might well have projected it into the hallucination. One greases a cart to make it move more easily and faster. What could be faster than a cart which flies under its own power?

The localization of the tale mentioned in the opening sentences ("here in this parish") is corroborated by the marks in the bog mentioned at the end. Perhaps the tale may also have been used etiologically, in explanation of the marks in the bog.

83. *Following the Witch*

Once there was a tramp who was going to be put up at a certain farm. And at that time the woman there was about to go to Blåkulla. "Up here and out here!," she said, and off she went through the chimney on a broom. Then the tramp thought he might like to follow her just this once, both for amusement and to see how they behave there. And so he got hold of a calf to ride on. He probably thought that if the going got tough on the curves he would be able to hold onto a calf more easily than a broom. But he hadn't heard right. He thought the woman had said: "Up here and down here!" So when he had got the calf up on the stove and was ready, he said: "Up here and down here," he did. But he went up and down the chimney instead, and the calf was bellowing, and they kept it up the whole night long, and so by morning they were half dead.

[N. Möre, Småland. Recorded by Hilda Lundell and Elise Lundell Zetterqvist, probably in the 1880s, and printed in "Folkminnen från Kläckebärga ock Dörby," *SvLm*, 9:1 (1889–1936), 407.]

A very popular legend, ML 3045, "Following the Witch," this is a more humorous version of the preceding story, one which was told all over Scandinavia. Misunderstanding and mispronouncing the magic formula are constant, but the consequences vary. Up and down the chimney is perhaps the most common in Sweden, but the luckless persons who would follow the witch also crash around inside of houses and barns, fly swiftly just *under* the level of the treetops, and so forth.

There may, too, be a realistic background to some of these stories. The uninitiated who got hold of the witch's salve and through its narcotic effects experienced hallucinations might well feel as though they were flying out of control around the room; those prone to claustrophobia might even imagine they were making hopeless journeys up and down in a chimney. The aftermath, too, of such a negative experience might approximate the physical discomfort humorously implied in these tales.

84. Milking Others' Cows

A

Magnus Tilda's mother was certainly an Easter-hag, she was. And she had two milk-hares, a big one and a little one. People said she had made them out of knitting-needles and heddle-withes and rags. They would milk other people's cows and then run home and spit up the milk. She had a kettle in the barn and every morning it was full. Once Sandberg ran into them in the forest and he shot both the little one and the big one. But it took him three shots to bring down each one. And dogs are usually not reluctant to claim their share, but Sandberg's dog was so frightened it didn't dare run up to them, for their guts ran off into the bushes like evil snakes, so anyone could see there was witchcraft involved.

B

TILDA's mother would make all sorts of trouble on Easter morning for Pettersson. Once snow had fallen during the night, and when people came out in the morning they could see the tracks of a cow going in and out of the fodder storeroom. Then they understood that the old hag had gone in there with her cow to drain the milk from Pettersson's cows for the coming year. There was nothing for him to do but to go to her, and what he said to her I have no idea, but he must have convinced her to return the milk, for otherwise his cows would not have produced any milk for the entire year.

[Tveta, Småland. Collected before 1905 by Bärnhard Karlgren from "Madame" Sandberg, from Hästbron, and printed in Karlgren, "Folksägner från Tveta ock Mo härader," *SvLm*, B2 (1908), 20–23 (*A*) and 22–24 (*B*).]

These are two short legends, among several, of the "witchcraft" thought to be practiced by a local woman. Both concentrate on one of the most frequently mentioned acts of alleged witchcraft, taking the milk from a neighbor's cow. This has been the subject of a migratory legend, ML 3035, "The Daughter of the Witch," about a girl who demonstrates her innocent command of magic by milking a neighbor's cow, often to death. In *B* the woman was thought to have gone herself with her cow to a neighbor's barn in order to drain the other's cows of their ability to produce milk by taking the essence (Swedish *must*) of their milk. The tale is a pure memorate, probably originating to explain some unusual marks in the new fallen snow. The narrator has extricated herself from the story rather nicely with her anti-climactic, noncommittal ending. Story *A* involves the use of one of the many devices thought to aid in milking neighbors' cows, the milk-hare. The legend is common in central Sweden and bears a close resemblance to other tales of hunting strange or supernatural animals, frequently affiliated with the *skogsrå*. Conceptions of the milk-hare, also sometimes known as *bjäran*, are rather old, as has been shown by John Pape, "Bidrag till belysande av föreställningarna om Bjäran-Mjölkharen i företrädesvis äldre tradition," *Folkkultur,* 5 (1945), 84–118. The earliest attestations are found in church paintings, of which the oldest are from Ösmo, Södermanland, from the mid-fifteenth century. This series of pictures shows two small rabbits, one red and one white, "milking" a cow, regurgitating the milk into buckets, and the subsequent production of butter. Various devils aid in the process throughout. From around the beginning of the sixteenth century the *bjäran* is encountered in literary sources. As in our legend *A,* these accounts tell of the fabrication of some sort of milk-sucking animal from ordinary household materials, a conception which has remained remarkably constant. Among the earliest recordings, fabrication of the animal from the parts of a loom, as in *A,* is attested, and other methods are very similar to other twentieth-century recordings. Informants from Norrland, for example, have described the interweaving of nine differently colored threads into a ball, on which one spilled a drop of one's blood while reciting a magic formula like "As long as you will run for me/ I will burn in Hell for thee." The result was a *bjäran* (Nils Eriksson, "Bjäran: Uppteckningar från Wilhelmina socken i Lappland," *FmFt,* 18 [1931], 147–150). Similar techniques are attested three centuries earlier.

85. Captain Eli

Somewhere in Småland—no one knows where—there lived once upon a time a witch who was known throughout the entire province. Her real name was forgotten long ago, but her nickname, Captain Eli, by which most people knew her, has been retained, along with the account of her evil and tragic death, in folk legends.

Among the other things she did, Captain Eli took milk from all the farmers in the area. Once a year, namely on "Holy Thursday," she went to Blåkulla, where the devil lived, with curds for the annual cheesemaking which the ruler of the evil spirits held there each year. All the troll-hags who took milk from the cows of others had in fact got their power from the devil, who in return got the curds from the witches for his cheese on "Holy Thursday" every year.

Captain Eli did not have a milk-hare in her service like other milk-hags. Instead she had two garters attached to the roof, which she milked as if they were the teats on a cow's udder.

In order to put a stop to Captain Eli's milking, all the farmers of the district came one day to her little cottage. After they had made clear their errand, the witch turned to them in anger and said: "If you don't get out of here I'll milk until I get blood." When the farmers drew back only with strong protests, Captain Eli put her threat into effect. She milked the garters so hard that blood was drawn. At the same time, all the cows in the neighborhood gave blood when milked.

Then people from throughout the district got together to decide what to do. It was decided that Captain Eli should be burned on the pyre. This was to take place in Ljunga parish in Västra härad. There a large pyre was prepared and Captain Eli was led up onto it. She was tied to an iron stake, and people were just preparing to gag her when someone remembered that before great sinners die they are usually given a last chance to convert. She was therefore given five minutes and urged to lighten her heart. And then Captain Eli shouted down from the pyre: "It is my wish that henceforth not a single green root shall grow here." In horror those present put the gag in her mouth and lit the pyre. As the flames licked wildly around the woman who had done such evil, however, their feeling of terror was changed quickly to joy at the prospect of being rid of that fearful woman. As the fire leapt up higher and higher and consumed its victim, they danced around the pyre and sang their most joyous songs.

For many of those present, however, the joy was not lasting. For when the pyre had burned down, the area around it was transformed into a huge bog where nothing would grow, which is still there. And on the spot where the pyre had stood, there ran from the ashes seven brooks which ran in the four cardinal directions.

And that was the origin of the bog at Ljunga, with its seven brooks running out from the center toward the edges.

[Östbo/Västbo, Småland. LUF 871. Printed in Olof Gjerdman, "Hon som var värre än den onde: en saga och ett uppsvenskt kyrkomålningsmotiv," *Saga och Sed,* 1941, pp. 67–68. No further information on recording is provided.]

Captain Eli(n) was one of the best-known Swedish witches, in part because of an extremely popular folk book about her which went through twelve editions during the early nineteenth century. The text printed here is of interest because it seems to be independent of the folk book, despite its very obvious literary stamp; it is almost certainly a conflation, by a man of some learning, of more than one tale about Captain Elin. The main point is etiological, and the tale does not otherwise depart from countless other legends of witches.

The origin of the name Captain Elin is still not fully clear. What is known is that she was the wife of a crofter from Mofikerud in Värmland. At the accusation of a twelve-year-old girl, who said she had been taken off to Blåkulla, Elin was tried for witchcraft and confessed to having entered a pact with the devil a few years earlier. She was apparently executed. For a full account see Bror Gadelius, *Tro och öfvertro i gångna tider* (Stockholm, 1913), 2: Chapter 8; reprinted in his *Häxor och häxprocesser* (Stockholm, 1963), pp. 138–151.

86. The Devil and Kitta Grå

ONCE there lived an old man and an old woman who had always agreed about everything. They had never, ever, quarreled. That annoyed the devil. He tried for seven years to get the man and woman to argue, but without success. Then he went to Kitta Grå and asked her to help him . . . and they struck a bargain, that she was to get a new pair of wooden shoes from the devil if she succeeded.

And so Kitta Grå went first to the old woman and told her that her husband was unfaithful to her and was seeing other women. But the woman refused to believe it. "Yes, it's true," said Kitta Grå. "He has been placed under a spell, but if you place some steel in your bed the spell will be broken. Put a knife in bed, then your husband will be cured and will have eyes only for you once again." At that the woman took her husband's razor and put it under the pillow in their bed.

After that Kitta Grå went to the old man and said to him: "Listen. Your wife has something against you. She intends to murder you."

"Oh no. We have never quarreled. I don't believe you," said the old man.

"Well, but it's true," said Kitta Grå. "Take a look around your bed and see if she hasn't hid a knife or something similar to stab you with while you are asleep." And when the old man looked in the bed he found the razor under the pillow, of course. And then they had a quarrel, those two.

And now Kitta Grå was to get a new pair of wooden shoes from the devil in payment for her services. But the devil was afraid of Kitta Grå, for she was even worse than he was! And so when the time came to give her the shoes, he put them out on a slick part of a frozen lake. Then when she went out on the ice to get the shoes, the devil took a long pole and gave her a shove, so that she and the shoes skidded far off on the ice. Then he had time to escape.

[Lenhovda, Småland. ULMA 2817:3. Printed in Olof Gjerdman, "Hon som var värre än den onde: en saga och ett uppsvenskt kyrkomålningsmotiv," *Saga och Sed*, 1941, pp. 54–55.]

This is the international wonder-tale, AT 1353, "The Old Woman as Trouble Maker," in Swedish guise. The name Kitta Grå, which perhaps means "Woman dressed in gray" (Gjerdman, op. cit., pp. 61–64), is centered in southern Sweden, whereas Titta Grå is more typical of central Sweden, and other names, among them Skoella and Captain Elin (as in story no. 85), are also found. Kitta Grå is prominent in two other tale types besides the one attested here: AT 1074, "Race Won by Deception: Relative Helpers," where Kitta Grå and her daughter outrun the devil; and AT 1170, "The Evil Woman in the Glass Case as Last Commodity," where Kitta Grå, tarred and feathered, sits in a glass case belonging to a man whose salesmanship was guaranteed by a pact with the devil. When the devil comes to claim him the case has still not been sold, and so the man goes free. The devil remarks of Kitta Grå: "No one who knows her would buy her." All the attestations of these tale types in Sweden are catalogued in Waldemar Liungman, *Sveriges samtliga folksagor* (Djursholm, 1952), 3, 466–536.

Of interest in our tale is that it was illustrated in sixteenth-century church paintings from Uppland and Västmanland, which show the devil passing an old woman a pair of shoes on the end of a long pole. Probably the shoes have replaced a more original sack of money, perhaps in Italy where the word *scarpa* at one time could mean both "pouch" and "shoe." At any rate, our informant has reinterpreted the motif in an interesting manner.

87. Werewolf and Nightmare

A WEREWOLF was a human who was transformed into the shape of a dog which walked on three legs, the other leg sticking up like a tail. The task of the werewolf was to tear the unborn child from pregnant women. If he did he was freed from being transformed into that shape. The change could come on at any time whatever. The person being transformed was not aware of it himself. And it happened to people because their mothers had taken the membrane from newborn foals. They put it up on stakes and ran naked under it three times while they were pregnant. If they did that, they were supposed to have an easy labor and a painless delivery. But if they did it, it would affect the unborn child. If it was a girl she would become a nightmare, if it was a boy he would become a werewolf. The nightmare usually takes the form of an invisible little thing that can go through keyholes and cover people's mouths when they lie asleep, and she can sit astride a horse's neck and braid the mane into the form of stirrups, and there she likes to sit and ride the horse. There are still people who believe in that today.

If somebody would say to them: "I think you are a werewolf" or "I think you are a nightmare," and if someone was willing to say that and someone else answered: "If I am, thanks for telling me," that one would be freed and would no longer have to be a werewolf or nightmare. But if the person said: "Now you can be a nightmare as long as I have been," that person was freed but the lot fell to the one who had spoken first.

A story has it that there was a man who was a werewolf, and his wife knew about it. One day they were out working in the field. They were getting in grain, for it was harvest time. In those days people used pitchforks. The man said to his wife—he had a hunch that he was sometimes transformed into a werewolf—"If something comes after you here, don't stab with the pitchfork, but hit it as hard as you can." And later he was changed into a werewolf and he returned. And she hit him to defend herself. But he tore at her skirt with his mouth, and a few threads were caught between his teeth. [Later] while they were having dinner she happened to notice the threads caught between his teeth. She said to him: "I think you are a werewolf."

"Well, if I am, thanks for telling me, for now I am freed from it," he said.

My parents had a neighbor here in Borrby whom people took for one of those.

And now a story about a nightmare, who entered through a tiny hole in a sleeping loft. She was in the habit of passing through there and going up to a man who lay asleep. One night he watched his chance and stuck a pin into the hole she had come in through. They have to get out the same way they come in, so when there was no way out she was left standing there. Then, naturally, she returned to the form of a woman, and she stayed with him and married him. After they had been married a long time, he asked her if she knew where she had come from. No, she didn't. Then he pulled the pin out of the hole she had come in through. Like a shot she was gone through the hole, instantaneously, and her clothes were left lying behind. Stories like this have been told, and people have believed them.

[Borrby, Skåne. Collected in 1915 by Louise Hagberg, from a man in his sixties. Printed in Hagberg, "Sägner och folktro från Borrby socken i Skåne," *FmFt*, 18 (1931), 173–174.]

Conceptions of werewolves are rather ancient in Scandinavia and abound, for example, in the oldest native literature, the sagas of medieval West Scandinavia. Without a doubt the most famous is Kveldúlfr, the grandfather of the saga hero Egill Skallagrímsson. Kveldúlfr means "evening-wolf," and the name refers to his ability to change his shape into that of a wolf. He was *hamrammr*, "possessing the ability to change one's shape," a characteristic he shared with a number of other figures from Old Norse literature. The wild ferocity which accompanied such a change was inherited by his son and grandson, whose tempers could flare up mightily, and spiritual heirs are the berserks, whose name literally means "bearskins"; they were also known as *úlfheðnar* ("wolf-coats"), which seems to reflect werewolf belief. Such belief was known to the ancient Greeks and Romans and has been found throughout the world. (A thorough comparative discussion is found in Nils Lid, "Til varulvens historia," *Saga och Sed,* 1937, pp. 3–25.) In Scandinavia, besides werewolves, we meet man-bears, which is not surprising considering the imposing role these two played as predators. A great many legends tell of the elimination of the wolves or bears, and some stress the joy of the population thereafter. Another group deals with the interaction between them and the human community; see Odd Nordland, "Mannbjørn: ein studie i heimfestingsproblemet ved vandresegner," *By og Bygd,* 11 (1956–57), 133–153. Regarding these predators as men in disguised shape is consistent with the anthropomorphization of nature characteristic of Scandinavian folk tradition.

The werewolf legend printed here is ML 4005, "The Werewolf Husband," the only truly migratory legend of werewolves attested in Sweden. It is also popular in Norway and Denmark. For a complete discussion of the werewolf in Swedish tradition, see Ella Odstedt, *Varulven i svensk folktradition* (Stockholm, 1943).

The complementary distribution of werewolves and nightmares by sex, suggested in the first paragraph, accords well with the sexual stereotypes of the culture. As aggressors men would be more suitable werewolves, and the silent nightmare is consistent with the role of women and also, of course, with traditional beliefs about witchcraft. The explanation offered for the cause of this phenomenon, typical of South Sweden, probably has to do with the belief that horses have an easy time at birth, but may also be associated with the partial homonymy between *märr*–"mare" and *mara*–"nightmare" (Lid, op. cit., pp. 11–12); note, too, the supposed "task of the werewolf" mentioned in the first paragraph—namely, tearing an unborn child from its mother.

The nightmare was thought to be able to "ride" either humans or cattle. The rationalistic explanation, long since offered, is that the concept of the nightmare is the product of dreams and problems sleeping. A heavy featherbed settles over a sleeper's face, or a sinus condition affects his breathing, and given the traditional belief in the nightmare, the difficulty is retroactively assigned to the nightmare. Unlike many other supernatural beings, the nightmare is seldom encountered, except in migratory legends; when the sleeper awakes to an empty room, it is assumed that the nightmare has vanished or turned itself into some small and insignificant object. It has sometimes been pointed out that living conditions of older Northern Europe may also have been a factor, since ordinarily several people slept in one room, which particularly in winter would be smoke-filled and ill-ventilated. When cattle, particularly horses, were sick or were found sweating in the morning (presumably from fever), belief in the nightmare provided a convenient explanation.

The story told about the nightmare here is the migratory legend ML 4010, "Married to the Nightmare," common to large areas of Europe. In introducing an erotic element it is typical of migratory legends, which to a certain extent tend to emphasize such matters more than most other legends. Erotic dreams, too, provide a rational explanation. The story of the swan maiden who first marries the man who seizes her swan coat and then vanishes as soon as he returns it has been suggested as a source for this migratory legend; see Helge Holmström, "Sägnerna om äktenskap med maran," *FmFt*, 5 (1918), 135–145.

A survey of the nightmare in English is C. H. Tillhagen, "The Conception of the Nightmare in Sweden," in Wayland Hand and Gustav Arlt, eds., *Humaniora: Essays Honoring Archer Taylor* (Berkeley, 1960), pp. 317–329.

88. *Becoming a Werewolf*

Once there was an old Finnish woman who came up to someone's house. She was not welcome there; instead she was greeted with words of scorn when she came through the door. "People like you," the farmer said, "would make good company for the wolves."

"You'll soon know about that," the old woman answered, slammed the door, and left. When evening arrived, the farmer disappeared into the forest. There he grew the skin of a wolf, and thus he became like a wolf and lived among the wolves. But the real wolves would have nothing to do with him; instead he had to roam on his own for the most part.

At one place where he intended to go in and claw someone, he stood with his front paws against the window. The people inside were frightened and addressed him and said: "Is it you, Johan?" They had no sooner got the words out when the wolf underwent a great change. The wolf coat fell from him and he became a man. He went inside and explained that he had been under a spell. He had been like that for many years, but no one had called him by his name before.

[Värmlandsnäs, Värmland, IFGH 5421:20, 21. Collected from Marit Nilsson, born in Kila in 1868. Printed in Bergstrand/Nilsson, *Värmlandsnäs*, 3:210–211.]

In areas, like Värmland, with large Finnish populations, lycanthropy was not uncommonly attributed to the magic spells of Finns; in northern areas Lapps were blamed. Many a werewolf tale begins: "A man had been in Finland and there he was transformed into a wolf. . . ." Such attribution is only part of a larger pattern in which Finns and Lapps were assumed to have magical abilities. In this legend the casting of the spell has been motivated by the man's scornful insult, and one assumes the legend was used didactically, as an inducement to charitable behavior. The breaking of the spell follows a very common story pattern: years of wandering as a wolf or bear are broken by the incidental mention of the victim's name.

89. The Identity of the Nightmare

A

On a farm both the cows and the horses were ridden by a nightmare. The one who owned the animals was then advised to keep watch so that nothing would get into the barn. But no matter, it was of no use. They suggested that he clean everything so carefully that nothing remained inside with the animals. And so he did.

And then one night—it was a Saturday night—he saw a piece of straw in the stall with a mare, and *that* piece of straw, he was quite sure, had not been there when he had cleaned everything up. So he took the piece of straw and set fire to it. But he put out the fire when there was still something left of the straw. And on Sunday morning half of the bedding of the daughter on the farm was found burned. And then she said that she never knew she had been the nightmare. But she had always felt tired and sick and had believed that she had been sleepwalking.

[Röra, Bohuslän. IFGH 5238:6–7. Collected in 1940 by Konrad Ekdahl from Olivia Johansson, born 1883 in Röra sn. Printed in Klintberg, no. 340, pp. 243–244.]

B

At a certain place a pair of shoemakers sat up making shoes until late into the night. A serving-girl lay on the oven, but suddenly a cat jumped down, and it said: "Ugh. It's a long way and cold." However, one of the shoemakers hit the cat with a last, and in the morning the serving-girl lay dead on the oven. She was the one who had been the cat. She was on her way out to ride people as a nightmare.

[Lerum, Västergötland. Collected by Helmer Olsson before 1936 and printed in Olsson, *Folkliv och folkdikt i Vättle härad under 1800-talet*, SKGAAF, 12 (Uppsala, 1945), p. 185.]

In many cases the nightmare was thought to be a local woman, "riding" people or animals, often without herself being aware of it. Folk belief attests various means of ascertaining the identity of a nightmare. One of the simplest was to bar all exit from the room and then begin naming names. At the correct name the nightmare could confess her identity and the spell would be broken. Of a more epic character are legends of the type printed here, which lead to a dramatic revelation the morning after. They are obviously closely related to stories like no. 79, "The Easter-Hag Put a Water-Trough in Her Place," and other legends of witchcraft. Indeed the line between nightmare and witch is not always clearly defined, and sometimes the "riding" of the nightmare seems to have been regarded as a kind of witchcraft. Story *B* seems to fall into that category, since no one expresses any regret at the death of the cat/serving-girl.

90. The Farm Hand Tied Sharpened Scythes over the Horse's Back

THIS happened in Morskoga in Ramsberg, and it was before I was born, but my father talked a lot about it, and it was surely true.

There was a horse there who was very badly treated by a nightmare. And the farm hand there on the farm, he was so worried about the horse, he did everything he could to protect it at night from the nightmare, since it stood in the stall dripping with sweat, half dead, practically every morning. And the farm hand took sharpened scythes and tied them over the horse's back one night to see if that would help, since nothing else had done any good.

When the farmer came down to the stable the next morning, the farm hand was lying dead in the stall next to the horse, cut all to pieces by the scythes. So he himself had been the nightmare, though he himself had no idea about it.

There must have been others involved, evil people who forced the boy to act as a nightmare even though he didn't know about it himself.

[Skinnskatteberg, Västmanland. ULMA 7377:4. Collected in 1934 by Ellen Lagergren from widow Maria Hansson, born 1853 in Ramsberg sn. Printed in Klintberg, no. 343, pp. 244–245.]

This is one of the most dramatic of nightmare revelations, because the nightmare is caught by his own trap, unaware that he is the nightmare. Klintberg (p. 343) notes that the legend demonstrates the tenacity of sex roles over folk belief: the nightmare is ordinarily a woman, but taking care of the horses was always man's work. (See further Max Lüthi, "Urform und Zielform in Sage und Märchen," *Fabula*, 9 (1967), 41–54.) It must be noted, however, that males as nightmares are far from unknown in genuine folk tradition.

91. A Haunting

My mother and sister once saw a revenant. There was a small crofter's holding a short distance from where I was born, and some people lived there, an old man and woman. They carried on shamelessly and could never agree about anything. When the man died the old woman didn't dare stay at home, so she moved in with my parents.

My mother saw him once before the funeral feast, as it took place near us. It had snowed during the night, and in the cattle-barn she saw him leaving through the gates—that old fellow's name was Erik Hansson—and she clearly recognized him. That may perhaps sound a bit doubtful, but in the morning, when she was on her way to get some beer from the cellar, there were no tracks in the snow.* He had no power to leave tracks, of course.

And how he carried on and haunted after the funeral feast! His old woman had a chest and some skins up in the attic. There he went and rattled during the night. It also sounded sometimes as if he were trying to drag the chest and throw it down. Then he would get on the woman and squeeze her. She screamed to my father, "Dear Master!"—my father was a tailor, of course—"please put on a light, for the old man is on me again." Well, father got up and lit a candle; he heard him well enough, too, did father.

One evening we sat up late. The woman sat on a sofa asleep. Father and mother also sat and pretended to sleep. We got permission to light some candles and have a fire. And all at once the old man came in and saw the woman sitting asleep. Then he got angry, of course, and struck the wall near where the woman was sleeping so that she jumped right up. And that is obviously the truth, it is, for my sister is still alive and she too can tell it the same way.

*This is particularly significant because it was the sort of snow well suited to leave tracks (Swedish *spårsnö*, literally "track-snow").

[Skuttunge, Uppland. Collected in 1896 by Elias Grip from an informant named Lundgren. Printed in Grip, "Skuttunge- ock Björklingemål: Folksägner," *SvLm*, 18:3 (1899), 30–33.]

This classic ghost story is told by a third party, present but not an eyewitness at a supernatural event, and hence is a memorate, despite some of the additional material it contains. A frequent aspect of Swedish (and other) ghost stories is that quarrels begun in life continue in death; in some tales the quarrels of the dead are so spirited as to disturb the living. In this story it appears that the man simply continues his persecution of his wife, but he apparently changed his tactics somewhat—besides the rattling in the attic, he employs the kind of squeezing typical of *gastar* and thus usually known as a *gastkram* or "ghost hug," not a very pleasant embrace, never given with affection, and usually leading to unpleasant consequences.

The supernatural experience, when the informant's mother and sister saw the revenant, took place late at night, in obscure light, when some of the party had been sleeping and others pretending to sleep (or pretending to pretend). Since they seem to have been awaiting the ghost, under those circumstances any sort of thump could make strong claim to the world of the dead.

92. *A Ghost Gets a Free Ride*

ONCE grandmother told a story about a ghost. An old man came and was riding on the parsonage road, but at last it was so difficult that he couldn't go forward. So he got down and looked between the bit and the horse's head, and then he saw that an old lady in a green jacket was sitting on the cart. He removed the harness pegs, and then she got so heavy that the cart rolled over down the hill and the woman fell out. But he took the horse and rode home.

[Essunga, Västergötland. Collected from Johannes Andreasson, born in 1854. Printed in C. M. Bergstrand, *Essunga i svunnen tid: vad de gamla berättat*, 2 (Göteborg, 1958), p. 12.]

Statistically, encounters with ghosts are probably more likely to follow the pattern of this story than any other; one of the most obvious ways for ghosts or *gastar* to manifest themselves was to make a cart heavy. A favorite subject is a cart transporting a coffin somewhere, but almost any kind of conveyance could be subject to such delay. Sometimes the extra weight of the cart was no doubt perceived through the extra effort of the horses to pull it, which might after all have been caused by any number of factors and thus could serve to strengthen the power of this aspect of folk belief. On the other hand, many memorates tell of a coffin which grew progressively heavier as the pallbearers neared the grave site.

Similarity to and crossing with devil legends is very apparent. Frequently, as in story no. 75, "The Devil as the Fourth Wheel," these are accompanied by the legend of making the devil carry the cart, and frequently, too, the *gast* is made to carry the cart after being discovered.

93. *Strand-Ghosts*

A

People talked about how bad the strand-ghosts used to be. They would scream, "Help us to hallowed ground!" People could hear the water streaming off of them. One night when the hired hand was supposed to go out and shut the door, there was one of those strand-ghosts hanging over the door—they used half-doors in those days. He said to the hired hand:

"Help me to hallowed ground, and you can have a chest which is buried in a hill in Söndrum."

He took the strand-ghost and carried him on his back to the Halmstad cemetery and threw him over the wall. Then he went out and looked for the chest; and he found it.

After that they made the beach Christian. My grandmother said she remembered it. Both clergy and laymen sailed a long way out to sea, according to her account. Afterwards there were no more strand-ghosts.

[Övraby, Halland. IFGH 4346:3. Recorded in 1939 from her own memory by Hanna Samuelsson, born in 1854 in Övraby sn. Printed in Carl-Martin Bergstrand, *Hallandssägner* (Göteborg, 1949), p. 161, and in Klintberg, no. 245, pp. 196–197.]

B

THERE was a ghost on the island Balgö. It was a corpse that had washed ashore, and someone had plundered it and thrown some dirt over it so it wouldn't be discovered. But nobody could get any peace from the ghost. They heard it enter the room, and it would take the bedclothes and cast them aside. Finally a man asked it what it wanted. "I want my socks and shoes, my red coat and buttons, and I want to be in hallowed ground," it answered. The man accompanied the ghost out, and when they reached the place where the corpse was hidden, the ghost vanished. They dug up the corpse and put it in the churchyard, and then the hauntings ceased.

[Kärra, Halland. IFGH 3943:40. Collected by Carl-Martin Bergstrand from Nelina Andersson, born in 1856, and printed in Bergstrand, *Gammalt från Nordhalland*, 1 (Göteborg, 1964), pp. 189–190.]

Limited for the most part to South Sweden, such legends illustrate the folk belief that some hauntings are caused by the overpowering desire of the dead to rest in hallowed ground. The largest single group denied that right was composed of those lost at sea. Until the beach was "Christianized," it was liable to haunting by uneasy corpses washed up there. The treasure used in *A* provided a plausible explanation for why anyone would want to get involved in the affairs of the dead, particularly the unhallowed dead. The lack of the explanation in *B* makes it somewhat less plausible. Indeed, other variants of the haunting on Balgö stress the fear and suffering of those beset by the haunting and omit the accompaniment of the ghost to its unhallowed grave; instead a "clever" person or clergyman is called in for advice and discovers the terrible secret. *B* differs from *A* in adding the motif of the plundering of the corpse, and like any crime, it, too, leads to a haunting. The main cause of the haunting in *B* as well as in *A*, however, is the magnetism of hallowed ground.

94. The Parson Could Not Say "Our Daily Bread"

THERE was once a woman in Ostmark who had a nine-year-old girl. She was engaged, and her fiancé said to her, "If only you didn't have that little girl—then we could get married."

She thought about what he had said for some time. Finally she locked the girl in a shieling shed and didn't return for seven days. But when she came back the girl was still alive. The woman was so cruel, however, that she still didn't let the girl out. And the girl died and was buried, and nobody knew what had caused her death.

When it was time to bury her, the parson could not recite the Lord's Prayer. When he came to "our daily bread," he couldn't say a word. It was impossible.

Naturally the people wondered why the parson couldn't get out the Lord's Prayer. It seemed so wrong that finally they dug up the girl's body. And they found that she had eaten the flesh off her arms as far as she could manage.

The woman was beheaded, of course.

[Nyed, Värmland. IFGH 1919:24. Klintberg, no. 417, p. 280. Collected in 1929 from a man born in Myed, in 1859.]

"Mordre wol out, certein, it wol nat faille." Any number of legends from Swedish oral tradition attest Chaucer's proverb, but few as interestingly, or gruesomely, as this one. Ordinarily one would have expected some kind of haunting, either in the shieling or in the woman's house. This legend, however, draws attention to the importance of the final rite of passage in the human life cycle. Because she has met an improper death, the murdered girl cannot pass directly into the world of the dead. This principle is seen even more clearly in another legend printed in Klintberg, in which the parson could not get past "Thy kingdom come" at a funeral service; on opening the coffin, those present found the man to be buried still alive (Klintberg, no. 193, p. 171). Our legend has put this notion to particularly grisly use, seizing imaginatively on the actual text of the prayer in relation to the supposed circumstances of the girl's death.

95. Peace in the Grave

THERE is a proverb here: "You ask questions as boldly as Vall-Lisbet's mother in Våtlaven." If someone hears something unusual and asks about it, the answer is likely to be: "You're doing what Vall-Lisbet's mother did."

Anyway, she lived in Fala and was on her way to town to find a cure for something that ailed her. In the evening she got lodgings with the farmer here. When she went out to give the horse its evening feeding she bumped into an old man standing outside the door. She asked: "Who are you?"

"I am the farmer's father. I have been dead for many years, but I get no rest in my grave," he said.

She asked more questions, and then he said that he would tell her everything, so that he might have peace. And so he did.

Vall-Lisbet's mother went to bed without telling the farmer about it. In the morning she said: "I ran into an old man here last night."

"Awful! We see him at once, as soon as we look out. But we've never dared ask him who he is or what he wants."

"But don't you see that asking questions is exactly what you should do with that sort of thing? Otherwise they can't say anything. And I asked questions, I did," said Vall-Lisbet's mother. "And he said he was your father and wanted to reveal that he had buried his money chest in the wall of the fireplace. And now I will show you where the wall is to be torn down."

The wall was torn down, and the chest of money was exactly where Vall-Lisbet's mother had said it would be.

Then the young farmer recalled that his father had been pretty well off but had never revealed where he had hidden his money before he died.

Because of her boldness in asking questions she got a barrel of rye, the old man got peace in his grave, and the young farmer got the money chest, and also the haunting stopped.

[Ljusdal, Hälsingland. Collected by V. Engelke from an informant named "Ros-Kersti" and printed in Engelke, "Hälsingesägner 2," *SvLm*, 7:10 (1892), 12–13.]

Among the numerous stories of hauntings, only one story pattern has become sufficiently epic and widely enough distributed to merit inclusion in Christiansen's catalogue of migratory legends, namely ML 4020, "The Unforgiven Dead," of which the story printed here is an unusual version. Christiansen cites only seven Norwegian variants, in many of which the dead man seeks to reveal that he had wronged a girl; it is clear that this migratory legend is based on a notion that all the dead man's affairs should be in order before he can rest comfortably in the world of the dead. This varies slightly from the more general notion that haunting is a result of moral or legal crimes in life. The unexplained silence of the old man concerning the whereabouts of his money before death was no crime, but it presumably disrupted the ordinary course of the inheritance process, and thus he becomes potentially loquacious after death. The nosy heroine taps his loquacity, and accordingly she has become the subject of a proverb. The interrelationship between various forms of folklore is demonstrated in the context of the variant recorded here, told to explain the proverb, itself the result of the legend.

96. The Hanged Man Seeks His Pine Tree

THERE was something a bit strange about that schooner, the Aagot. When they were building her at Södra Garn in 1890, I was there to watch over the work; and it was slow and hard, as it always is at a shipyard. I was lodging with the foreman, and when we had eaten supper one Saturday night, I just couldn't go straight to bed, so I went down to the shipyard and looked around again. The ribs of the ship had been put up by then. When I got there, there was an old man in among the frame timbers. I had never seen that old man before, but I thought he was an ordinary person, so I spoke with him. I asked what he wanted, and he answered and said, "I only wanted to see what you did with my pine tree." Then he was gone.

Sunday morning, when the foreman and I were supposed to go to church at Gammelös, I told him about it. "Oh, Good Lord, is Jonte going around here looking for the pine tree he hanged himself from?," the foreman responded. That pine tree which Jonte had hanged himself from was the ship's stem, at the forestay. The pine had been the pride of the man's farm, but his widow could not stand to look at it and cut it down, and so it became the ship's stem.

[Näs, Värmland. IFGH 3530:24. Reported by Anders Fröjdendahl, from Skipper Ängdal på Liljendal, born 1842. Printed in Bergstrand/Nilsson, *Värmlandsnäs*, 3:179.]

Suicide was regarded as one of the most serious crimes, one which led to forfeit of one's right to rest in hallowed ground. Accordingly suicide victims could be expected to haunt, and that they did. The obscure, often unmarked grave where a suicide lay would always be regarded as a dangerous place, perhaps in part because it would generally be situated in some out of the way place in the forest, not near human habitation; under the wrong circumstances a person wandering in such a place would be more likely to meet the ghost buried there than some other supernatural being. A second site liable to haunting was the place where the crime had occurred. The memorate printed here shows how persistent suicides could be in seeking the scene of the crime. Indeed, that seems to be the point of the story, for neither the narrator nor the foreman appears to have been particularly concerned at the apparition.

97. The Power of Sorrow

This tale is taken from a diary entry from May 15, 1666. The diarist recounts a tale or legend included by the bishop in a sermon on the occasion of the burial of the diarist's daughter.

In the same sermon was also included a story or legend—namely, that a woman once lost through death her only child, for which reason she mourned and wept about it that she would accept no consolation. And in the midst of her grief, weeping and mourning she went into a green meadow thinking she might find solace there. Then she caught sight of a group of small children dressed in white; they sang, danced, and played, and among them she also saw her own child dressed in white, who was very distressed and hanging her head in sorrow, and had a jug in her hand. The mother asked why she was not singing and dancing like the others, but was so mournful. The child answered, "Dear Mother, as long as you weep and mourn so much, I too can do nothing but weep and mourn; I have here in a jug all your tears. When I see them, then I must grow sad and apprehensive. Therefore, dear Mother, do not deny me the heavenly joy I now possess, and weep no more over me, so that I may sing and dance."

[Quoted, from the *Diarium* of Petrus Magni Gyllenius, by R. Bergström, "Strödda bidrag till svensk folklore," *SvLm*, 6, Smärre meddelanden (1885), p. cxii.]

The story pattern is that of the ballad *Sorgens makt* ("The Power of Sorrow"), whence the title. This ballad is well-known in Sweden, appearing as no. 6 in the collection of Geijer and Afzelius, and is also included in Grundtvig's famous Danish collection ("Aage og Else"). It is Child's "The Unquiet Grave." The ballads are based on the all but universal folk belief that excessive mourning can disturb the repose of the dead.

This diary entry is useful in illustrating the assumption that clergymen recounted legends from the pulpit and thus played an important role in the dissemination of oral traditions in Scandinavia; see Introduction, pp. 9–10. Additionally, it reveals an obvious social use for such a legend—namely, calming or reassuring the bereaved; the dead are fairly well off and one must not mourn them too much. In cases of extreme grieving this tale must have been frequently heard.

Some attempt has been made in the translation to render the seventeenth-century flavor of the original.

98. *The Dead Bridegroom*

There was a girl who was engaged to a man who went off to war, and she promised she would never marry another. He could come and take her, alive or dead.

He was away for seven years, and then he came back, and it was Christmas Eve, naturally. He came riding up, and the girl had just bathed and washed her hair, which wasn't dry yet, and she ran out to welcome him home. But when she gave him her hand, he pulled her up onto the horse and took off at a furious gait. He was dead, you see, and now he was going to take her to his resting place.

They rode through nine parishes, and in each church he had to go in and make a payment on his behalf. But when they had reached the ninth parish and he had gone into the church, she saw an open door and ran in. And that was a tomb, for once inside she crawled behind a corpse. Then her fiancé returned, and he was in a tremendous hurry, since his time had almost run out during his various delays. "Is there someone alive among the dead in here?," he asked. "No," the corpse answered.

And that was what rescued her, for after that he left. But by then they had come so far that she couldn't understand the language and was unable to speak with anyone there. And yet they had been traveling so fast that she hadn't noticed the cold, even though she was so lightly dressed. It took her ages to get home, several years, and she had to find work along the way to support herself, but at last she got home in the end.

[Junsele, Ångermanland. ULMA 2064:7. Collected in 1928 from "A.B.," a woman, by Ella Ohlson, and printed in Ohlson, "Sagor från Ångermanland," *SvLm*, 1931, pp. 15–16.]

This tale is best known from the German poet Gottfried Bürger's famous poem "Lenore" (1773), (which has become a tag for both folktale and ballad), and was also included in Arnim and Brentano's *Des Knaben Wunderhorn* (1806–08). As an international wonder-tale, AT 365, it has been collected all over Eastern and Western Europe and is said to have originated in Russia. German variants frequently contain a snatch of verse, "Der Mond scheint hell, die Toten reiten schnell," which is repeated in Bürger's *Kunstballade*. (See Will-Erich Peuckert, *Lenore*, FFC, 158 [Helsinki, 1955].) A closely related folk ballad is "Sweet William's Ghost" (Child, no. 77), also found in slightly different form in Denmark and Sweden. Some have argued that the second *Helgakviða hundingsbana* of the Old Norse *Poetic*

Edda is related, but there the visit to the grave is not tinged with horror, and clearly the story has more to do with ballads recounting the power of sorrow (cf. the preceding story).

The variant printed here is a fine example of vigorous narrative tradition, a wonder-tale still told effectively in 1928. It is only slightly less elaborate than some of the fullest variants from Eastern Europe, and the style is smooth and flowing. This is perhaps all the more striking, given the relative infrequency of the tale in Sweden. On the Swedish and European distribution, see Waldemar Liungman, *Sveriges samtliga folksagor,* 3 (Djursholm, 1952), 101–102 and 474–477.

99. The Christmas Service of the Dead

People say that long ago the dead held a service in the church on the night before Christmas. Once a woman arrived too early for Christmas service. When she entered the church she found it lit up and full of dead people, singing:

> Here we sing, our bones all bleached,
> Here we sing with beautiful voice,
> When shall the day of judgement come,
> What yet have you to say?

The woman recognized her dead sister among them. She came and urged the woman to hurry out and leave something behind her in the church; otherwise the dead would take her life. The woman went out, leaving her shawl behind. When the churchwarden came and put the lights on, the shawl had been torn into small pieces.

[Sillerud, Värmland. VFF 1212:3. Printed in Carl-Martin Bergstrand, "De dödas julotta i västsvensk folktradition," *FmFt,* 24 (1937), 119. Informant not stated.]

Probably the best-known Scandinavian variant of this migratory legend, ML 4015, "The Midnight Mass of the Dead," is in Asbjørnsen's "En gammeldags juleaften" ("An Old-fashioned Christmas Eve"), which localizes it to Vor Frelsers Kirke in Oslo.

The story is widely spread in Europe and extremely old, having been set in Autun, Burgundy, by Gregory of Tours in his *De Gloria Confessorum.* The variant printed here is distinguished primarily by the singing of the dead, which might be understood as their attempt at a hymn. Their concern with Judgement Day is typical of all otherworlders, but particularly appropriate for the dead in simple Christian theology.

In most variants the human, usually a woman, comes to the church too early. This was apparently not an uncommon sort of mistake, since most households did not have clocks until fairly recently. Bergstrand, op. cit., p. 121, cites a parish meeting from 1673 in Västergötland in which it was decided to hold Christmas service just after sunrise so that all would know when to come to the church. Brynjulf Alver, "Dauinggudstenesta: ein europeisk førestellingskrins i norsk tradisjon," *Arv,* 6 (1950), 145–165, cites a few Northern Norwegian variants in which someone who falls asleep at a church service awakens to find himself at a service for the dead. Klintberg attributes this to Lappish shamanism, but it would seem equally likely that such variants might stem from a time when the notion of arriving too early at church had become rather outlandish, although the didactic import of such a beginning must not be overlooked either.

The climax of the story is the escape from the threats of the dead, often at the advice of a friend or relative among the congregation of the dead. The most frequent means employed is the one found in the text printed here—namely, leaving behind a piece of clothing. Bergstrand has suggested that the escape is effected either by an offering or by a kind of *pars pro toto,* whereas Alver sees some sort of ruse. The latter seems more likely.

The Norwegian variants are surveyed by Alver and in Christiansen under ML 4015. Bergstrand examines the West Swedish variants, and a thorough discussion of the European distribution of the legend is found in B. Deneke, *Legende und Volkssage: Untersuchungen zur Erzählung vom Geistesgottesdienst* (dissertation, Universität Frankfurt, 1958).

100. A False Ghost

Our parson was named Lundell, and he had been in the parish where what I am about to tell you about happened. The parson there used to go and pray over the altar every Saturday night. His wife didn't like it and decided to scare him into stopping.

One evening she dressed up the hired hand in some white cloth and sent him to the church. When the parson saw that ridiculous white object in the church, he went up to it and asked it what it was. Apparently the fellow did not answer. The parson asked him once again, but still the man kept silent. After asking the question three times without getting an answer, the parson went up to the altar and started praying, and it wasn't long before the man's feet had sunk beneath the floor. And after some more praying, he was sunk up to his waist. Then he was frightened and cried out to the parson what was going on. "It is too late now," the parson said.

Well, the man died, and now a stone stands on the floor of the church where he sank down. That certainly was a skillful parson, since he could pray with such force that the man sank into the floor.

[Skuttunge, Uppland. Collected by Elias Grip in 1896 from "Mother Gelin" and printed in Grip, "Skuttunge- ock Björklingemål: Folksägner," *SvLm*, 18:3 (1899), 66–67.

This migratory legend, ML 3005, "The Would-be Ghost," is attested sporadically in all the Scandinavian countries. In Sweden it was among the earlier legends to be printed in the nineteenth century (Afzelius, *Svenska folkets sagohäfder*, 3 [Stockholm, 1842], 17).

The obvious didactic point of the legend is that ghosts are serious business, not something to joke or pretend about. One is reminded of a similar Icelandic legend in which a girl mistakes a genuine ghost for her brother in a sheet and insults him by snatching his nightcap. On trying to return it to him she violates an interdiction of silence and dies (Jón Árnason, *Íslenzkar þjóðsögur og æventýri* [Leipzig, 1863], 1:239. English translation in Jacqueline Simpson, *Icelandic Folktales and Legends* [Berkeley, 1972], pp. 113–115).

Equally important to our story, however, is the skill of the parson. What makes the story somewhat unusual is that the hired hand dies not at the hands of a supernatural being but those of a skilled human whose talents are misdirected. The parson's skill even led the informant to add an admiring last sentence to the account.

It is possible that this variant of the story was localized to Skuttunge in order to explain the large stone on the church floor referred to by the informant.

Abbreviations

AT	Aarne and Thompson, *The Types of the Folktale.* (Classification system).
FFC	Folklore Fellows Communications. 1910 et seq. (Publications series).
FmFt	*Folkminnen och Folktankar.* Lund, 1914–44. (Journal).
hd.	Swedish *härad* ("district").
IFGH	Institutet för folkminnesforskning vid Göteborgs Högskola. (Archive housed in Institutet för Folklore, Göteborg).
Klintberg	Bengt af Klintberg, *Svenska folksägner.* 1972.
LUF	Folklivsarkivet, Lund. (Archive).
ML	R. Th. Christiansen, *The Migratory Legends.* (Classification system).
NM EU	Nordiska Muséet, Etnologiska undersökningen. (Archive).
NM HA	Nordiska Muséet, Hammarstedtska arkivet. (Archive).
SKGAAF	Skrifter utg. av Kungliga Gustav Adolfs Akademin för Folklivsforskning. (Publications series).
Skogsrået	Gunnar Granberg, Skogsrået i yngre nordisk folktradition. 1935.
sn.	Swedish *socken* ("parish").
SvLm	*Svenska Landsmål och Svenskt Folkliv.* Stockholm, 1878 et seq. (Journal).
ULMA	Landsmåls- och Folkminnesarkivet, Uppsala. (Archive).
VFA	Västsvenska Folkminnesarkivet. (Archive housed in Institutet för Folklore, Göteborg).

VFF	Västsvenska Folkminnesförening. (Archive housed in Institutet för Folklore, Göteborg).
Värmlandsnäs	C. M. Bergstrand and Ragnar Nilsson, *Folktro och folksed på Värmlandsnäs,* 3. 1962.

Bibliography

THE bibliography is in two parts, "Editions" and "Studies." "Editions" contains most of the more important editions of Swedish legends, whether they have been used in this book or not. It also contains editions from other countries or of other kinds of material when these have been cited in the text. "Studies" lists the secondary references cited in the text. There is of necessity some overlap; some editions are also studies, and many studies contain texts of at least a few legends. In choosing the category for a given reference I have made my own, sometimes arbitrary assessments.

In alphabetizing, Swedish conventions have been followed: å, ä, and ö/ø are the last three letters of the alphabet.

I. Editions

Afzelius, Arvid August. *Swenska folkets sagohäfder,* 1–11. Stockholm, 1844–68.

Afzelius, Arvid August, and E. G. Geijer. *Svenska folkvisor från forntiden.* Stockholm, 1814.

Arill, David. "Folksägner från Sanne." *FmFt,* 5 (1918), 118–126.

Árnason, Jón. *Íslenzkar þjóðsögur og æventýri,* 1–2. Leipzig, 1862–64.

Arwidsson, August Iwar. *Svenska fornsånger: en samling af kämpevisor, folk-visor, lekar och danser, samt baron- och vall-sånger.* Stockholm, 1834–42.

Asbjørnsen, P. C., and Jørgen Moe. *Norske folkeeventyr.* Christiania, 1843–44.

Bergstrand, Carl-Martin. *Bohuslänska sägner.* Göteborg, 1947.

______. *Dalslandssägner.* Göteborg, 1951.

______. *Essunga i svunnen tid: vad de gamla berättat,* 2. Göteborg, 1958.

______. *Gammalt från Kind: 3. Sagor och sägner.* Göteborg, 1961.

______. *Gammalt från Nordhalland,* 1. Göteborg, 1964.

______. *Gammalt från Orust.* Göteborg, 1962.

______. *Hallandssägner.* Göteborg, 1949.

______. *Våra gamla berätta.* Göteborg, 1944.

______. *Värmlandssägner.* Göteborg, 1948.

______. *Västgötasägner.* Göteborg, 1944.

Bergstrand, Carl-Martin, and Ragnar Nilsson. *Folktro och folksed på Värmlandsnäs: 3. Sagor, sägner, visor och övrig folkdiktning.* Göteborg, 1962.

Bergström, Richard. "Strödda bidrag till svensk folklore." *SvLm,* 6: smärre meddelanden (1885), i–xii, cviii–cxxiii.

Bergström, Richard, and Johan Nordlander. "Sagor, sägner ock visor," *SvLm,* 5:2 (1885).

Bohuslänska folkminnen utg. av Västsvenska Folkeminnes Förening. Uddevala, 1922.

Bore, Erik. "Sägner och händelser upptecknade i Västmanland." *SvLm,* B31 (1934).

Bringéus, Nils-Arvid. *Folkminnen från Örkelljungabygden.* Skrifter utg. av Örkelljungabygdens hembygdsförening, 4. Lund, 1953.

______. "Folksägner från Värend uppteckande av Gunnar Olof Hyltén-Cavallius." *Kronobergsboken,* 1968, pp. 39–128.

Cederschiöld, Vilhelm. "Ur Olaus Olssons sägensamling." *FmFt,* 19 (1932), 99–124, 186–196.

Celander, Hilding. "Närkiska folkminnen från Lillkyrka och Vinön." *SvLm,* 16:3 (1922).

Dahllöf, Sigurd. "Västsvenska skepparsägner." *FmFt,* 16 (1929), 125–127.

Djurklou, Nils Gabriel. *Sagor och sägner,* 1–2, ed. Jöran Sahlgren. Svenska sagor och sägner, 5–6. Uppsala, 1943, 1953.

______. *Sagor och äfventyr, berättade på landsmål.* Stockholm, 1883.

Engelke, V. "Hälsingesägner 2." *SvLm,* 7:10 (1892).

Ernvik, A. *Folkminnen från Glaskogen: Sägen, tro och sed i västvärmländska skogsbygder,* 1–2. Skrifter utg. genom Landsmåls- och Folkminnesarkiv i Uppsala, B12, Uppsala, 1966–68.

Floyd, Donald. *Attitudes toward Nature in Swedish Folklore.* Dissertation, University of California, Berkeley, 1976.

Granström, Matts Magni. "Soldaten Karl Snyggs levnadshistoria." *SvLm,* B30 (1933).

Grip, Elias. "Skuttunge- ock Björklingemål: Folksägner." *SvLm,* 18:3 (1899).

Götlind, Johan. *Saga, sägen och folkliv i Västergötland.* Uppsala, 1926.

Hagberg, Louise. "Sägner och folktro från Borrby socken i Skåne." *FmFt,* 18 (1931), 163–177.

Harbe, Daniel. *Folkminnen från Edsbergs härad*, 1-2. SKGAAF, 19. Uppsala, 1950, 1956.

Hjelmström, Anna. "Från Delsbo: Seder och bruk, folktro och sägner, person- och tidsbilder." *SvLm*, 11:4 (1896).

Hyltén-Cavallius, Gunnar Olof. *Wärend och wirdarne: ett försök i svensk etnologi*, 1-2. Stockholm, 1863-64.

Hyltén-Cavallius, Gunnar Olof, and George Stephens. *Svenska folksagor och äfventyr*. Stockholm, 1844-49.

______. *Svenska sagor*, 1-4. Stockholm, 1964-66.

______. *Sveriges politiska och historiska visor 1: Från äldre tider intill år 1650*. Örebro, 1853.

Ingers, Ingemar, ed. "Några folksägner från Bara härad." *Skånes Hembygdsförbunds Årsbok*, 1939.

______, ed. "Texter från Skåne." Part 2 of Lundell et al., "Sagor, sägner, legender" (q.v.). *SvLm*, 3:3 (1945).

Johnsson, Pehr. "Folksägner från Hälsingland." *FmFt*, 6 (1919), 97-119.

Kalén, Johan. *Halländska folkminnen: Lokalsägner och övertro från Fagered*. Stockholm, 1927.

Karlgren, Bärnhard. "Folksägner från Tveta ock Mo härader." *SvLm*, B2 (1908).

Klintberg, Bengt af. *Svenska folksägner*. Stockholm, 1972.

Langer, Thur L., ed. *Dalsländska folksägner*. Uddevala, 1908.

Linnarsson, Linnar. *By, bygd och gård: gammal bygd och folkkultur i Gäsene, Laske och Skånings härader*, 2. Skrifter utg. genom Landsmåls- och Folkminnesarkivet i Uppsala, B4. Uppsala, 1950.

______. *Mäster Hults Värmlandshistorier: minnen och äventyr från västra Värmland*. Stockholm, 1952.

______. *Så berätta gamla: sägner och folkminnen från gamla västgötabygder*. Uppsala, 1938.

Liungman, Waldemar. *Sveriges sägner i ord och bild*, 1-7. Stockholm, 1957-69.

Lundell, Hilda, and Elise Lundell Zetterqvist. "Folkminnen från Kläckebärga ock Dörby." *SvLm*, 9:1 (1889-1936).

Lundell, J. A., Manne Eriksson, Gunnar Hedström, et al., eds. "Sagor, sägner, legender, äventyr och skildringar av folkets levnadssätt på landsmål." *SvLm*, 3:2 (1881-1946).

Löfgren, Emil. *Folktro, sed och sägen från Njurunda socken i Medelpad*. Malmö, 1918.

Modin, Erik. *Härjedalens ortnamn och bygdesägner*. 3 uppl. Stockholm, 1949.

Molbech, Christian. *Udvalgte eventyr og fortællinger*. Copenhagen, 1843.

Nordin-Grip, Ingeborg. *Tro och sägen i Stora Malm*. Katrineholmsortens Hembygdsförenings skriftserie, 12. Katrineholm, 1966.

Nordlander, Johan. "Mytiska sägner från Norrland." *Svensk Fornminnesförenings Tidsskrift,* 5 (1881–83), 3–70.

______. "Norrlands äldsta sägner." *Norrland,* 1:6 (1907).

Ohlson, Ella. "Sagor från Ångermanland." *SvLm,* 1931, pp. 5–53.

Olsson, Edvard. *Värmländska folkminnen.* Göteborg, 1932.

Pettersson, O. P. *Sagor från Åsele lappmark.* Svenska sagor och sägner, 9. Stockholm, 1945.

Rothman, Sven. *Östgötska folkminnen.* SKGAAF, 8. Uppsala, 1941.

Rääf, Leonhard Fr. *Samlingar och anteckningar till en beskrifning öfver Ydre härad i Östergöthland,* 1. Linköping, 1856.

Segerstedt, Albrekt. *Svenska folksagor och äfventyr.* Stockholm, 1884.

Simpson, Jacqueline. *Icelandic Folktales and Legends.* Berkeley, 1972.

Sköld, P. E. *Blekingesägner om skogsnuvor, drakar, gastar m.m. samlade i Tvings socken.* Malmö, 1917.

Ståhle, Carl-Ivar. *Rannsakningar efter antikviteter,* 1 et seq. (Vitterhets-, historie- och antikvitets- akademien.) Uppsala, 1960–.

Svensén, Emil. "Sagor från Emådalen." *SvLm,* 2:7 (1881).

Svensson, Sigfrid. "Folksägner om de underjordiska uppttecknade i södra Skåne." *FmFt,* 9 (1922), 117–126.

Swahn, Sven Öjvind. *Folktro och gammal dikt.* Lund, 1926.

Säve, P. A. *Gotländska sägner.* Ed. H. Gustavson and Å. Nyman. Svenska sagor och sägner, 12. Stockholm, 1959–61.

Thiele, J. M. *Danmarks folkesagn,* 1–2. Copenhagen, 1843.

Waltman, K. H. "Lidmål." *SvLm,* 18:1 (1894).

______. "Lidmål: ny samling." *SvLm,* B39 (1939).

Werner, Hilder. *Westergötlands fornminnen.* Stockholm, 1868.

Wigström, Eva. *Folkdiktning, samlad och upptecknad i Skåne.* Copenhagen, 1880.

______. *Folkdiktning, samlad och upptecknad i Skåne: andra samlingen.* Copenhagen, 1881.

______. "Folktro och sägner från skilda landskap (folkdiktning, 3:e samlingen)." *SvLm,* 8:3 (1898–1914).

______. *Folktro och sägner upptecknade i Skåne.* Malmö, 1914.

______. "Sagor och äfventyr upptecknade i Skåne." *SvLm,* 5:1 (1884).

Åström, Elis. *Folktro och folkliv i Östergötland: uppteckningar.* SKGAAF, 39. Uppsala, 1962.

II. Studies

Aarne, Antti, and Stith Thompson. *The Types of the Folktale.* FFC, 184. Helsinki, 1961.

Ahlman, Hans W:son et al., eds. *Sverige: land och folk,* 1–3. Stockholm, 1966.

Alver, Bente Gullveig. *Heksetro og trolddom: et studie i norsk heksevæsen.* Oslo, 1971.

Alver, Brynjulf. "Dauinggudstenesta: ein europeisk forestellingskrins i norsk tradisjon." *Arv*, 6 (1950), 145–165.

Andersson, Ingvar. *A History of Sweden*. Translated by Carolyn Hannay. London, 1955.

Andersson, William. "Folktro från Blekinge skärgård." *FmFt*, 7 (1920), 113–126.

Bergstrand, Carl-Martin. "De dödas julotta i västsvensk folktradition." *FmFt*, 24 (1937), 118–132.

Bergstrand, Maja. "Näcken som musikaliskt väsen." *FmFt*, 23 (1936), 14–31.

Boberg, Inger M. *Baumeistersagen*. FFC, 151. Helsinki, 1955.

______. *Sagnet om den store Pans død*. SKGAAF, 2. Copenhagen, 1934.

Bringéus, Nils-Arvid. *Gunnar Olof Hyltén-Cavallius som etnolog: en studie kring Wärend och wirdarne*. Nordiska Muséets handlingar, 63. Stockholm, 1966.

______. *Människan som kulturvarelse: en introduktion till etnologi*. Handböcker i etnologi. Lund, 1976.

______. *Årets festseder*. Stockholm, 1976.

Broderius, John R. *The Giant in Germanic Tradition*. Chicago, 1932.

Bull, Edvard, and Sverre Steen. *Byer og bebyggelse*. Nordisk Kultur, 18. Oslo, 1933.

Celander, Hilding. "Oskoreien och besläktade föreställningar i äldre och nyare nordisk tradition." *Saga och Sed*, 1943, pp. 71–175.

Christiansen, Reidar Th. "The Dead and the Living." *Studia Norvegica*, 1:2 (1946).

______. "Kjætten på Dovre." *Videnskapsselskapets skrifter, II. hist.-filos. kl.*, 6. Oslo, 1922.

______. *The Migratory Legends: A Proposed List of the Types with a Systematic Catalogue of the Norwegian Variants*. FFC, 175. Helsinki, 1958.

Dannell, Gideon. "Folklivet i en gammal svensk by." *FmFt*, 12 (1925), 33–41.

Deneke, B. *Legende und Volkssage: Untersuchungen zur Erzählung vom Geistesgottesdienst*. Dissertation, Universität Frankfurt, 1958.

Dundes, Alan. "Texture, Text and Context." *Southern Folklore Quarterly*, 28 (1964), 251–265.

Egardt, Brita. "De svenska vattenhästsägnerna och deras ursprung." *Folkkultur*, 4 (1944), 119–166.

Ehrenberg, August. *Allmogen i Albo härad under 1880-talet*. Kristianstad, 1945.

Ejdenstam, J. "Är tomten ett dragväsen?" *FmFt*, 30 (1943), 8–17.

______. "Omfärd vid besittningstagande av jordegendom." *SvLm*, 69 (1946), 86–114.

Enqvist, Arvid. "Två folksägner från Hälsingland i äldre och nyare uppteckningar." *FmFt*, 17 (1930), 123–130.

Ericsson, Olav Algot. "Sägnen om Hårgadansen och dess rötter." *FmFt*, 15 (1928), 92–98.

Eriksson, Nils. "Bjäran: uppteckningar från Wilhelmina socken i Lappland." *FmFt*, 18 (1931), 147–150.

Erixon, Sigurd. "Svensk byggnadskultur och dess geografi." *Ymer*, 42 (1922), 249–290.

Feilberg, H. F. *Bjærgtagen: studie over en gruppe træk fra nordisk alfetro*. Danmarks Folkeminder, 5. Copenhagen, 1910.

______. *Dansk bondeliv, saaledes som det i mands minde førtes, navnlig i Vestjylland*. Copenhagen, 1889.

______. *Nissens historie*. Danmarks Folkeminder, 18. Copenhagen, 1918.

Fernholm, H. "Fiskelycka: studier över valda delar av fiskets folklore." *Folkkultur*, 3 (1943), 242–283.

Fossenius, Mai. "Sägnerna om trollen Finn och Skalle som byggmästare." *Folkkultur*, 3 (1943), 5–144.

Gadelius, Bror. *Häxor och häxprocesser*. Stockholm, 1963.

______. *Tro och öfvertro i gångna tider*, 1–2. Stockholm, 1912–13.

Gentz, Lauritz. "Vad förorsakade de stora häxprocesserna?" *Arv*, 10 (1954), 1–39.

Gjerdman, Olof. "Hon som var värre än den onde: en saga och ett uppsvenskt kyrkomålningsmotiv." *Saga och Sed*, 1941, pp. 1–93.

Grambo, Ronald. "Verse in Legends: Some Remarks on a Neglected Area of Folklore." *Fabula*, 11 (1969), 48–65.

Granberg, Gunnar. "Memorat und Sage: einige methodische Gesichtspunkte." *Saga och Sed*, 1935, pp. 120–127.

______. "Skogsrået: en folkminnesgeografisk orientering." *Rig*, 1933, pp. 145–197.

______. *Skogsrået i yngre nordisk folktradition*. SKGAAF, 3. Uppsala, 1935.

Hagberg, Louise. *När döden gästar: svenska folkseder och svensk folktro i samband med död och begravning*. Stockholm, 1937.

Handwörterbuch des deutschen Aberglaubens. Berlin and Leipzig, 1927 et seq.

Hartmann, Elisabeth. *Die Trollvorstellungen in den Sagen und Märchen der skandinavischen Völker*. Tübinger Germanistische Arbeiten, 23. Stuttgart-Berlin, 1936.

Hauge, Hans-Egil. *Levande begravd eller bränd i nordisk folkmedicin: en studie i offer och magi*. Stockholm Studies in Comparative Religion, 6. Stockholm, 1965.

Hecker, J. F. C. *Die grossen Volkskrankheiten des Mittelalters: historischpathologische Untersuchungen*. Berlin, 1865. English translation by B. G. Babington, *The Black Death and the Dancing Mania*. New York, 1888.

Hildebrand, Emil. *Sveriges historia till våra dagar,* 1-15. Stockholm, 1919-45.

Holmström, Helge. "Sägnerna om äktenskap med maran." *FmFt,* 5 (1918), 135-145.

Honko, Lauri. *Geisterglaube in Ingermanland,* 1. FFC, 185. Helsinki, 1962.

_____. "Memorates and the Study of Folk Belief." *Journal of the Folklore Institute,* 1 (1964), 5-19.

Hultkranz, Åke. *The Supernatural Owners of Nature.* Stockholm, 1961.

Hyltén-Cavallius, Gunnar Olof. *Vocabularium vaerendicum.* Uppsala, 1837-39.

_____. *Wärend och wirdarne: ett försök i svensk etnologi,* 1-2. Stockholm, 1863-64.

Höttges, Valerie. *Die Sage vom Riesenspielzeug.* Jena, 1931.

_____. *Typenverzeichnis der deutschen Riesen- und riesischen Teufelssagen.* FFC, 122. Helsinki, 1937.

Jakobsen, D. "Den onde i kyrkan." *Skånska Folkminnen,* 1926, pp. 92-130.

Johannesson, Gösta. *Skånes historia.* Stockholm, 1971.

Johansson, Levi. *Bebyggelse och folkliv i det gamla Frostviken.* Skrifter utg. genom Landsmåls- och folkminnesarkivet i Uppsala, B3 (1947).

Jörberg, Lennart. *The Industrial Revolution in Scandinavia.* The Fontana Economic History of Europe, 4:8 (London, 1970).

Kalén, Johan. "Hämndegåvan: några ord om en sägentyp." *FmFt,* 22 (1935), 107-120.

_____. "En typ av Pansägnen i västsvenska uppteckningar." *FmFt,* 23 (1936), 89-92.

Klintberg, Bengt av. " 'Gast' in Swedish Folk Tradition." *Temenos,* 3 (1968), 43-56.

Kullander, A. "Några drag ur det forna skogsbyggarlifvet i Edsvedens skogstrakter." *SvLm,* 11:10 (1896), 3-50.

Levander, Lars. *Övre Dalarnas bondekultur under 1800-talets förra hälft.* Stockholm, 1943.

Lid, Nils. "Til varulvens historia." *Saga och Sed,* 1937, pp. 3-25.

_____, ed. *Folketru.* Nordisk Kultur, 19. Stockholm, 1935.

Liestøl, Knut. "Kjetta på Dovre." *Maal og minne,* 1933, pp. 24-48.

Lindow, John. "Personification and Narrative Structure in Scandinavian Plague Legends." *Arv,* 29-30 (1973-74), 83-92.

Linnarsson, Linnar. *Bygd, by och gård.* Skrifter utg. genom Landsmåls- och folkminnesarkivet i Uppsala, B4. Uppsala, 1948.

Liungman, Waldemar. "Finnsägenproblemet." *FmFt,* 29 (1942), 86-113, 138-154.

_____. "Jätteleksaken." *FmFt,* 18 (1931), 83-90.

_____. *Sveriges samtliga folksagor: 3. Varifrån kommer våra sagor?*

Djursholm, 1952. German translation by Elsbeth Umlauf, *Die schwedischen Volksmärchen*, Berlin, 1961.

Lloyd, L. *Peasant Life in Sweden*. London, 1870.

Lüthi, Max. *Märchen*. 5 Aufl. Sammlung Metzler, 16. Stuttgart, 1974.

______. "Urform und Zielform in Sage und Märchen." *Fabula*, 9 (1967), 41–54.

Martin, Alfred. "Geschichte der Tanzkrankheit in Deutschland." *Zeitschrift des Vereins für Volkskunde*, 24 (1914), 113–134.

Mead, William Richard. *An Economic Geography of the Scandinavian States and Finland*. London, 1965.

Meisen, Karl. *Die Sagen vom wütenden Heer und wilden Jäger*. Volkskundliche Quellen, 1. Münster, 1935.

Millward, Roy. *Scandinavian Lands*. London, 1965.

Møller, J. S. *Moder og barn i dansk folkeoverlevering: fra svangerskab til daab og kirkegang*. Danmarks Folkeminder, 48. Copenhagen, 1940.

Möller, P. "Allmogeliv i Göingebygden vid adertonhundratalets början." *FmFt*, 3 (1916), 179–190.

Nicolovius, Nils Lovén. *Folklifvet i Skytts härad*. 3rd ed. Lund, 1908.

Nilsson, Albert. "Övertro och häxprocesser." In *Svenska folket genom tiderna*, 5 (Stockholm, 1939), 161–174.

Nilsson, Martin P:n. "Byalaget i sydsvensk kultur." *Saga och Sed*, 1943, pp. 54–63.

______. *Tideräkningen*. Nordisk Kultur, 21. Stockholm, 1934.

______. *Årets högtider*. Nordisk Kultur, 22. Stockholm, 1938.

Nilsson, Yngve. *Bygd och näringsliv i norra Värmland: en kulturgeografisk studie*. Meddelanden från Lunds universitets geografiska institution, avhandlingar, 18 (1950).

Nordland, Odd. "Mannbjørn: ein studie i heimfestingsproblemet ved vandresegner." *By och Bygd*, 11 (1956–57), 133–153.

Norlind, Tobias. *Skattsägner: en studie i jämförande folkminnesforskning*. Lunds Universitetets Årsskrift, N.F., Avd. 1, 14:7. Lund, 1918.

______. *Studier i svensk folklore*. Stockholm, 1911.

______. *Svenska allmogens lif: 1. folksed, folktro och folkdiktningen*. Stockholm, 1912.

Nylén, Anna-Maja. "Svensk landsbygd i omvandling." *Rig*, 47 (1964), 1–9.

Odstedt, Ella. *Varulven i svensk folktradition*. Stockholm, 1943.

Ohlson, Ella. "Naturväsen i ångermanlänsk folktro: en översikt." *FmFt*, 20 (1933), 70–112.

Olsson, Helmer. *Folkliv och folkdikt i Vättle härad under 1800-talet*. SKGAAF, 12. Uppsala, 1945.

______. "Sägnen om jätteleksaken." *FmFt*, 22 (1935), 35–41.

______. "Tomten i halländsk folktro." *FmFt*, 24 (1937), 100–117.

Pape, John. "Bidrag till belysande av föreställningarna om Bjäran-Mjölkharen i företrädesvis äldre tradition." *Folkkultur*, 5 (1945), 84–118.

Pentikäinen, Juha. "Grenzprobleme zwischen Memorat und Sage." *Temenos*, 3 (1968), 136–167.

______. *The Nordic Dead Child Tradition: 1. Nordic Dead Child Beings.* FFC, 202. Helsinki, 1968.

Peuckert, Will-Erich. *Lenore.* FFC, 158. Helsinki, 1955.

Phil, Carin. "Livet i det gamla Överkalix." *SvLm*, 1955, pp. 83–187.

Piaschewski, Gisela. *Der Wechselbalg: ein Beitrag zum Aberglauben der nordeuropäischen Völker*, Deutschkundliche Arbeiten, A, 5. Breslau, 1935.

Reichborn-Kjennerud, Ingjald. *Vår gamle trolldomsmedesin*, 1-5. Oslo, 1928–42.

Rooth, Anna Birgitta. *Folkdikt och folktro.* Handböcker i etnologi. Lund, 1973.

______. "Saga och sägen." In Rooth, *Lokalt och globalt*, 1. Lund, 1969.

Röhrich, Lutz. *Erzählungen des späten Mittelalters und ihr Weiterleben in Literatur und Volksdichtung bis zur Gegenwart*, 1–2. Bern, 1962–67.

______. "Die Frauenjagdsage." *Laographia*, 22 (1965), 408–423.

______. *Sage.* 2 Aufl. Sammlung Metzler, 55. Stuttgart, 1971.

______. "Teufelsmärchen und Teufelssagen." In *Sagen und ihre Deutung.* Göttingen, 1965.

Sahlgren, Jöran. "Strömkarlen spelar (Nordiska ortnamn i språklig och saklig belysning, 10)." *Namn och Bygd*, 23 (1935), 42–55.

______. "Sägnerna om trollen Finn och Skalle och deras kyrkobyggande." *Saga och Sed*, 1940, pp. 1–50; 1941, pp. 115–154.

Sandström, Anna. *Natur och arbetsliv i svenska bygder: Götaland.* Stockholm, 1948.

______. *Natur och arbetsliv i svenska bygder: Norrland.* Stockholm, 1924.

Schier, Bruno. "Die Sage vom Schrätel und Wasserbären." *Mitteldeutsche Blätter für Volkskunde*, 10 (1935), 164–180.

Scott, Franklin D. *Sweden: The Nation's History.* Minneapolis, 1977.

Ström, Folke. *The Sacral Origin of the Germanic Death Penalties.* Stockholm, 1942.

Strömbäck, Dag. *Folklore och filologi: valda uppsatser.* SKGAAF, 48. Uppsala, 1970.

______. "Kölbigk och Hårga I." *Arv*, 17 (1961), 1–48.

______. "Kölbigk och Hårga II." *Arv*, 24 (1968), 91–132.

______. "Näcken och förlossningen." *Varbergs Museums Årsbok*, 1963, pp. 77–85.

______. "Den underbara årsdansen." *Arkiv för Nordisk Filologi*, 59

(1944), 111–126. Reprinted in Strömbäck, *Folklore och filologi*, 54–69.
______, ed. *Leading Folklorists of the North*. Oslo, 1971. Reprint of *Arv*, 25–26 (1969–71).
Sundblad, Johannes. *Gammaldags seder och bruk*. Stockholm, 1917.
Svensson, Sigfrid. *Bondens år: kalender, märkesdagar, hushållsregler, väderleksmärken*. Revised ed. Stockholm, 1972.
______. *Introduktion till folklivsforskning*. Stockholm, 1966.
Sydow, C. W. von. "Iriskt inflytande på nordisk guda- och hjältesaga." *Vetenskapssocieteten i Lund, Årsbok*, 1920, pp. 26–61.
______. "Jättarna i mytologi och folktro." *FmFt*, 6 (1919), 52–96.
______. "Kategorien der Prosavolksdichtung." In von Sydow, *Selected Papers*, q.v., pp. 60–88.
______. "Naturväsen: en översikt till ledning för samlare." *FmFt*, 11 (1924), 33–48.
______. "Om folkets sägner." In von Sydow, ed., *Folksägner och folksagor*, q.v., pp. 96–112.
______. *Selected Papers on Folklore*. Copenhagen, 1948.
______. "Studier i Finnsägnen och besläktade byggmästarsägner." *Fataburen*, 1907, pp. 65–78, 119–218; 1908, pp. 19–27.
______. "Övernaturliga väsen." In Lid, ed., *Folketru*, q.v., pp. 95–159.
______, ed. *Folksägner och folksagor*. Nordisk Kultur, 9B. Stockholm, 1931.
Sømme, Axel, ed. *A Geography of Norden*. Oslo, 1960.
Taylor, Archer. *Northern Parallels to the Death of Pan*. Washington University Studies, 10. Seattle, 1922.
Thompson, Stith. *The Folktale*. New York, 1946.
Thorsén, Edvin. *Uppländsk torparliv*. Stockholm, 1949.
Tillhagen, Carl-Herman. "The Conception of the Nightmare in Sweden." In Wayland Hand and Gustav Arlt, eds., *Humaniora: Essays Honoring Archer Taylor*. Berkeley, 1960, pp. 317–329.
______. "Folklore Archives in Sweden." *Journal of the Folklore Institute*, 1 (1964), 20–36.
______. "Sägner och folktro kring pesten." *Fataburen*, 1967, pp. 215–230.
______. "Was ist eine Sage? Eine Definition und ein Vorschlag für ein europäisches Sagensystem." In G. Ortutay, ed., *Tagung der Sagenkommission der International Society for Folk-Narrative Research, Budapest, 14–16 Oktober, 1963. Acta Ethnographica Academiae Scientiarum Hungaricae*, 13:1–4 (1964), 9–17.
Troels-Lund. *Dagligt liv i Norden i det sekstende århundrede*, 1–7. Copenhagen, 1879–1901.
Tufvesson, Theodore. "Bäckahästen i svensk folktro." *FmFt*, 3 (1916), 161–176.
Turner, Victor. *Dramas, Fields, and Metaphors: Symbolic Action in Human Society*. Ithaca, N.Y., 1974.

Visted, K. *Vår gamle bondekultur*, 1–2. Kristiania, 1971.

Wadman, Vidhelm. Review of N. G. Djurklou, *Sagor och äfventyr, berättade på landsmål* (Stockholm, 1883). In *Svenska Landsmål*, 6: smärre meddelanden (1885), xxxvi–xlii.

Wigström, Eva. "Allmogeseder i Rönnebergs härad i Skåne på 1840-talet." *SvLm*, 8:2 (1891).

Wikman, K. Rob. V. "Förskrivning till djävulen." *Fataburen*, 1960, pp. 193–199.

______. *Livets högtider*. Nordisk Kultur, 20. Stockholm, 1949.

Wildhaber, Robert. "Die Stunde ist da, aber der Mann nicht." *Rheinisches Jahrbuch für Volkskunde*, 9 (1958), 23–58.

______. *Das Sündenregister auf dem Kuhhaut*. FFC, 163. Helsinki, 1955.

Woods. Barbara Allen. *The Devil in Dog Form*. University of California Publications in Folklore, 11. Berkeley, 1959.

Index of Tale Types

Type number	Story number
AT 365	98
AT 701	17
AT 826	77
AT 1161	25
AT 1165	23
AT 1179	76
AT 1353	80
ML 3005	100
ML 3010	75
ML 3045	83
ML 4005	87
ML 4010	87
ML 4015	99
ML 4020	95
ML 4050	4
ML 4055	52–53
ML 4090	49
ML 5015	17
ML 5050	50
ML 5060	45
ML 5090	38
ML 6000	39–40
ML 6015	25
ML 6045	35–36
ML 6070A	33
ML 6070B	34
ML 7005	60
ML 7010	63
ML 7065	22
ML 7095	13
ML 8010 f	14–15

General Index

"Aage og Else", 191
Achilles, 112
Africa, 83
Afzelius, Arvid August, 20, 21, 124, 191
Agriculture, 4, 15–17
Archives, 24
Arwidsson, August Iwar, 21
Asbjørnsen, Peter Christian, 21–22, 90, 130, 193
Asgard, 86–87
Assizes, 157

Baldr, 66
Ballads: early editions, 20–21; and ghosts, 53; *näck* in, 97, 118; patterns in, 126; parallel to a text, 191
Baltic countries, 90
Baptism: protective power of, 11–12, 13, 49; of a changeling, 93; in a story, 164
Bear, 178
Beggars, 7
Beowulf, 33–34
Bergtagning: and marriage, 30–31; and trolls, 33; defined, 34; as explanation for human problems, 41; in a story, 96–99; location, 98; the re-exchange, 99
Berserks, 178
Birth, 11, 67
Bjäran. *See* Milk-hare
Black Book, 10, 46, 157
Black Death. *See* Plague
Black Mass, 16, 47, 48–49. *See also* Blåkulla
Blåkulla: discussed, 47, 165, 174; and witch's salve, 48; in a story, 162, 163, 167, 169, 172
Blind motif, 136
Bonde. *See* Peasantry
Brentano, Clemens, 20
Broadsides, 89
Bürger, Gottfried, 192
Bäckahäst, 39, 119, 120–121. See also *Näck*
Bönder. *See* Peasantry

Calendar, 15–16
Catechism, 13
Catholic Church, 9
Cattle, importance of, 42
Ceaseless dance, 44, 149–152. *See also* Dancing
Changeling: explanation, discussion, 12; variety within story tradition, 34; as explanation for human problem, 41; influence on other tales, 65; in a story, 91–94; didactic value, 92; and baptism, 93
Charles XII, 6
Children, role and rights of, 5

Christening, 88
Christianity: power against supernatural beings, 11–13, 34, 47, 90, 95, 98, 103, 113, 119–120, 129, 154; role of, in legends, 33, 34, 42; opposition of *skogsrå*, 37; and folk belief, 54–55, 56; and giants, 80, 83; church doctrine and supernatural beings, 144
Christmas: discussed, 17, 194; and supernatural beings, 33, 54; in a story, 79, 89, 138, 141, 161–162, 192, 193
Church, 5, 9
Church paintings, 172, 176
Church service, 159–160, 193, 194
Churchwarden, 10
Clergy. *See* Parson
Communion, 44, 155; in a story, 95, 103, 155
Confirmation, 13–14
County (*län*), 8
Craftsmen, 7
Cycles. *See* Legends, cycles

Dancing, 44; in a story, 117–118, 148, 150, 151–152
Dancing sickness, 149
Dead, the. *See* Ghosts
Dean, 10
Death, 15. *See also* Ghosts
Denmark, tales and belief in, 37, 73, 93, 101, 116, 124, 130, 141, 192
Des Knaben Wunderhorn, 192
Devil. *See* Satan
Dietrich von Bern, 116
Dísir, 70
District (*härad*), 8
Djurklou, Nils Gabriel, 23
Dräng, 6
Dragon, 31, 76–77
Draugar, 15

Easter: and witchcraft, 16; in a story, 163, 166, 171
Easter-hag. *See* Witchcraft

Edda, Poetic. See *Poetic Edda*
Edda Snorra Sturlusonar. *See* Snorri Sturluson, *Edda*
Education, 13
Egils saga Skallagrímsonar, 177
England, 101–102
Entertainment. *See* Legends, as entertainment
Environment: investigation of, 30, 59–60; formation of, 32, 84–88 *passim*; anthropomorphization of, 178
Eoten, 33
Etiological folklore, 27. *See also* Legends used etiologically
Exemplum, 116, 160
Exorcism: of a *tomte*, 42, 144; of Satan, 43, 148, 153; in a story, 143, 147

Fairy, 35. *See also* Troll
Fairy-tale. *See* Wonder-tale
Family, 5
Farm, 5
Fate, 30–31, 64–66
Fenno-Swedish language, 4
Fetch, 70
Fictional folktale. *See* Wonder-tale
Finland, 4, 86, 110
Finn-legend, 86–88
Finns, 8, 30, 179–180
Fishing, 4, 126–132 *passim*
Folk belief: pregnancy, birth, baptism, 11, 13; iron and steel, 12, 13, 96, 119; and supernatural experiences, 28–29; relation to legends, 28; bibliography, 29; comparison with a text, 91; and household spirits, 142–143, explanation of disease, 179. *See also* Changeling, Fate, Milk-hare, Plague, Portent, Supernatural beings, Witchcraft
Folk festivals, 16
Folklore collection, 20–24
Frame of reference, 29
Freyja, 87
Frigg, 66

Funeral, 15, 52–53, 185, 187; in a story, 69–70, 183, 187
Fylgja, 70

Gast. *See* Ghost
Gautreks saga, 66–67
Geijer, Erik Gustav, 20, 124, 191
Genii, 70
Genre divisions and terminology, 24–28
Germany, tales and belief in, 81, 86, 90, 93, 116, 119, 139, 149, 192
Ghost: described, haunting, 15, 52–54; *gast*, 15, 52–53, 80; bibliography, 52; and Christianity, 52, 55, 56, 74; *spöke*, 53; as explanation for the unusual, 55; discussed, 184–195 *passim*; in a story, 183–195 *passim*
Giant: decline of, 27; description, role in legends, 32–33; etymology, 33; as collective beings, 35; in a story, 79–88, 97; individualized and localized, 80; size, 81; subject of popular humor, 82; fear of Christianity, 83; *jättekast*, 32, 84–85; and Satan, 156
Godparent, 13, 92, 164
Gregory of Tours, 194
Grimm, Jakob and Wilhelm, 20, 21, 25
Gustav Adolf Academy, 23
Gustav Vasa, 63
Gypsies, 7
Gårdsrå. See *Skogsrå*; *Tomte*

Hallowed ground, 185–186. *See also* Christianity
Haunting, 15, 41. *See also* Ghost
Heinrich von Freiburg, 91
Heliand de Froidmont, 116
Herbs, 109–111
Holiday, 20, 90. *See also* Assizes; Christmas; Easter; New Year's Eve; Whitsuntide
Hunters, 105–106, 112
Hyltén-Cavallius, Gunnar Olof, 21–24 *passim*
Härad. *See* District
Höðr, 66

Iceland, 120, 195
Industrial Revolution, 4, 8
Innocence VIII, 48
Interest Dominance, 34, 71
Ireland, 116

Jacques de Vitry, 160
Judgement Day, 194
Julian calendar. *See* Calendar
Järteckensbok, 160
Jätte. *See* Giant
Jättekast. *See* Giant
Jötunn, 33

Kalevala, 67
Kinder- und Hausmärchen, 20
Kloka, de, 30
Kvarngubbe, 124–125
Kyrkotagning, 13, 94

Landnámabók, 120
Lapps: and magic, 8, 152, 180; social position, 30; in a story, 108
Lares, 70
Legends: didactic value of, 12, 30–31, 38, 41, 44, 92, 127, 139, 140, 143, 153–154, 156, 195; described, 25; contrast with wonder-tale, 25–26, 136; subdivisions, 26–28; used etiologically, 27, 68, 75, 98, 150, 169, 174, 196; relevance to population, 28; origins, 46; structural patterns, 46, 76, 95, 125–126, 128, 180; background in reality, 154, 170; and broadsides, 89; as entertainment, 140, 142, 154, 159, 160–161; cycles, 167. *See also* Local legend; Memorate; Migratory legend
Lemminkäinen, 67
Life cycle, 11–15

Linnaeus, Carolus (Carl von Linné), 124
Local legend, 27-28
Loki, 66, 87
Lord's Prayer, 13, 83; in a story, 153, 161-162, 187
Lübeck, 61-63
Lundell, J.A., 23
Lutheran Church, 9, 13
Lycanthropy. *See* Werewolf
Län. See County
Länsman. See Sheriff

Magic: practiced by gypsies, Lapps, Finns, 7-8, 180; at birth, 11; and witchcraft, 47-48, 163; invisibility, 99; dealing with *skogsrå,* 107; formulae, 118, in fishing, 130; in a story, 168
Maríu saga, 160
Marriage, 97
Masterbuilder. *See* Finn-legend
Mattsson, Sten, 158
Maundy Thursday, 166, 172-173
Mayday, 17
Maypole, 17
Memorate: defined, 28; and supernatural experiences, 28-29, 143; reference to a text, 76, 91, 171; and ghosts, 185
Merman, 130
Midsummer, 16
Midwife, 11
Migratory legend: defined, 26; classification, 26-27; structural patterns, 46; and ghosts, 53-54, 189; humor, 122; characters, 158; erotic elements, 179
Milk-hare, 50, 171-173
Moe, Jørgen, 21, 90
Molbech, Christian, 21
Monarchy, 9
Murder, 187
Music, 117-123 *passim,* 150, 193. *See also* Ceaseless dance; Dancing
Märchen. See Wonder-tale

Nature-beings. *See* Giant; *Näck; Sjörå; Skogsrå;* Supernatural beings; Troll
Nessos, cloak of, 84
Newborn infant, 11-12
New Year's Eve, 114, 115
Niccor, 38
Nightmare: described, 51-52, 181-182; discussed, 178-183 *passim;* in a story, 176-177, 180-181, 182
Nihhus, 38
Nisse. See *Tomte*
Nobility, 5
Norway, tales and belief in, 37, 90, 93, 101, 110, 116, 130, 139, 141, 189, 194
Nykur, 38
Näck: threat to infants, 12; defined, conceptions of, 38-39; etymology, 38; as explanation for the unusual, 55; relationship to a giant, 80; in ballads, 97, 118; and Satan, 118-119; helps farmer, 119-120; ridden, 120-121; hopes for salvation, 123-124; and *kvarngubbe,* 125; "binding", 129-130; in a story, 117-119, 123. See also *Bäckahäst; Sjörå*

Oden, 114-116
Oden's hunt. *See* Wild hunt
Óðinn. *See* Oden
Oikotype, 102, 141
Óláfr Haraldsson. *See* Saint Olaf
Óláfs saga helga, 139
Olaus Magnus, 127
Omen. *See* Portent
Oral tradition: dissemination of, 6-8, 11; collection of, 20-24; in formation of legends, 28; and history, 30, 63; tenacity of, 30, 63; dissolution of, 60-61; and plague legends, 72; typical narrative elements, 109; fluidity of, 163; skillful narrator, 171
Oskorei, 33, 37

Other world, 31–32

Pan-legend, 20, 100–101
Parish (*socken*), 8
Parson: in society, 9–11; as adviser, 95; as hero in legends, 144, 151; lays ghost, 186, recounts legend, 191; and magic, 196
Peasantry, 5
Peddlars, 7
Peer Gynt, 90
Plague, 31, 71–74
Plutarch, 20, 100
Poetic Edda, 126, 192–193
Portent, 30, 70 74; in a story, 68–72 *passim*
Predestination, 30
Pregnancy, 11, 176
Proverb, 139, 153, 189

Reformation, 9
Revenant. *See* Ghost
Ritual: for possession of land, 130; for fishing, 132
Romanticism, 20
Russia, 192
Rå. See *Sjörå*; *Skogsrå*
Rääf, Leonhard Fredrik, 20–21
Rückert, Friedrich, 81

Sabbath, violation of, 115, 149, 155
Saint Birgitta, 160
Saint Olaf, 87, 139
Saint Valborg (Walpurga), 17
Saints' days, 16–17
Satan: encounters with clergy, 10; as musician, and *näck*, 38, 118–119; jokes about 41, 82; in folk belief and narrative, 43–47; nomenclature, 44; pact with, 45–46, 157, 175; origin of legends about, 46; and Christianity, 56, 154; and infertility, 65; in improper statements, 68; in disguise, 148; and dancing, 149, 152; and cardplaying, 153; exorcised, 153; interdiction violated, 159; and ghosts, 185; in a story, 147–162 *passim*, 174–175
Scotland, 90
Seasonal help, 6
Seelentrost, 149, 160
Sermon, 9–10, 190. *See also* Parson
Servants, 5–6
Sex roles and stereotypes, 178, 182
Sexton, 10–11
Shamanism, 194
Sheriff (*länsman*), 8–9
Shieling, 4, 187
Siegfried, 112
Siælinna Thrøst, 149, 160
Sjörå: defined, etymology, role in narrative, 39–40; as explanation for the unusual, 55; relative familiarity to humans, 55; relationship to a giant, 80; as horse, 121; mistreatment of, 128; "binding", 129–130; encounter with, 136; in a story, 60, 126–129, 132–134. See also *Bäckahäst*; *Näck*
Skogsnuva. See *Skogsrå*
Skogsrå: described, 36–37; bibliography, 37; as explanation for the unusual, 55; relative familiarity to humans, 55; in a story, 105–114 *passim*; in folk belief, 106–107; and wild hunt, 116; changes appearance of something, 167; associated with hunting, 171
Slavic countries, 90. *See also* Russia
Snorri Sturluson, *Edda*, 66, 86–87
Socken. *See* Parish
Social system, 6, 8
Soldier, 6, 82–83
Spöke. *See* Ghost
Stagnelius, Erik Johan, 124
Stephens, George, 21
Strömkarl, 121–122. See also *Näck*; *Sjörå*
Sturluson, Snorri. *See* Snorri Sturluson, *Edda*

Suicide, 154, 190
Supernatural beings: abroad at Christmas, 17; in legends, 28; distinction between collective and solitary, 35; as explanation for the unusual, 54–55; relative familiarity to humans, 55–56; dissolution of, 112; desire for salvation, 123, 144; respect for, 131; life style, 132; results of encounters with, 136; and Christianity, 144; and Satan, 148. *See also* Giant; *Näck*; *Sjörå*; *Skogsrå*; *Tomte*; Troll; Witchcraft
Supernatural experience: as actualized folk belief, 28–29; and narrative, 29, 143; *bergtagning* as, 34; with *skogsrå*, 36–37; and treature, 77; and ghost, 184
Svenska Landsmål, 23
Swan maiden, 179
Sweden; geography, 1–3; map, 2; culture areas, 3; social classes, 5; ethnographic bibliography, 17–20
"Sweet William's Ghost", 192
Sydow, Carl Wilhelm von, 28

Tannhäuser, 123
Thiele, J.M., 22
Thor, 32, 89
Tibast-legend, 110, 111, 112
Tithe, 10
Tomte: described, 40–42; and Satan, 42; bibliography, 42; dairy farming, 50; relative familiarity to humans, 55–56; in portent, 71; and *kvarngubbe*, 125; characteristics, 138, 141; disrespect for, 139, 142; and household animals, 142–143; and exorcism, 144; on ships, 145; and witchcraft, 167–168; in a story, 71, 98, 136–145 *passim*, 162, 166
Tradition-bearer, 25, 29, 56, 60
Traditional society, 30, 55
Treasure, 31, 186; in a story, 75–77, 83, 88, 185
Trickster, 7
Troll-hag. *See* Witchcraft
Troll: decline of, 27, 103; described, 33; and *bergtagning*, 34–35; bibliography, 35; as collective beings, 35; and *sjörå*, 39; as explanation for the unusual, 55; relative familiarity to humans, 55; in local environment, 60; subject of popular humor, 82; and *vättar*, 104; and Satan, 156; troll-food, 167; in a story, 59, 72, 75–76, 85, 89–92, 94–102 *passim*, 128

Ulfheðnar, 178
University, 10
"Unquiet Grave, The", 191

Vantevän, 102, 126–128
Verse in narrative, 103, 126; in a story, 86
Village, 4, 6
Vincenz de Beauvais, 116, 160
Vittror, 35–36
Von Sydow. *See* Sydow, von.
Västgöteknalle, 7
Vättar, 35, 100, 103–104

Wadman, Vilhelm, 23
Water spirit. See *Näck*
Wedding, 94–95, 96
Werewolf: described, 51; in a story, 176–177, 179–180; in Old Norse literature, 177
Whitsuntide, 155
Wild hunt, 37, 115, 116
William of Newbury, 102
Witch's salve, 48–49, 165, 168–170
Witchcraft: and cattle, 42; description, 47–51; social background, 48, 56; and dairy farming, 50; in narrative, 50, 171; bibliography, 50–51; as explanation

for the unusual, 55; and trolls, 94; in a story, 162–175 *passim*; and magic, 163, 167; trials, 165; in a folk book, 174; related to nightmare, 181–182
Wolf, 108, 178. *See also* Werewolf
Wonder-tale: defined, 25; traditional ending, 31, 46; ghosts in, 53–54; and legend, 76, 136; compared with a text, 85, 91, 168; compared with devil legends, 154; style, 163, 193
World view, 30, 46, 55
Wärend och Wirdarne, 22

Design:	Dave Comstock
Composition:	Freedmen's Organization
Lithography:	Braun-Brumfield, Inc.
Binding:	Braun-Brumfield, Inc.
Text:	Compugraphic Paladium
Display:	Jetsetter Palatino Italic
Paper:	Warren's 1854, basis 50